ADVANCE PRAISE FOR STRUGGLES AGAINST TIME

Struggles Against Time: Memories and Musings is a philosophical and deeply reflective memoir by Ted Shigematsu. Ted shares his experience of feeling like he didn't belong as a child with Japanese genes in Genova, Italy. He couldn't wait to migrate with his family to the USA while preparing to do so in 1963. Unfortunately, he still felt out of place with his heavy accent and his "old jalopy", which influenced his decision to drop out of Imperial Valley College. Fortunately, he couldn't resist the call to learn and ended up becoming a professor and getting several degrees, including an Associate of Science degree in respiratory therapy. From war to art, travel, COVID-19, education, the passage of time, loss, and love relationships, Ted Shigematsu presents his thoughtful views on different memories and moments from his past.

Ted Shigematsu's memoir stands out with a third-person perspective that allows readers to follow the story from an all-encompassing viewpoint. I enjoyed reading the book from the first page to the last. It's one of the few times I got to see an author refer to himself as "the old man" and "the young man", and I loved how unique it felt. Fans of philosophy and historical texts will love the book since it covers these topics vividly, including Hesiod's work. An important lesson I learned is that the years go by faster than you think, which is gleaned from impactful statements like, "One moment it had been the sixth of January 1958; the next moment it was 2020." Struggles Against Time, a philosopher's journey through life, is nothing short of amazing. It's brimming with adventure, profound philosophical quandaries, and relatable, evocative experiences.

Readers' Favorite 5-star review

STRUGGLES AGAINST TIME

STRUGGLES AGAINST TIME

MEMORIES & MUSINGS

TED SHIGEMATSU

KONSTELLATION PRESS

Copyright © 2024 by Ted Shigematsu

All rights reserved.

Konstellation Press, San Diego

www.konstellationpress.com

No part of this book may be reproduced in any form or by any electronic or mechanical means, including information storage and retrieval systems, without written permission from the author, except for the use of brief quotations in a book review.

Cover: Scarlet Willette

ISBN: 979-8-9868432-8-5

For Stephanie,

Let's "...pluck till time and times are done,
The silver apples of the moon,
The golden apples of the sun."
W.B. Yeats

1

The boy opened his eyes to the warm early-morning light blazing through the window. He lay still listening to voices coming from below—his aunt had traveled the night before from Genova to visit them, and now her voice and laughter danced in the air. He jumped up from the old army cot and ran out of the room, down the stairs. His grandmother sat on a chair in the kitchen, her eyes closed and lips slowly moving, as she recited the rosary she held in her trembling hands. Out on the terrace, Sandrina, his sister, sat on the floor and played with a doll as his mother and aunt, wearing robes, lounged on deckchairs, drinking coffee. "Here's my little guy, come give me a kiss," his aunt said. He walked up to her, and she hugged him close to her blue robe and kissed him on the cheek, her long black hair tickling his face. She smelled of coffee and cigarettes. "Good morning," he mumbled, rubbing his eyes. His mother smiled as she hugged and kissed him. As they went in the house to fix breakfast followed by his sister, he lay down on the warm cement propped on his elbows and took a deep breath. The scent of newly cut grass was in the air; someone was probably swinging a sickle nearby, clearing the trail that led down to the village. He turned to look at the tall fig tree that stood by the left side of the house, then gazed into the distance. The green mountains seemed like the folds of a blanket, and the highway a faint white string on which tiny beetles slowly climbed. He often gazed at those mountains—so far away and at times shrouded in mist or haze. He was only six years old but knew that the whole world was beyond them, and his future.

AN OLD MAN stared back at him from the mirror as he brushed his teeth. How did it happen? What artifice had transformed him into such a wreck? Despite the passage of time, it seemed strange, uncanny, to see himself like that, the high brows sagging, eyelids threatening to overflow, brown spots on the cheeks the early manifestations of a rot soon to expand and blot him out of existence.

He had looked forward to writing, reading and traveling after his retirement, but the pandemic changed everything. The virus was deadly, especially for the old, and he was old. He chuckled. It would have been the perfect cosmic joke, to have looked forward for so many years to the culmination of his life's goals, only to be snuffed out by a virus.

A background hiss and the beating of his heart in the left ear. "Oh, it's just tinnitus; it happens at your age." Spiders and flies crawling inside his eyes—and if he looked up on a bright day, innumerable black dots swam in the blue sky. "Vitreous detachments," the ophthalmologist had said, "quite common as people get older."

In bed at night he often wondered if there were scents he could no longer detect, sounds he couldn't hear, tastes his tongue couldn't savor. His eyes reminded him of the television set his parents-in-law used to have, so old that the picture had lost color and detail. Since they watched it every day, they had gotten used to the slow deterioration of the CRT tube. It was the same with his senses. The thought made him feel enclosed in a box, locked in, distant from the vibrant, clear, exuberant way trees and sky, mountains and seas asserted themselves when he was young. Maybe that was the reason he fought going to bed at night. He would sit in his study and, too tired to read, watch videos on YouTube until he could not keep his eyes open and then drag himself to bed.

After what seemed an interminably long time he fell asleep, but in the middle of the night he woke up. His sinuses felt slightly congested; his neck ached. He took a drink of water from the bottle he kept on the bedside table and walked out of the bedroom. He sat in his easy chair in the study, surrounded by books. The glow of the lamp on the end table brought to life the colorful backs of the volumes lining the shelves. He looked up at the *Expulsion from the Garden of Eden* by Masaccio, a print bought decades earlier in Florence, at the Santa Maria del Carmine gift shop, after standing for an hour in the Brancacci Chapel, enthralled by the frescoes. He had framed it and put it on the wall facing his reading chair. It seemed to him now that the red angel with the flaming sword had cast him out of his youth. It had happened slowly, imperceptibly, until he had looked at his hands one day—wrinkled skin, blue veins protruding underneath parchment paper skin, the tips of his little fingers bent by arthritis.

But had he really been exiled? His youth after all was not a place where he had lived; he had lived his youth, consumed it. He understood this, and yet Masaccio's image of the *Expulsion* spoke to him. Adam hid his face in his hands; Eve covered her nakedness, her face a mask of anguish. They ate of the fruit of knowledge and knew death.

Would he be willing to give up awareness in order to have the immortality implicit in not knowing? Could he have relinquished subjectivity, his inner life, memories and dreams, for blissful ignorance? No, he could not, would not. He had to accept his exile, if that is what it was, had to accept that he had used up his youth and could never have it back.

His youth hadn't been a paradise, after all; it had been full of fear, dread, failures and disappointments. But when he had gotten out of bed in the mornings he hadn't felt any pain; when he had looked in the mirror he hadn't been repulsed. The future had been a field of possibilities extending beyond the horizon. Now the horizon was a rapidly approaching cliff, and soon he would tumble into oblivion. In youth, when he had looked at attractive women on the street or in other public places, it would have been within the realm of possibility to imagine he could have a relationship with them; now when he saw attractive women, they could have been his daughters. Even to older women, he was just a walking memento mori.

As a child he had read with fascination the encyclopedia, and even though he didn't like school, what he learned told him that he lived in a coherent, stable reality where intelligent human beings, guided by reason, sought to understand the world and make it better. Then when he discovered philosophy, he assumed that human beings were ultimately rational, open to factual evidence. Surely, in those thick books, Plato, Aristotle and other thinkers would reveal to him knowledge and truth. And it was with such hopes that he had approached his university years.

As a student, he came across the writings of Sartre and Camus. He remembered how he stayed up nights to finish books like *Nausea* and *The Stranger*, and how they had shaken him to his foundations. And then came other books that ignited his imagination and sense of wonder. But his intellectual life was untethered from his miserable daily existence.

His study was small, the left wall covered with philosophy books, the right with psychology, religion and Italian literature, dictionaries and references, piles of volumes rising from the floor like thick stalagmites. He pushed back on the chair so it would recline.

As he gazed at the colors of the volumes' spines, he was struck again by the realization that the world presented itself only through his experience. Nature, history, art—everything existed only as filtered and made sense through his body and his subjectivity. The world was not something "out there"—he was part of it, had "come out" of it, but it was through his consciousness and experience that he had retroactively given it reality.

What did that mean? That the world was not a creation of his mind in a crude solipsistic sense, but it was only through his body, his genetic possibilities, the specific linguistic, historical and environmental strands that made up "his life," that whatever was out there took form and appeared as a world. And there were nights when it cracked deep inside and spilled all over, the realization that it was only through his feelings and thoughts, memories and dreams that everything that existed, the whole world, had reality only through himself and would die with him. Of course, the same was true for other human beings, but how they experienced the world he had only an indirect idea. Often this realization became unbearable. It felt like a terrifying weight, a monstrous form of claustrophobia, of loneliness. And to think that when he first became interested in philosophy, he had taken for granted that there was an objective world out there that could be known through reason and exploration.

He had been a naive realist, had assumed an external objective point of view. Of course, that was before he studied Kant, Nietzsche and Heidegger. He realized now that Nietzsche was right: there was no cosmic third-person point of view. The world was not a simple creation of his mind; he had been born into it, lived in it and would soon die, and then it would be as if he and his world had never existed. He had always considered awareness the most important thing. Perhaps that was the reason it had always been difficult for him to fall asleep. Once he died, his awareness, subjectivity and memory would be extinguished. "But you will live on in the memories of others, in how in myriad ways you interacted with the world," some people would reply. But in time everyone he had known would die; at some point in the future, there would be no trace of his ever having been. And what difference did it make to him, once dead, if some people still remembered him?

He thought of vernal pools, those depressions in the ground that after heavy rain fill up with water, and for a few weeks or months become worlds populated by living things—tadpoles, fairy shrimp, daphnia, all busily going about their lives—until summer, when the pools dry up. Wasn't the earth just a vernal pool? Pondering this, human life appeared devoid of any meaning. But you still had to brush your teeth and take a shower, go to work and pay your bills, go to the grocery store and try to satisfy your needs. And then there were other people.

How could human beings think themselves free? They spent most of their lives in the pursuit of food, sex, power and prestige, like any other primate. They were a mutant primate species with their heads full of fantasies, who strutted around convinced of their superiority and self-importance.

He had been brought up a Roman Catholic, but as he reached adulthood, he'd abandoned religion, became an atheist. In middle age he had reconciled with the Church, became religious again in a spiritual sense, but it did not last long. The more he thought about it, the more implausible religious beliefs became, especially the Judeo-Christian narratives. There is an all-good Supreme Being that created all things, including you. He knows you absolutely and loves you. You have a body but you are not your body, you are an eternal, immaterial soul, and if you live according to His will, when your body dies you will live in bliss for all eternity in God's presence, reunited with all your loved ones. It was a comforting tale, but how could anyone accept it as true?

What did life turn out to be but a continuous stream of losses? He woke up in the morning and yesterday was gone. He had fallen asleep as a child one night as his mother kissed him good night and had woken up an old man, his mother a faint memory. The teachings of the Buddha made more sense. All things are impermanent, there is no essence or independent core to things, to live is to suffer—the three marks of existence.

We are not our egos; our inner lives, our memories, our feelings, our thoughts, our sense of self—they are all parts of an illusion. We must identify not with that, but with the energy, the force that runs through everything. If we do so, then there is no birth and there is no death. Nonsense. What the hell did he care about the energy that ran through his body, about sunyata or brahman? *I am the illusion*, he thought. He was an organism with memories, thoughts, feelings and awareness, a product of particular genetic, social and historical events. Yes, he was an ephemeral illusion, and as he thought about it, he began to feel better.

∼

HE REMEMBERED the Sunday when more than twenty years ago he begrudgingly went to church with his wife and son. They had arrived just as the mass began, which put him in an even worse mood. He liked to get there fifteen minutes early so they could find seats up front. His five-year-old son behaved well but kept fidgeting and people trickled in, disturbing the rite, as two ushers helped them find seats. Infants cried. He could not concentrate on the mass, and as he watched the priest go through the motions, he began to feel that the whole thing was an exercise in futility. After communion, as he knelt in the pew, he thought, *God does not exist, and Jesus was just a man.*

As he continued thinking in this vein, the priest wiped the chalices, the eucharistic ministers placed the leftover hosts back in the tabernacle and a tender movement played on the organ. As he gazed at the scene, at Jesus on the cross behind the altar, God the father above him, the statues of Mary and the saints, the paintings, a wave of joy passed over him. Everything became luminous. God did not exist, Jesus never rose from the dead and the whole thing was meaningless, but precisely because of this, that moment, the celebrants sitting or kneeling, the priest in his vestments wiping the chalices, the altar boys behind him, the music rising from the choir in the back of the nave, the light, became a mandala, a rapturous moment suspended in nothingness. And even if God did not exist, his presence was in that moment; and even if Jesus was only a man, in that instance he was the son of God; and even if everything had no meaning, that moment was full of tenderness and beauty.

2

SAN DIEGO, 2020

The old man's existential claustrophobia was exacerbated by the pandemic, which made even going for a walk problematic and trips to the stores troubling excursions. He had to wear a mask, which fogged his glasses, make sure to keep six feet from others, and either wear gloves or treat his hands with sanitizer before getting in the car. Going to buy groceries was like a military mission: you did not know if you were going to become infected with the virus and die.

Every day the news was bad. People were dying all over the world by the tens of thousands, more getting infected every day. Covid-19 was primarily a respiratory disease; it attacked the lungs and often resulted in pneumonia, so people drowned in their own secretions. As a child he had been afflicted with chronic asthmatic bronchitis, so he knew full well the awful feeling of being congested, unable to breathe normally. His phobia of nasal congestion made him dread getting a cold. If his sinuses ever felt stuffed, he panicked, had to take a tranquilizer. And now this damn virus threatened him with what he feared most. When he finally went to bed and after an hour lying there wide awake, he fell asleep.

He saw himself wandering through a hospital until he went down a long staircase and stepped into a dimly lit cavernous room. A strong smell of rubbing alcohol and iodine assailed him, along with a cacophony of mechanical swooshes. When his eyes adjusted to the low light, he saw statues in different poses, dozens of them standing around a platform. As he moved closer, he realized the statues were monks, nuns and priests, dressed in robes, breathing through machines. As he approached the platform, a wooden cross stood out from the darkness. Jesus, nailed to it, seemed asleep. Blue corrugated hoses connected to a tracheostomy tube protruded from his neck. With every inhalation pumped into his lungs by a Bennett MA-1 ventilator, Jesus's chest rose, and with every exhalation, fell, as the bellow in the clear plastic spirometer went up and down. His long hair matted, his naked body covered in sweat, Jesus opened his eyes and screamed silently through them.

What a nightmare! No wonder he didn't like going to bed.

THE PRESIDENT on TV tried to minimize the seriousness of Covid-19, saying it's not that bad, it'd go away soon, don't worry. The morning after the election he woke up in a different country. Decency, open-mindedness, reliance on cogent reasoning and factual evidence, tolerance and compassion, the values that he had associated with America from childhood, were openly negated by Trump's inauguration. But had those ever been the values of America?

As a child growing up in Italy, he had had a naive, romantic view of the United States, primarily acquired from Hollywood movies. He abandoned that view at the university when he read about the genocide of American natives, slavery, the exploitation and oppression of Asians, robber barons and manifest destiny, of the United States' interference in the democratic elections of other countries, the rampant greed of American corporations and increasing inequality. But he had retained the hope that with education, people would be able to go beyond dogmas, shed blind beliefs, become more open-minded. The 2016 presidential election had extinguished that hope. Every day, in the media, from news programs to talk shows, on Twitter and Facebook, he could not escape the latest attacks on the ideals of fairness, open-mindedness, truth and objectivity.

The decay of America, of his ideal of it, was reflected in his body. When he opened his eyes in the morning and got up to go to the bathroom, he was glad to still be alive, but later in the day the dread began to seep into his consciousness: he was still trapped in an aging body.

When his wife retired, one of her projects had been to organize the garage, and she asked him to clean up the books and folders he had stashed in boxes. He sat on the old La-Z-Boy he had moved into the garage when he'd gotten a new one for Christmas and opened a thick folder full of clippings from thirty-year-old Italian newspapers. On his visits to Tuscany to see his parents he would buy *La Repubblica*, *La Stampa*, *L'Unità*, the *Corriere della Sera* and peruse the reviews of films, the articles on culture and politics.

The clippings were in surprisingly decent shape, considering their age. The paper had yellowed in varying degrees and had lost its crispness, but the print was clearly legible, and the black-and-white photos had not faded. As he flipped through the pages, his eyes rested on an ad for the TV show of Paolo Guzzanti, a journalist and politician, who smiled at him from thirty-one years earlier. That smile brought him back to the cage of time where he was condemned to remain, never to return to the day when he bought that paper at a newsstand in Albinia.

One morning more than thirty years ago he had walked to that newsstand. He had passed the bar The White Goose and the Coral Hotel, and said good morning to a couple of passersby, the air cold, already full of Christmas. And now, all that remained of that day was a yellowed paper clipping. Wasn't that why he hung on to photos and journals, kept notebooks and mementos? To try desperately to hold on to what time would erase? He went on vacation and brought back souvenirs, maybe a refrigerator magnet, so that years later he'd remember the trip.

Later that night, the old man, unable to sleep, got up and went back to the study, sat on the new La-Z-Boy and gazed at Masaccio's *Expulsion*. He thought, *so that's how the human story begins: in pain and shame, thrown out and condemned to die.* Did Adam and Eve experience regret? The deep pain of irreversibility? Did they wish they had not eaten of the tree? Was it seared in their being forever, the realization that once done, an action cannot be undone?

Was there freedom, besides the limited one of a prisoner locked up in a cell for life? The prisoner was free to stand, sit or lie down, to read or sleep or listen to music, but not to leave the cell. We were determined by genetics and environment, by time and space. We were not free not to grow old; we were not free to travel back to an earlier time. "But that's a fantastic idea of freedom, that's not human freedom," someone might say. Exactly. Human freedom was limited to the prisoner's possibilities within the cell. He could only venture outside the cell in his imagination, and what he could imagine was limited by his physical and historical parameters. He could fantasize about a reality where he didn't grow old, or where he could go back to relive his childhood or university days. Infantile, stupid musings. There were laws of physics; entropy, the arrow of time; get real. You were free to steal or not, go for a walk or watch TV, go to college or join the army, kill yourself or live. *Well*, he thought, *aren't we back in the cell?* He wanted out, but there was no out. A metaphysical claustrophobia began to take hold of him.

Human beings, an animal species whose exploding population threatened the planet. They puffed themselves up with fantasies of having been created by God—who they believed made them immortal—and with their minds full of fantasies and beliefs, they went on flattening hills and forests, covering more of the planet with concrete and steel, polluting it with their presence and activities.

They took delight in torturing and killing each

other and employed their intelligence and ingenuity in devising more elaborate forms of torture, from the Chinese one thousand cuts to iron maidens, to "advanced interrogation techniques." Full of hate and distrust, fear and anger, they delighted in attacking the other, all the while convincing themselves of being children of God, to whom even the angels must bow.

Still sitting in his chair in the study, sinking in gloom, he turned to look at his philosophy books. On the top shelf he noticed a volume bound in dark blue cloth, gold lettering on the spine. He got up to retrieve it and sat down again. *Outlines of the History of Greek Philosophy* by Eduard Zeller. At the bottom, also in gold, was the image of two trees, labeled "Arbor Scientae" and "Arbor Vitae," and below, the publisher, Routledge & Kegan Paul. He flipped through the pages—thick ivory paper; he could not identify the font, but it was dark and appealing—printed in Great Britain. The paper had a texture reminiscent of fabric and when he put his nose in the gutter of the volume, a rich scent he associated with the olfactory patina of scholarship pleased him. He had bought the book years earlier at the Adams Avenue Book Store but had just recently finished reading it. He pictured himself on the sofa on a lazy afternoon when he had nothing to do but read that book and felt buoyed.

Yes, there was something special about humans—they had memory and language, self-consciousness and feelings—and some of them brought forth art and music, philosophy, literature and science. Unfortunately, most human beings were not thoughtful creatures driven by intellectual curiosity and fairness.

Didn't they kill Christ? That weak, poor *other* who preached forgiveness and love? But that was what they did best: kill the weak, the different, those who did not belong to their tribe. Even the followers of Christ burned down pagan temples, destroyed their art and killed those who believed in other gods—in other words, those who did not belong to their tribe.

They had killed Hypatia, and he would never forgive them. Hypatia, a Greek philosopher and scientist who lived in Alexandria in the fourth and fifth centuries, had many pagan and Christian students. She was respected and loved by the community, yet she was murdered by a mob of Christians who dragged her in the street, stripped her flesh with seashells, cut out her eyeballs and chopped her body to pieces. So much for Christian love.

Now the naked apes had electronic devices and traveled in jets, but they were still just murderous primates intent on satisfying their real and imagined needs, eager to strike and kill those they considered a threat. He recalled what Joseph Campbell had said in an interview with Bill Moyers. The well-known professor of mythology narrated a story of his meeting with the guru Sri Atmananda. Campbell had asked how it was possible to embrace life in the face of so much hate, misery and violence, and the guru had answered, "For you and me, we must say yes."

Could he say "yes" and accept it all with equanimity? No, he could not. He needed to relax so he could go to sleep; it was almost two o'clock. He took deep breaths and flipped the book's leaves as he read the headings: "The Athenian School," "The Later Stoics," "Epicurus and His School," "Aristotle," "Plato,"

"Socrates," "The Sophists," "The Pre-Socratics." Holding the volume, running his fingers along the cover and the leaves, eased his breathing and relaxed his muscles. Just a short outline of ancient Greek philosophy, but it became a precious object in his hands. He read a few more pages until his eyes started to close. It was time to get up from the chair and go to bed.

BOLTS OF PAIN shot from his lower back as he got up. He lay flat on the floor and did a couple of exercises, then took a long, hot shower. He stretched his neck under the hot water, and afterward he felt nimble, more awake; the pain receded. He made a pot of coffee and read newspapers on his iPad. More than 100,000 people had died of Covid-19 in the United States, and people were hoarding toilet paper, hand sanitizer, gloves and food. Hospitals followed triage protocols, deciding not to treat patients they thought would not survive.

That night, he sat in his chair surrounded by books and the consoling yellow light of the table's lamp. His wife slept, but he fought going to bed. It had been a surreal day. They'd tried to find a place to walk, but all the parks and trails were closed. At Vons, most of the grocery shelves were bare. He was beginning to feel more closed in, locked in a cell, the only way out inward, back in time. Why not take stock of his life, to relive it, in case he caught the virus and died? He glanced at the print of the *Expulsion* and closed his eyes.

3

SELLA, 1954

As he lay on the terrace enjoying the warmth radiating from the floor, his mother called and he dashed inside. The kitchen was small and bare, with a propane range set on a narrow wooden counter next to the sink. He sat at the table and ate a soft-boiled egg with a slice of bread.

The two-story house perched on a hill, with a terrace at ground level and a fig tree growing on the left side, was the first house they had ever lived in. In Genova, they had stayed in rented rooms or apartments. They began to call it the House of the Fig. After breakfast, the boy took the trail not far from the house and soon found himself in the forest, where he often went, imagining himself a warrior. As he walked through ferns, on pine needles and moss-covered rocks, he did not feel alone. He picked up a handful of chestnuts from the ground and bit into one, tore pieces of the leathery skin with his teeth, spit them out, and with his fingernails scratched the rust-colored fuzz off. He walked chewing the white nuts, savoring their crunchy flesh, now chasing a lizard through the brush, now trying to catch a tree frog, and came to the ravine. He climbed down and saw them—the mushrooms, white tall stems, red caps. His heart began to race, and a tingle ran down his back as he knelt. Where were they, the little people that lived under the mushroom caps? His whole body had filled with electrifying wonder and certainty, and he sat and waited for a long time, but they never emerged. He got up and walked back home. A light breeze flowed through the trees and as he looked up, a few white fluffs lazily moved in the azure sky.

He came to the stream, took off his shoes and socks and waded in the cold, transparent water up to his knees, smooth clay under his feet. He bent over and tried to catch a minnow, but it darted away. Suddenly he rose up and listened to the flowing water, to the wind passing through the branches. The sun seemed to melt on the pines, on his skin, on the crystalline stream, and he took a deep breath. He stood still and his thoughts disappeared to make room for the whisper of the flowing creek, the cool breeze, the trees' branches lazily stirring, the sun's light and warmth. Why couldn't this moment last forever? But it was time to go back, so he began to walk home.

"After lunch Grandma is going to church to pray for the priest, so don't go wander about. You need to go with her," his mother said, so he climbed on the fig tree by the side of the house, sat on a branch and gazed toward the hazy mountains. He wondered about his father. His mother told him he worked on a ship. Where was he now? New York? Calcutta?

Athens? Istanbul? He sent letters and photos from all those places. The boy vaguely remembered him. In the evening, before going to sleep, he would say his prayers and look at the photos on the bedside table. In the dim light they were just grainy shadows swirling into forms, congealing into an American soldier catching a baseball frozen in midair, smiling next to his mother on a bridge, ruins of buildings in the background.

In early afternoon he went with his grandmother. She lived in a *cantoniera,* or roadman's house, in Orbetello, a town with Etruscan roots, rising on a strip of land in a lagoon in Tuscany. Sometimes she visited his family and stayed for a few weeks. His grandfather, Giovanni, a tall, intimidating man with a handlebar mustache, didn't like to be away from his vegetable garden and rarely traveled. Five hours on the train "*é troppo*," he would say, "it's too much."

His grandmother, short and stocky, dressed in black, with a scarf on her head, would show up with two bags full of olive oil, wine, sausages, smoked eels and cheese. She had reddish wrinkled skin, brown spots on her hands, and she smelled of food—she reminded him of a big black bird. As he walked next to her, he lost himself in the scent of wild daisies and newly cut hay, in the chirping of birds, the tepid warmth of the sun. As they climbed down the steep trail, stepping carefully on the rocks, his grandmother steadied herself by holding his hand. Nettles and ivy growing on the sides brushed against his legs. Hazelnut trees full of white nuts grew in clusters, and even though he knew they were not ready, he took a nut and bit into it, immediately spitting out the bitter pulp. Once on the main road, they walked close to the steel parapet on the right side. Honey locusts and ailanthuses thrust their branches heavy with white-yellowish flowers over the parapet, the fragrance strong and insistent. On the left, roots showed through the steep mountainside. Sudden piercing trumpet blasts from behind announced that the bus was just around the curve, so they walked closer to the barrier. The blue bus passed by them in a rush of dust and air. As they walked, he saw *Viva Coppi!* scribbled in black paint on a gray wall, and he wondered if the champion bicyclist had ever passed by on that road.

Now they could see the church. It stood out white among green fields and hills, but as they got closer, the color seemed to change into sandalwood. The campanile leaned slightly to the left, as if the four greenish bells at the top had proven too heavy. He liked to look at the rose windows above the brown wooden doors—they reminded him of rainbows. He went to the church every Sunday afternoon to watch old black-and-white films that the priest showed to the children. He also fed them little snacks—a few crackers and cheese, an apple, a chocolate.

As they entered the rectory, the priest greeted them and led them into a small white room where a younger priest dressed in a black cassock lay on the bed. His hair neatly combed, eyes closed as if asleep, his folded hands grasped a black rosary. The boy stood with bowed head by the door while his grandmother knelt and kissed the dead priest's hand. She took her rosary from her pocket and began to pray, head bowed, eyes closed. The boy stood in the stuffy room trying to listen to outside sounds—birds, rustling leaves, the breeze—but all he could hear were the paternosters and Ave Marias, a whispering that reminded him of the mountain stream. As he stood watching his grandmother's hands tremble slightly, he wiped the sweat from his forehead and leaned against the wall. The priest lay there, just a thing, like the dead little animals he saw sometimes on the side of the road. The priest was a young man doing God's work; why did he die? God is a good, loving father, he was told, but if that was true, why didn't God help the young priest? Images and thoughts scuttled across his mind like squirrels and lizards until his grandmother laboriously got up. She made the sign of the cross, and they left. Outside, fresh air and warm light revitalized him. They stopped at the small village store and his grandmother bought him a candy. He took deep breaths as he unwrapped the sweet from the red cellophane paper, popped it in his mouth and held her hand.

THE OLD MAN opened his eyes to the angel with the flaming sword, took three Tums out of the container and started chewing them. His heartburn was getting worse. Sixty-five years had passed, but he still saw the dead priest on the bed, still felt the relief as he tasted the candy and walked back home holding his grandmother's hand. How did they wind up in that mountain village behind Genova?

His mother received money from his father sporadically and could no longer afford to rent in the city. It was 1953; he was five years old, Sandrina an infant. His father had come to Italy in 1944 with the 442nd, the Japanese American U.S. Army regiment, and after the war he was stationed in Livorno to guard German prisoners of war. At a dance he met Luisa, a woman with long brown hair, an oval face and a Roman nose; he thought she was the most desirable woman at the dance. They became a couple. Then in March of 1947 he had to return to California to be formally separated from the Army. He visited with his family for three months, then returned to Italy. He and Luisa lived in a rented room in Rome, and the boy was born in 1948. They didn't know where to put the baby, so they laid a blanket in a drawer and placed him in it. A year later they moved to Genova, where his father began to study Italian at a private language school. They rented a room behind Piazza de Ferrari.

The old man closed his eyes and forced himself to recollect days now more than seventy years past, but only a few faint, blurry images appeared. Just a few years old, he climbed a palazzo's stairs and squealed in delight—he was holding a new tricycle. In another memory he strolled with his mother in a park with white marble statues along the path. A statue slowly began to move; the head turned to look at him.

The old man saw himself playing on the floor in the kitchen and as a woman moved a pot of boiling water from the stove to the sink, a handle came off and the water fell on the boy's back. But he could not have seen the scene from a third-person point of view. He must have constructed the memory based on what his mother told him later. He could only remember fragments, images, short scenes. In a hospital, his mother sitting on a chair next to him; days spent at home in bed; the excruciating pain when a doctor who came to the house poured acid on his back to treat the scars.

As a child he was often in bed with bronchitis, and the doctor would come to give him shots of penicillin. What was his name? Doctor Enrile, tall, slim, middle-aged. The boy's mother was wringing her hands. A woman came to give him injections and once he developed an abscess, so the doctor came and cut it open without any anesthetic. His mother and his aunt Avia held him down as he cried at the top of his lungs, "Jesus! Jesus, help me!"

They moved often, to different neighborhoods of Genova, and then Sella—a small village on a mountainside 640 meters above sea level, with fewer than one hundred inhabitants. Only fifteen miles from Genova, but to get there they had to use a narrow, treacherous, winding mountain road.

Soon after they moved there, his mother bought him a new suit. As he went out to play with a couple of local children, she had warned, "Make sure not to get your suit dirty." The boys walked to a grassy field, and they pushed him in the mud. He did not want to go home, so he walked around for a long time. When he returned, his mother, enraged, beat him and made him stay under the stairs in the dark. He sobbed uncontrollably.

How old was he? Six? His sister was one year old, his half-brother twenty-two. Tall and wiry, with a dimple in his strong chin like Humphrey Bogart, Noé was born in 1933, when the Great Depression was in full swing, Hitler had been appointed Chancellor of

Germany, and Mussolini ruled Italy. Noé had belonged to the Balilla, the Fascist youth movement, as every child was required to, and grew up admiring Mussolini. But when war came to Italy, his world began to disintegrate. Following his mother, who was a clerical worker for the government, he found himself in a truck on the way to Lake Garda with a Fascist contingent. On the way they were attacked by American planes and he, his mother and others jumped out of the trucks and sought cover in a wheat field. His face pushing in the dirt, the smell of wheat in his nostrils, he must have felt his mother's heart beating madly on his back as machine-gun rounds whistled by his head. Then, as things began to fall apart for Mussolini and the Fascists, his mother paid a truck driver to take them from Lake Garda to Tuscany. He hid with his mother for long hours among barrels of wine in a truck on the way to Pisa.

Once in Livorno, his brother spent long months in a boarding school, wondering if he had been abandoned. Where was his mother? What happened to his father? Noé's father was in an institution, his brain ravaged by advanced alcoholism, but he didn't know it. His mother had been sixteen when her father gave her in marriage to Pietro, who was an alcoholic. When Pietro was a little boy, his father gave him wine to drink and then laughed when the child walked unsteadily and bumped into the furniture. Pietro had become a terminal case, and after squandering his wealth, had been institutionalized.

Noé's mother returned to the boarding school with a strange man, an American, and a Japanese-looking one at that. He probably wondered why his mother was with an enemy soldier, but he took a liking to the American who always had chewing gum and candy bars.

Then his mother had two children, and Noé found himself with a brother and a sister. He apprenticed as a house painter, and after learning about paints and varnishes, and how to create decorations and antique effects, he began working in Genova. When they moved to the mountains behind the city, he bought a motorcycle so he could commute.

Noé took the young boy for rides on his Ducati 175 Sport motorcycle over the winding mountain roads. The boy held on to him as they flew through ailanthuses, pines and firs, the engine screaming around the high-speed curves. "Don't sit straight in the curves—lean in as I do," his brother told him.

On the boy's first day of school, he was led, crying, dressed in a black smock with a white plastic collar and a blue ribbon tie, by his mother, who dragged him by the hand down the path, just a trail that led from the house on the hill to the school below. He was being pulled toward something painful and frightening. The school was a single room with ten or fifteen children sitting at desks. The teacher was a young woman who greeted him smiling. He was still crying when his mother left, but after a while he calmed down as he watched a boy writing on the blackboard. As time passed, he became less afraid, and he liked to write and listen to the teacher. Each desk had an inkwell, and the pupils had to buy their own nibs that fit in the wooden pens. The teacher read them *The Adventures of Pinocchio*, which he enjoyed. He felt a kinship with the puppet who yearned to be accepted as a real boy.

Later, some of the children began to call him "little China man" and laughed at him. The boy couldn't understand why they called him this, or why it would have been a bad thing. One morning, when he arrived at the front door of the school, he could not bring himself to turn the knob. The muffled voices of his tormentors came from inside and he turned around. There was a three-foot-wide gap between the building and the hill's retaining wall, and he hid there. It was quiet, and he took deep breaths in the shade. He wished he could have stayed there, but he knew he couldn't, so he forced himself to walk home. He told his mother there was no school that day, but she did not believe him and took him back, saying, "You're lying! Why do you keep telling lies? What's wrong with you? You better go, or else!" He found himself back in his seat in the classroom, the bigger boys who usually taunted him staring at him with smirks on their faces.

And so it went on, week after week. At the end of the school day, the boy's spirits lifted as he walked home. At times he saw the priest pass by on his bicycle. "Hey, Chou En-lai!" the priest greeted him.

When the boy started second grade a new teacher arrived, and she was not as friendly as the first. In winter, the classroom was heated by a wood-burning stove, and on a cold morning the new teacher said the students needed to go outside and bring more logs in. The boy was on his way out when he went back to get his coat, because it was freezing outside, but the teacher saw him and said, "It's true what they say about you people. You are lazy. Get back outside and help!" She made him sit in the back of the room, but that wasn't far enough; he wished he could have hidden someplace so no one could see him.

For carnival day the teacher had asked the children to come to school dressed up in a costume, but the boy's mother could not afford to buy or make him one, so he put on his rubber rain boots and tucked the ends of the pant legs in and went to school believing he was a cowboy. "And what are you supposed to be?" asked the teacher scornfully. "Nothing," he replied.

His aunt Avia was always kind to him and protected him from his mother's bad temper. Avia, an unusual name of Hebrew origins. Tall and slim with long brown hair, his aunt was a free spirit who ran away from home as a young girl to follow a German soldier she had fallen in love with. When he died, she wound up in a concentration camp. "I'm not Jewish," she kept repeating to the guards, "I'm not Jewish," but no one listened, no one cared. After all, wasn't Avia a Jewish name? When she showed up back home after the war, her mother didn't recognize her at first—emaciated, missing teeth, who was the scarecrow standing at the door? "I'm Avia," she whispered, "Avia, your daughter." After a few months she went to stay with her sister in Livorno, and there they both met Japanese American soldiers. Avia married Tam, who promised he'd come back or bring her to California, where he lived, but the years passed. Her sister, the boy's mother, also married a Japanese American soldier, who promised to come back and did.

His aunt often came from Genova to stay with them. When he saw her, the boy felt lighter, less alone. She was a ray of warm sun in his gray world. His mother, left alone to raise the boy and his sister, not receiving a letter or money from his father for months, was often nervous, in a bad mood.

One late afternoon, Avia took him for a walk on the trail behind the house. The sun had sunk below the peaks, but the top of the chestnut trees shone with an inner light. He took a deep breath and gazed at the hills and mountains. They accepted him, didn't judge; they offered themselves to him, gifted him with their presence. It was people he was afraid of. The air had quickly turned colder, and the boy raised the collar of his jacket. Avia walked ahead, with hands in her sweater's pockets. She lived in the city, and when she came to visit she grew bored after a few days. Up there in the mountains they didn't even have a radio, and she didn't like to read, so she talked to her sister, smoked cigarettes, and drank coffee, and to get out of the house would take the boy for a walk up the trail, a meandering path up grassy hills, past trees and scattered houses. "You like school?" she asked him without turning around.

"No," he replied.

"I didn't either, but you have to learn how to read and write. After school, your mom and I played with the other kids a game with pen nibs. The one who threw a nib closest to a marker won all of them. Your mom was the champ. Look, a chicken!" A brown bird, pecking and scratching, was coming down the hillside. "Get it! Let's get that chicken," she cried, and they began to chase it. The bird, startled, turned around and began to run, followed by Avia. As the chicken rushed down the slope, the boy ran sideways to intercept it. Seeing him coming toward it, the bird stopped for an instant, and the boy grabbed it. "Bravo!" said Avia, with a smile on her face.

"Here, hold it," said the boy as the bird began to squawk and struggle. It was getting darker now and the air colder, and as they ran home, Avia holding the chicken close to her and the boy following, the stars began to appear in the still pale sky.

"Look at what your son caught," said Avia to the boy's mother as they walked in the house. He smiled, and that evening they had a good dinner.

In the early 1950s, Avia lived a sporadic life. Her husband didn't return for her, and with no education or skills, she relied on boyfriends. Once she showed up with Piero, and they stayed for a few weeks. His aunt's friend was a short, stocky man who had been a security guard. One afternoon he had come home and caught his wife in bed with another man. Piero shot the man and spent time in jail. The boy liked to watch Avia's friend wash his face in the bathroom sink. Piero lathered his hands, then covered his face with the white suds, rubbing the back of his ears and neck. Then he rinsed for a long time and dried himself with a towel. He wore a sleeveless white cotton tee shirt, and big vaccination marks, like large coins, marked his big, hairy arms. The boy was entranced by the meticulous washing; it seemed a sacred ritual.

One afternoon, the boy went for a walk behind the house with a different boyfriend of his aunt's. On the way up the hill, they sat on a boulder as the man smoked a cigarette. A lizard lay on a rock. "Hey, look at this!" said the man as he put the cigarette's tip in front of the lizard's mouth. The lizard inhaled the smoke and became bigger and bigger until it burst like a balloon. The man laughed. The boy said nothing, but the event had seared itself in his psyche. That a man could laugh in amusement at the destruction of a defenseless living being—what did it say about the world he found himself in?

The boy was captivated by the *teleferica,* a steel cable strung from a wooden support in the center of the village to the top of a mountain. The villagers hiked to the top with hatchets and rope, cut wood and made bundles they sent down with rollers. Before this technology, the villagers had to carry the bundles of wood on their backs all the way down. When he gazed up at the towering mountain far in the distance covered with trees and at the steel cable that curved downward as it reached its support at the bottom, he felt a bond, a connection with something far away, much bigger than himself.

His brother Noé woke up early when it was still dark and rode his motorcycle to Genova to work. In winter he put newspapers under his leather jacket, to ward off the gelid wind. One spring he fell in love with Bruna, a girl who lived in the village, and on Sundays, he took her on rides. Bruna's mother, Giula, used to tell the boy stories about the partisans who fought the Germans in the mountains. She told him about the day the Germans dragged Luigi, the owner of the restaurant in the adjacent village of Moranego, into the street because they suspected him of being a partisan. They were going to shoot him when his wife ran outside, knelt in front of the commander and gave him all the gold jewelry she had, swearing that her husband was not a partisan, and begged for his life. The German officer accepted the gold and left with his squad.

"Where are they going?" the boy asked Giula when his brother and Bruna left on the motorcycle. "Oh, they're going to make love!" replied Giula. The boy pictured his brother and Bruna sitting on a blanket under a tree, intent in making something with sticks and leaves.

The boy watched the bundles of wood come down on the cable, the roller making a high-pitched whistling sound, and Giula told him to stand farther back, because it was dangerous. Then she told him about the day a man on the peak, while sending a bundle of wood on the cableway, had gotten a leg caught in the logs and had been dragged in the air all the way down until he was smashed against the base down below.

She told him the names of the mountains, and how to say things in the Genovese dialect. Genova was called Zena. Eugenio, her husband, was a tall, quiet man who tended his plot of land and occasionally went to the city to work as a laborer. They lived in a small house with a wood stove in the middle of the room, and sometimes Giula would put a potato on top, and when it was cooked, give it to the boy with some salt sprinkled on it.

The boy lived in Sella for three years, but in various places. His mother usually found problems with each apartment or house they moved to. After living on the hill in the "House of the Fig" they lived in a small apartment next to the house where Giula, Eugenio and Bruna lived. There was an alleyway that ran from the main road through the cluster of seventy buildings that comprised the village, many of them built with bricks of tuff. The alleyway was paved with stones, and in early morning and late afternoon, villagers passed by with oxen—huge, docile beasts that in the evening lumbered stoically to their stalls to finally rest for the night. The boy liked to listen to them trudge on the stones. He sat on top of the wall and heard the oxen before he could see them—faint, slow rhythmic sounds that became louder as the animals appeared down the path. They passed in front of the boy—the alley wide enough for only one ox and a man. It was a sign that the day was coming to an end, that it was time to eat and rest.

The apartment, right next to Giula's house, had a cement patio elevated from the alleyway, and the boy would lie down on top of the wall by the stairs that led to the rocky path, his head propped up on the adjacent wall, and gaze at the trees that covered the mountain facing him. Why was he there? Not in that particular place, but there, in general? Why did he have to go to school? That room with old desks in rows, the blackboard, the other kids who mocked him, the teacher sitting in front, stern, judging—they were manifestations of a world that had nothing to do with the mountains, the stars, the sound of the brook or the dances of the fireflies on summer nights.

To get him out of the house, his mother sent him at times to accompany one of the neighbors, Giorgio, when he had to work down in his field. Sella was built on the side of a mountain, but below the road the ground flattened, and fruit trees, small vineyards and vegetable gardens needed to be tended. Giorgio was a quiet man who lived with his sister, Maria. She hiked up the mountain early in the morning to fill a huge basket that she carried on her back with grass, to feed their cow. While Giorgio worked in his field, the boy passed the time by running around or climbing trees. One winter his mother asked Giorgio if he could bring her a little tree for Christmas, and after he finished working, he chopped a small pine, and the boy helped him carry it to their house. His mother had no money for presents that year, but on Christmas Eve she baked all night, and the tiny kitchen was full of light and the scents of cookies, biscotti and sweet breads.

THE OLD MAN rose from the chair and limped to the bathroom. He wondered why he had so many memories of those three years he lived in Sella and few of other periods of his life. Even after more than sixty years, when he thought of that period of his childhood, what passed through his mind first was holding on to his brother as the motorcycle banked left or right on the curves. The red Ducati whined angrily, and he held on tight and buried the side of his face on his brother's back to keep the wind from slapping him. The roar of the engine, the cold air, the warm bike's sides, the smell of hot engine oil and deep forest, holding on to his brother. The vibrant reality, the sparkling sensations, were now faint, ghostly memory traces. His brother was dead, and the boy was an old man. *Fucking time.*

The old man sat back on the chair and glanced at

the watch propped up on the side table—it was 1:30 a.m. He needed to go to sleep, or he would feel groggy the following day. He plugged in his iPad and shuffled into the bedroom. His wife was asleep. He pulled the covers over his shoulder and adjusted the pillow, memories of Sella still swirling in his head. What happened when they moved back to Genova? *I'll go back to that time tomorrow*, he thought. After all, he didn't dare go out much now that the pandemic was in full swing.

4

SAN DIEGO, 2020; GENOVA, 1950S

Images of a policeman kneeling on a man's neck. "I can't breathe, I can't breathe!" the man says as the officer glares defiantly at the bystanders. Raging fires burning swaths of California as more people die of Covid-19. The old man no longer goes for a walk because he can't keep a social distance of six feet on the sidewalk. Beaches and parks are closed. The box gets smaller.

That night, in his study—or was it a bunker?—he picked up one of his favorite art books and flipped through the pages until he came to the first panel of the *Gates of Paradise*. Every time he went to Florence, he walked to the east door of the Baptistery and stood enthralled in front of the twenty-foot-tall gold-plated bronze doors. In the book, he finally found the first plate and his eyes rested on it.

Thick golden mist, pure Being before time and space, before the beginning, before the Word. And then, out of the golden wall bursts forth God followed by his angels: the regal principle of actuality sweeping over the void, Plato's Idea of the Good, Aristotle's Pure Form, the One of Plotinus, Jung's Ultimate Archetype, He appears through a mandala, a communion's host, the circle of perfection, the cosmic womb; He wears a magician's hat, holds a rod in his right hand, and in a big bang, an eruption, an emanation, an ejaculation, He creates heaven and earth. On rocky ground adorned with large star-like flowers He pulls Adam out of the earth, just as Ghiberti seemed to have pulled God out the gilded bronze plate. Adam is an unwilling, fearful creature who resists, wishing to remain safely within the womb of the earth. With his right hand raised in a blessing, bent toward the drowsy creature, God imparts to it a spark of divinity. With his left hand He raises Adam up, a pull lasting millions of years, from the inanimate rock to a living, breathing mammal endowed with intelligence and self-consciousness. A metamorphosis through countless forms until dust became able to say, "I am." Locked in the loneliness of his manly strength, Adam grows desolate, secretly wishing for an embrace, a rose, for the power to create life and nurture it, a desire unknown to himself, but manifest in his dreams. And God, out of animal life, brings forth woman. Eve, still partly dream, is held up by angels as she faces Yahweh. Now brute strength and calculating intelligence are no longer alone; sensitive strength and nurturing intelligence complement them.

Adam and Eve in the Garden of Eden pass their timeless days amid cool, flowing waters and luxuriant vegetation, and birds perched on crowns of towering trees fill their world of undifferentiated consciousness with song. They are one with the song, the birds and the whole Garden, until they eat the fruit of the tree of the knowledge of good and evil. The serpent is coiled around the tree trunk, its human head bald on top like a professor's; the snake is an intellectual who has been around a long time and knows that with knowledge come duality and doubt but wants to bring everyone up to an educated level. Adam and Eve become aware of themselves as separate from the environment, and death enters their world. Paradise is forfeited, just as it is lost for every one of us when we are thrown out of our mother's womb and are forced through the gate into a cold, dangerous world. And so, Adam and Eve leave the Garden, frightened as much by what awaits them outside as by the angel's fiery sword. It took the Italian sculptor Lorenzo Ghiberti more than twenty-five years to complete the doors in the first half of the fifteenth century.

The old man's gaze remained on the book's illustrations. When, years later, he discovered the original doors were in the Museo dell'Opera del Duomo, he went to see the actual restored plates. He stood in reverence admiring the magnificent golden door that had taken Ghiberti decades to finish. It was a rainy January day and only a few people were there. Yes, cold, rainy winter days were best for visiting Florence. He wandered for hours in the museum and spent a long time gazing at Donatello's wooden statue of Mary Magdalen. He walked all around her, mesmerized by the bent body, long hair, ragged clothes, gaunt face and hands almost united in prayer. How could a wooden statue possess such a powerful spiritual essence, bring forth from deep within it fascination, sorrow and tenderness? It was just a six-foot-tall piece of wood carved more than five hundred years earlier, and here it was, in front of him, transformed into an old, emaciated woman who turned away from the world to devote herself to something beyond. Time. The time it took Donatello to turn the wood into Mary Magdalen, the time it took him to learn the art, the time it took for the techniques and the story to arrive at his epoch, the time it took for the seed to turn into the tree from which the wood was taken. It was in moments such as this that he thought of Shakespeare's words, "What a piece of work is man, how noble in reason! How infinite in faculty!"

Florence on a cold, rainy winter's day. As the old man sat in his chair at two in the morning, the thought lifted him up. Long walks by the Arno with drizzle washing his face, Ponte Vecchio in the distance, green hills rich with villas and ancient towers, hot shots of espresso in bars full of coffee aromas, the tinkling of spoons and cups, voices, the huffs and puffs of espresso machines. Everywhere he turned, art and architecture brought joy to his heart. To live in Florence, to spend every day in contemplation of centuries of art. The old man rested his head on the soft fabric of the reclining chair, closed his eyes and put himself there, walking along the Arno, the surface awakened by rain, chilly air on his face, his heart open to the brooding sky and dark jade hills. He kept walking, busts and statues looking indifferently at him as he passed, until he opened his eyes and was back in the study. Drowsy, he put the book down on the side table and got up. He slowly made his way to the bedroom.

HE HAD several strange dreams that night. He was alive for another day—perhaps. *Day and night, to be awake and to be asleep. Our whole lives, our existence, shaped by the rotation and revolution of the planet; we are born, go around the sun eighty or ninety times, and poof, we're gone. Imbedded in biological, historical, social and linguistic structures, we live out our days. We wake up, go to work, eat, talk and amuse ourselves until we retire to our bed to sleep until the next day, when we do it all over again.* Trite, common musings, and yet, if he pondered them enough, they acquired density, force, began to squirm restlessly deep inside.

The old man went through his daily routine—breakfast, trying to do some writing, lunch, a nap, reading, taking the dog around the block, dinner, a couple of hours watching a movie or TV with his wife, reading, then the struggle of letting go and retiring to bed. Back in the study, flipping through a photo album, going back to his Italy of so long ago.

In the late 1950s, apartment buildings sprang up like mushrooms on the hills hugging the center of Genova, and he lived with his mother, brother and sister in an apartment on Via Biga. The building had just been finished; there were still bags of cement left in front and he could smell the fresh white paint on the walls. Other edifices rose from the hill below them, signs of the economic boom that had begun to transform Italy.

It was a long walk down the steep road to the school, a rectangular building with two wings at the ends, the left one with the entrance for the boys, the right one for girls. The ten-year-old boy was in fourth grade, his sister Sandrina in the first grade.

They had a bowl of hot milk with coffe, sugar and pieces of old bread dipped into it for breakfast, sometimes a soft-boiled egg with a slice of bread and a banana. Then his mother walked them to school, and afterward picked them up, until later he went home by himself. The male teachers dressed in suits and ties, the woman who taught music always in a black dress; the pupils marched to classes like little army recruits. Professor Massone would tell them stories about his exploits in the Great War, the math teacher slammed his stick on the desk and never smiled, and toward the back, the meanest boy in the class masturbated under his desk to the amusement of the other pupils. During the religion hour, a priest came to tell them about God and Jesus. One day in class, the boy asked the teacher if he could go to the bathroom. Professor Massone let him go and when he returned, the tall man stood in front of him.

"Why did you write on the bathroom wall?" asked the man angrily. The boy didn't know what to think.

"I didn't write anything!" he replied, but Massone looked at him and said, "Don't lie! I can read your mind, and I know you did it." But the boy hadn't written anything on the wall, and if the man could really read his mind, he would have known the truth. He learned an important lesson that morning: adults lied and could not be trusted.

~

His uncle Libero showed up in summer with what to the boy seemed a big, fancy car. It was a used Opel. Libero had gone to Germany to work in a factory, and he had a few weeks of vacation. He stayed with them for a while, and one day he picked the boy up at school. As he hurried down the stairs and dashed outside, he saw Libero waiting. The boy had always liked his young uncle and beamed as he stood next to him in his black smock, his book bag in one hand and the other in Libero's pocket, searching for candy. Libero wanted to go to Orbetello, the town in Tuscany where he grew up, to visit his parents and brothers. "We'll surprise them, go to the beach. Don't you want to get out of Genova for a few days?" he asked the boy's mother, who was happy to see her younger brother. After long periods of unemployment, he had finally found a good job in Germany. She prepared sandwiches with Milanese beef cutlets, made potato salad, bought ripe peaches and plums, and in the early morning, they left.

The boy sat in the backseat of the Opel with his sister, Libero at the wheel and his mother in the passenger seat. It was a long drive, past Cinque Terre, the towns like drops of cream on pandoro cake, and Massa-Carrara with its white marble mountains, where his father fought retreating Germans during the war. It was an adventure for the boy, who kept looking out the window as if mesmerized. In Livorno, Libero parked off the road next to a line of trees and they had a picnic. As they sat on a blanket eating sandwiches and drinking sparkling water, a cool breeze passed through the trees, and under the branches' shade, two butterflies flittered above the grass while farther back, on the road, cars, trucks and motorcycles seemed to fly by in a continuous swoosh.

Once in Orbetello they stayed at his grandparents' house, the *cantoniera*. His grandfather had been a railroad man who maintained and managed a section of rail line. Whenever a train approached, he had to lower and raise the safety gate, then had to push heavy levers to divert the approaching train to another line. After the war, that part of the railroad went out of commission and his grandfather retired. Segments of rails, hidden partly by weeds, had been left in front of the house, and when the boy came with his mother and sister to visit, he amused himself by seeing how far he could walk on a rail before losing his balance. The boy's mother had two brothers who lived in Orbetello with their wives. Angiolino was the oldest, a serious man with a big black mustache and Gaetano, shorter and stockier. Angiolino and his wife, Iliana, had a daugher, Anna Maria.

When Libero parked the Opel in front of the *cantoniera* they were greeted by the boy's grandparents, who were surprised to see them. His grandmother took the boy and his sister to the vegetable garden, where they filled a basket with ripe tomatoes. Back in the kitchen, she grabbed a dagger-like knife and a loaf of Tuscan bread as long as the boy's arm, and holding the loaf with her left hand close to her chest she carved two huge slices. Then she cut the tomatoes and arranged thick slabs on the bread, sprinkling salt and olive oil as in a blessing, and offered them to the children. Even more than sixty years later, the old man remembered how the chewy, tangy flavor of the bread, the acidic sweetness of the ripe tomatoes, the soothing greenness of the olive oil and the brightness of the salt blended with his grandmother's wrinkled face, with the sound of her voice.

They went to the beach in Feniglia, near Porto Ercole. Libero, his mother and sister were accompanied by his aunts Lilia and Iliana and his cousin, Anna Maria. After walking over a wide swath of warm sand, the boy reached the water with his sister and his cousin. It was shallow, so they could wade a long way out, and the calm waves only reached the waist. He dived below the surface and the everyday world disappeared. The sandy bottom reflected sunlight, and in the fluid brightness he watched Anna Maria's shapely legs sparkle, like two magical marine creatures that beckoned to him, speaking in a silent, mysterious language.

As the old man reclined in the chair he was also diving deep, hoping to recover his past life, but he surfaced with only fragments and shards. And yet he had lived thousands of days in Genova. What was the sense of living, when as time passed he forgot most of it? Those days were gone. He knew that he had awakened early, gone to school, played in the afternoon, done homework and eaten dinner. But he could not remember the details, could not *feel* what it was like to be himself at that age. What did he eat and what did he do after dinner? They had no TV. Did he draw, read comic books? All the moments that form the rich material of daily life—the words spoken by his mother, brother and sister in the kitchen as they sat at the table eating dinner, the way the air felt as it entered the open window, the sounds from the courtyard, the smell of freshly washed clothes drying on the lines outside, the people on the sidewalk, the aroma of coffee, the yells of the fishmongers in the markets advertising fresh seabream, the scents of pastries and bread wafting from bars and bakeries as he walked to school, the warm rush of air as a bus accelerated from a stop—that rich, palpable fabric unraveled, came apart; only a few faded, flimsy strands remained. Many of his memories were disconnected images and scenes, like pieces of a vase that could not be put together again, could not even be visualized.

A memory fragment: having to dress up in his gray shorts, white shirt, tie and jacket and with his mother and sister, take the bus to Sella for his brother Noe's wedding. His and Bruna's mothers looking miserable and teary-eyed, as if they were going to a funeral. Why were they so sad, he wondered.

Another memory fragment: he's watching *On the Beach* at the Capital Theater; the crew of a submarine is searching for signs of human life on the West Coast of the United States after an atomic war devastated the planet. No one is found, and as lethal radiation covers the whole planet, the last survivors are doomed. In one scene, a calendar shows that the year is 1964. As he left the theater, the boy wondered if there was going to be a future for him.

When the ship his father worked on docked in Genova, his father invited a colleague to dinner. Don was a tall, blond middle-aged man who showed up wearing a white shirt, tie and suit, but after stuffing himself with homemade ravioli, his shirt had large red sauce stains. He looked like he had been stabbed in the chest. Don gave the boy and his sister a dollar each, and to the boy it was a precious bit of America, a tangible sign of the dream.

It was May of 1956, time for his first communion. The boy had been sick, so a woman came to the apartment to teach him the catechism. He had to pass a test, then go to the tailor to have a gray suit fitted. His mother bought him white gloves, a pearl-bound prayer book and the little gifts traditionally given for the occasion, then took him to the photographer to have a portrait taken. The mass at the church was an elaborate affair, with priests and a bishop. The eight-year-old boy felt important. His father was there, and in the afternoon they went to see *Guys and Dolls* at the Capital Theater.

The boy also began to read and collect weekly installments of an encyclopedia called *Conoscere* (To Know). It had illustrated entries on a variety of topics, and every few months the installment came bundled up with a hard cover, which his mother took to an office supply store, where the weekly issues were sent to be bound in a volume.

Whenever he went for a walk in the city with his mother and sister, he stopped in front of bookstores and gazed spellbound at the volumes on display behind the glass windows. They were precious objects beyond his reach, since his mother seemed never to have the money to buy him books. The books' covers, with their illustrations of rockets, monsters, pirates and ships, tantalized him with promises of exciting adventures, mysteries and the unknown.

As their financial situation improved, his mother bought him a few books and had a carpenter make him a bookcase. He would sit on the floor and admire the simple unfinished shelves with the volumes of the encyclopedia, the few books he had collected and copies of the two magazines he bought every month. He read avidly *Underwater World* and fantasized about being a scuba diver. He saw himself with two tanks on his back, a shiny regulator with double corrugated rubber hoses dispensing air in the mouthpiece, exploring the world below the surface, just like Captain Nemo and his crew did in the movie with James Mason and Kirk Douglas. The boy also liked *Four Wheels*. He read about cars, studied the pictures and then stood on the balcony overlooking the street, admiring the cars driving by. He wanted a white Ford Thunderbird. Every week he looked forward to the day his favorite comic book, *The Intrepid,* came out. He rushed to the newsstand, bought it, and ran home to read it. Did it come out on a Thursday? The old man couldn't remember. Why care? Such a small, inconsequential detail of his childhood, and yet it bothered him. He had looked forward to that day every week for years. He lost himself in *The Intrepid*'s adventures set in Africa and the American West, the mythological past of musketeers and medieval knights, but now the stories and illustrations had dissolved.

He went to the movies often, sometimes two or three times a week. The Capital, the Supercinema. Sitting in the dark movie houses as rockets, monsters, ancient Romans or cowboys came alive on the screen, he felt free. There was no one who stared at him, his mother wasn't on his back and he didn't have to think about school. He liked science fiction and westerns best of all, then war movies and comedies. John Wayne and the Marines, Laurel and Hardy, Alberto Sordi, Totò. One afternoon he saw *Supergiant*, a black-and-white Japanese science fiction film starring Starman. He liked to watch the Japanese superhero in his white costume fly; he could see part of the wire that held him up. He didn't know why, but he liked that part best of all.

A film that caused him nightmares was *Killers from Space*, a B movie from 1954 about aliens who plot to conquer the earth from a cave. The aliens wore black overalls with hoods so that only their faces showed: thick eyebrows and huge white eyes with big black pupils. For years, often when he closed his eyes, he saw those eyeballs staring at him from the darkness.

One afternoon his mother took him and his sister to see *Ben-Hur*. He was frightened by the scenes of the lepers and was scared for days. The thought that such diseases existed made life tentative, precarious, darkened the horizon.

His aunt Avia's husband had returned to California after the war with the promise that she would join him soon. It took twelve years, but he finally sent her a plane ticket, and she flew to Los Angeles to begin her life in America. It was 1958. The boy was ten years old. Earlier, rummaging through a shoe box full of old photos, the old man had found a card that his aunt had sent them. It was postmarked August 28, 1958, and it showed Hancock Park in Los Angeles. On the back she had written "...and here children go on the grass to play!" What a marvelous place America was—children could play on the grass. The old man ran his fingers across the postcard. His aunt had chosen it, had written on it, touched it, more than sixty years earlier. After a few months, she had sent a package. What was in it?

As we get older, the old man thought, *we forget more and more; then if senility kicks in, if we wind up with dementia, we're even going to forget how to eat and how to wipe our asses. But wasn't living itself a form of dementia? When we're ten we don't remember the first few years of our lives, when we're adults we have forgotten much of our childhood; we don't recall all the days we lived, just bits and pieces. That's the way the brain works, that's how memory functions, a psychologist would say. And even if we had a perfect memory and remembered every detail of every day, once we die we are completely erased, so what is the point? Maybe there is no point. Maybe we find ourselves in a rushing stream, trying to keep our heads above water, birds flying in a blue sky, black against lazy clouds, pines lining the banks, the sun's warmth on our skin, until we plunge down the waterfall and it's all over.* So, what was in the package his aunt sent? Mickey Mouse hats, he remembered that. Candy, pencils and key chains probably, but of the latter he didn't have a visual representation, only a subterranean feeling of sorts. A year later his aunt showed up at the door— she didn't like America, she said, and she missed Genova.

The old man remembered his aunt in front of the door, but nothing else of that day. Just an image torn from a book, and how ephemeral it was. He closed his eyes and tried to see it but couldn't. What did his aunt wear? How many suitcases did she have? What did his mother and sister say? What was that memory made of? Biochemical electrical activity of neurons in his brain, vague, unclear—more of a feeling than a vivid image; he could see it and yet not see it—his aunt at the door, the surprise of his mother, the living room, the marble floor. What did the floor look like? His mother would wax it and then he and Sandrina had to walk on it by dragging squares of cloth under their shoes, to keep it shining. But he could not see that floor now—sixty years had effaced it.

One Sunday, after having been sick for several days with bronchitis, his mother and his aunt Avia took the boy and his sister to see *The Ten Commandments* at a big theater in Via Venti Settembre, in the city center. It was very crowded, and Angelo, his aunt's new boyfriend, had to sit on the step, next to the seats. Angelo was a serious, hardworking man, and would later marry Avia. They were all dressed in their Sunday best. He was impressed when Moses's staff turned into a snake and he parted the Red Sea. What happened after the movie? Did they go for a walk to the fountain in Piazza de Ferrari? How did they get home? By bus? Tram? Taxi? He hated how only bits of his past were available to him, and even those were vague, unclear. How did the rest of the day unfold?

Forgetfulness, like an expanding acid, was the essence of death itself—for wasn't death at its core a kind of forgetting? Cells no longer able to repair themselves, neurons and synapses degrading over time—forgetfulness dissolved his recollections. He heard it often: "Old people live in the past; they spend so much time dwelling on their memories." But wasn't that what we all were, our memories? If we had no memories, we would not know our name, where we lived, or who we were. *The future is not yet, and the moment is here and gone, so aren't we made of the past?*

HE HAD FLUNKED the examination for entrance to the sixth grade, so his mother enrolled him in a private school run by religious brothers of the Marist Order. A bus took the boy to school and dropped him home in the early evening. Before class began, they had to kneel on the marble floor and pray the rosary. The teacher, a stern young man in his thirties, wore thick eyeglasses and a black cassock. They ate lunch in a dining room at long tables covered with white tablecloths. The teachers had a glass of red wine in front of their plates. In the afternoon he had to sit in study hall and do his homework. Once, he spoke to the boy who sat next to him, and the brother who walked back and forth through the aisles slapped him on his right ear. Another time, the teacher gave him a black book and told the boy to write on it whenever he had a bad thought. What gave him bad thoughts was seeing Brigitte Bardot at the movies. On the big screen, she seemed a goddess, and he couldn't stop thinking about her sultry eyes, full lips, and shapely white legs.

For a class assignment, he had to write an essay on what he would like to be when he grew up. He wrote that he would have liked to become a missionary. The teacher liked the essay, and soon after the boy received several letters written by boys from different schools, praising him and encouraging him in his vocation. He didn't know what to make of all this attention. He was thirteen. One morning, sitting by a window on the bus on the way to school, the boy noticed on the sidewalk a woman in a green dress. Her skirt was short, and she wore fishnet stockings and black high-heeled shoes. As she walked by, he knew deep down that he didn't want to become a missionary. The idea of becoming a priest or a brother, dedicating his life to God and going to Africa to proselytize, filled him with dread. Why had he written that essay? He retreated from activities connected to his old desire of becoming a missionary, to the disappointment of the teacher.

At the end of the school year it was time to take the test again—the test that would determine whether he could go on to the sixth grade or not. His mother bought him a new fountain pen and dressed in a nice shirt, dress pants and jacket, the boy walked to school to take the examination. The test involved the students standing in front of tables with teachers behind them who asked questions. For the math test, he sat with other students in a classroom while a teacher wrote a problem on the board. No matter how hard he tried, he could not solve it. Other pupils had difficulties also, and the teacher explained on the board how to arrive at the answer. But in spite of the helpful hints, he could not solve the problem. He walked home knowing he had flunked the test. What would his mother say? After all the money spent on a year of private school, he had failed a second time. When the official results arrived, the boy did indeed flunk the test. "How could you not pass? Didn't you study? What are you going to do now?" asked his mother in dismay.

When his father's ship stopped again in Genova, his father went to talk to Vittorio Serra, the director of the private school where after the war he had studied Italian. The director suggested that if the boy was not cut out for academic work, he could embark on a course of study to become an accountant. First, however, he had to finish three years of junior high, so in the fall of 1961 the boy took courses in Italian, Latin, geography and math at the Istituto Serra.

Italian literature was his favorite subject, taught by a young blond woman with whom he fell madly in love. He sat in the front row and occasionally dropped his pen so he could watch her legs as he bent down to pick it up. There were perhaps ten or fifteen pupils in the class and he befriended Giulio, who lived in a spacious apartment in Corso Sardegna with his parents and older brother. The boy would occasionally go to visit Giulio, who showed him his model airplanes, Meccano set and collection of soccer players' cards.

One evening, his mother and aunt dragged him to see a film he found boring and one scene scary and disturbing. An old man is seen on an empty street. The sun is high in the sky and no one is around. The old man looks at a clock with no hands. He sees someone up ahead, but the man doesn't turn around when addressed, and as the old man touches the man's coat, it crumples to the ground. A funeral carriage pulled by a horse appears, the carriage's wheel hits a rock, it comes off its axel, the carriage drops, a coffin falls on the street and the cover partially comes off. The old man gets closer, moves his hand toward the coffin, and the corpse's hand grabs his. The old man pulls back his hand in horror, and the cover falls off completely to reveal the face of the corpse, which is the same as the old man's. The following day in school, he mentioned to the teacher that he had gone to see *Wild Strawberries* and he hadn't liked it. She replied that it was a very worthwhile film and that maybe one day he would appreciate it. She had been right. As a young man, he saw *Wild Strawberries* at the Unicorn Theatre in La Jolla and had been spellbound by it, and as time passed, he bought it as a VHS tape, a DVD and a Blu-ray disc. The older he got, the more poignant the movie became. He used to identify with the two young men who catch a ride with the old man and his daughter-in-law, then years later, he identified with the old man's son, but lately, he identified with the old man.

A memory appeared somewhere in the old man's brain from the year 1961, self-contained, disconnected from what came before and after: he and Giulio carrying a box not far from the school, beyond a bridge crossing the Bisagno River. They passed a huge billboard of Fellini's film *La Dolce Vita*, but what was in the box? Why were they carrying it and where were they to deliver it? He held one side and Giulio the other, and as they walked past a newsstand, they saw their teacher, Signorina Ornella D'Amato. She stopped and smiled. She wore an elegant dress and high heels, and her blond hair seemed like a cascade of gold. She greeted them, and he had felt ashamed of being a fourteen-year-old boy.

Another floating memory. He was waiting outside on the sidewalk as his brother was buying a used Fiat 600. Through the large window he could see his brother talking to two men in suits, and after a long time, Noé came out with a smile on his face. Then the boy was riding in the car, his brother at the wheel. What did Noé say? The details, the density, texture and smell of that day, were gone forever.

THE OLD MAN turned his eyes toward the bookcase on his left. The book he wanted was on the very top, a few inches from the ceiling. He got up, climbed the two steps of the ladder to reach the volume, picked it up and sat down again. It was the textbook for the course in literature. Ornella, his teacher, assigned poems to memorize and short prose pieces to read. The 900-page tome had been paperbound, but after the leaves began to detach, he had convinced his mother to have it hardbound. It amazed him that he still had it, sixty years later. He opened it and smelled the pages—the faint chemical and musty scent—was that how the book smelled in 1961, or how the years had made it smell.

The old man flipped through the yellowing leaves of the text. Ornella had marked the poems they needed to memorize, and the blue pen marks were still next to some of the poems' titles: "Saint Martin and Before San Guido" by Giosué Carducci, Giovanni Pascoli's "The Kite," Giacomo Leopardi's "Saturday Night in the Village," and many more. The textbook turned out to be one of his favorites, and years later, he would not only reread the poems he had memorized, but the pieces he had never read before.

It was getting late. He went to bed, but a few

minutes after lying down he felt some resistance in his sinuses. He began to think of the virus, the pandemic. Hundreds of new cases every day in the county, as well as several deaths. He rose as pain shot up his sides from his lower back and returned to the study. The dog slept peacefully in his little bed. The old man took a diazepam and sat down in the chair. He noticed the other books from his childhood that had survived all the moves, all the ups and downs of his life, and now rested at the very top of the bookcase. He got up, retrieved them, and sat down again. He held the first book his mother gave him. The occasion had been the day of the Epiphany, in 1958. It was an illustrated hardbound copy of *The Boys of Paul Street*, by Molnár, in Italian translation. The boards were detached and the spine was missing. The first time he held that book he had been ten; now he was an old man. The sixty years that passed between the two events were gone. One moment it had been the sixth of January 1958; the next moment it was 2020. As he ran his fingers across the pages and looked at the illustrations, the radical disconnection between the two time frames threatened his grounding in reality. Then he took a look at *Rockets Through Space* by Lester Del Rey. How excited he had been when his mother bought him that book, a white rocket with red fins on the front cover! He loved stories and movies about space travel, but his mother told him men were never going to the moon, it was just make-believe, and all that fantasizing was not good for him. And now, thought the old man, men had gone to the moon more than half a century in the past. It had seemed to his mother and so many others an impossibility, the stuff of science fiction, yet now it was just another event mentioned in history books.

He began to feel sleepy, so he put the books away and shuffled back to the bedroom.

THE OLD MAN woke up early. His painful back made it hard to get up, but he rolled on his right side, pushed up with his elbow and swung his legs downward. He went downstairs to pick up the mug of moka coffee with soy milk his wife had left for him on the counter. She had gone swimming at La Jolla Shores.

Back in bed, he began reading the newspapers on his iPad as he sipped the coffee. He scanned the *San Diego Union-Tribune* before carefully going over the comics, which he considered the most important part, then he flipped the virtual pages of the *Washington Post* and *The New York Times*. In his youth he had carefully read most of the articles dealing with current affairs and politics, but as he got older, world events and politics became sources of anger and frustration. Either things remained more or less the same or they changed for the worse. The big-brained primates constantly fought over territory and dominance, strutting arrogantly in their expensive clothes, flaunting their status. They talked in platitudes and worn-out ideological doublespeak, uttering words like *our democracy, freedom, liberty, national security, the sacredness of life, free enterprise.*

If he had not retired, he would have been in the classroom, talking about philosophy. Then he remembered that with the pandemic in full swing, he would have been on Zoom. Could philosophy be done on Zoom? No. At least not well. He was glad not to be in the classroom, not in these times, when people were so easily offended, when he would have to be constantly on the alert, making sure he did not say anything that could be construed as offensive by someone.

One semester, some students went to complain to the dean that he had questioned the existence of God. And this was after he had patiently explained at the beginning of the course that in philosophy, beliefs are questioned and arguments analyzed. He challenged their assumptions, questioned their most cherished beliefs, especially in the critical thinking class. Most of them clung to religious dogmas, holding conventional views; some were invested in conspiracy theories. Many of them did not read the assignments, did not ask questions or make comments. But there were the students who were serious and studious, and they made it all worthwhile. Chris Edwards had been a wiry nineteen-year-old who had taken his Intro to Philosophy course in 1994. A serious young man eager to learn, he took all the courses the middle-aged man taught, and when he transferred to Fullerton State University he majored in philosophy. Chris had gone on to earn a degree in library science, and was now a librarian for the Orange County Library System. Throughout the years, Chris and the middle-aged man kept in touch, and when the old man thought of him, he realized that his teaching had been fruitful.

Now, due to the pandemic, he would have conducted the courses long distance, on the computer. What would Socrates or Plato have thought? The philosopher could have been in his underwear sitting at the kitchen table, talking about the existence of God or free will, while the students could have been sitting in bed or on their living room sofas. They could have had the video turned off and texted their friends or watched clips on Instagram or TikTok. To wake up early, get cleaned up and dressed, go to a particular place and sit in a classroom with others, the professor in the flesh, there was something to be said for that; something could be created in such a space, something that evaded Zoom classes.

After a long hot shower, he felt better. As he was going downstairs, he heard a whine. It was Berry. A seventeen-year-old poodle and Lhasa apso mix, the little black dog was standing at the top of the stairs. Lately, Berry had become deaf and couldn't see very well. The vet cardiologist had said Berry had leaky heart valves, so he had to take medication twice a day for it. He also had arthritis, was prone to pancreatitis, and choked and coughed occasionally due to a trachea problem. "Come on, Berry, I'll take you outside," the old man said to the dog, and he carried him downstairs. He let him out and began to make some drip coffee. He had received a bag of special Colombian beans from a local roaster and was eager to try it. And so the day unfolded.

AT 10:30 P.M., he kissed his wife good night and went back into the study. Berry would now be asleep in his little bed by the philosophy bookcases, next to the lowest shelf, the one with the Wittgenstein and

philosophy of language books. The dog had plush, comfortable beds in the family room and the bedroom, but lately, he preferred the one in the study. He remembered Billy, the Brittany Spaniel they had welcomed in the family when his son Joseph was four years old. An energetic, playful dog, Billy died after a battle with cancer and chemotherapy treatments. It had been a painful loss, and now Berry was nearing the end. Entropy, impermanence, life cycles, those were common words, easily understandable concepts, but abstract. It pained him to see them embodied in living beings.

There was a time when the old man could stay up until one or two in the morning and read, or when he was a student at the university, write a term paper. But now, soon after dinner, he felt drowsy, too sleepy to read or write. But he resisted going to bed—he knew he would not fall asleep, so he'd stay in the study until his eyes began to close, and then he'd force himself to go to bed. As he lay in darkness, he felt oppressed by the weight of his years, as if time had begun to squeeze him. Half a century earlier, striding down the sidewalk, shoulders back and spine erect, feeling no pain, he had basked in the knowledge that he was young. Ascending, the world his to explore, the future extending indefinitely ahead, he had at least half a century in front of himself, but now it was gone. He was still in the present moment, but now he was an old man. That was the trick, the subterfuge. It was always the present moment, but while there had been a moment when he was young, now he was old. *Panta rei*. Everything flows. Here today, gone tomorrow. Yes, it was a cliché, but he liked some clichés. Dust in the wind. Riding on the Ducati through trees and curves on the mountain roads behind Genova, holding on to his brother. It had been so real, so vivid, and now those moments were gone. Yes, he had the memories, but they were ghostly, fleeting representations of what had been lived experience. That's the nature of things, a Buddhist would say; you suffer because you are clinging to the past. Cherish it but let it go. But he didn't want to let it go.

His wife already in bed, the dog sleeping next to the bookcase, the old man sat in his chair and wasted time on the iPad until midnight, then went to bed. But soon after he rested his head on the pillow, he thought his sinuses were getting congested, felt like he could not breathe freely. It was happening again: Kronos, the god of time, was holding him in his hand and squeezed. The old man got up and went back to the study.

He turned on the lamp with its warm yellow glow, sat in the chair and rested his eyes on the *Expulsion*. He reached behind the side table and retrieved the H&K P30 9-millimeter pistol, released the magazine, took the rounds out one by one, then put them back in. They didn't look that big, but they were hollow points. Then he inserted the magazine and racked the slide. Now there was a round in the chamber, and all he had to do was make a swift movement, point the pistol in his ear or mouth and pull the trigger. Then the pain, the anxiety, the inescapable truth that he was old and falling apart, the raw truth that he had lived most of his life and what awaited was more pain and suffering—after all, the wear and tear on his body was only going to get worse—the dreadful feeling of an eternal damnation would be gone.

But he was not going to blow his head off. There were others to consider: his wife, children, relatives. "Let us not speak falsely now, for the hour is getting late..." The old man remembered the Bob Dylan song, and how often he used to think of suicide when young. Granted, he had flirted with it, only flirted. He took the magazine out of the pistol, pulled the slide and the round popped out. He inserted it back in the magazine, then put the pistol behind the table again. Berry curled up in his bed slept peacefully, but his side moved up and down a little too fast. *I hope he's okay*, the old man thought as he leaned back and closed his eyes. He wanted to go back to 1962.

5

GENOVA, 1962–63

As the fourteen-year-old boy stood on the roof of the apartment building in Corso Sardegna looking out over a sea of edifices, campaniles and rooftops, a longing sparked deep inside him and expanded to encompass not only his body but the whole city. The green dome of the Church of Holy Faith loomed in the foreground; several blocks past the church was the private school. He imagined Ornella sitting at her desk, discussing a poem, the literature anthology open in front of her. He had stopped going; he wasn't doing well in math and Latin, and his mother didn't want to waste more money. He had seen an advertisement in a magazine for a correspondence course that led to a license for repairing electrical appliances. It wasn't a bad way to make a living, to sit alone at a table in a shop surrounded by blenders and toasters, not having to talk to anyone. It would have been just like hiding in the dark space between the school and the wall, with no one to mock, laugh, throw rocks, insult or stare.

Solitary peace, no eyes to scrutinize him except for the eye of God, always looming above, eager to judge and punish. And he could make a living, buy his bread and books. He talked his mother into it, and so he began to receive thick envelopes with lessons on the theory of electricity and some simple electrical components that he had to work with, then send back the homework.

But the boy pined for Ornella and reread poems in his anthology of literature. Ornella. Tall, blond, slim, smart. He would picture her smiling from behind the desk, a goddess on the run, hiding from Zeus. Feminine principle, warm, nurturing, erotic. She was the portal to mysteries, salvation, eternal life and love.

He bought a book by Giacomo Leopardi; he especially liked the poems "To Silvia" and "Infinity." He read and reread "To Silvia," about a girl the poet listened to as she sang from afar. At times Leopardi got up from his desk where he spent hours studying, went to the terrace and listened to her voice, but she abruptly died in the "flower of youth." His companion of sweet innocence gone, Leopardi ended the poem by telling her that "at the appearance of truth you unhappy one fell, and with your hand from afar pointed to cold death and a naked tomb." Is truth death? Are the stories that comfort us at their core just lies we tell ourselves to shield us from the truth?

"Infinity" is a short poem, where the poet, sitting by a hedge, gazes at the horizon obstructed by plants and trees and imagines unending spaces, superhuman silences and a deep quiet that make him think of eternity and the passing of ages. In that immensity his thinking drowns, and it's sweet to founder in that sea, he says. Maybe that was what the boy longed for as he looked beyond the roofs and church domes toward the hazy horizon. Perhaps in Ornella he longed for an unending space, a superhuman silence and a deep quiet. Yes, he would happily have drowned in the immensity of Ornella; he would have found it sweet to founder in that sea.

In the summer they went to the beach, where the boy spent hours in the water, looking at the sandy bottom with a mask and snorkel, dreaming of going deeper with a scuba tank, like the divers he read about in *Underwater World*. When he needed to take a break from snorkeling he lay on a towel and read science fiction novels, as his sister looked for shells and made sand castles.

The year was coming to an end. His grandmother came to visit for Christmas, bringing smoked eels from the Orbetello Lagoon, salami and cheeses. Noé and Bruna came to visit with baby Fabrizio; Avia and her boyfriend Angelo, who lived in a nearby apartment, brought panettone and bubbly wine.

IT WAS NOW EARLY 1963. His father took him to the American Consulate so he could apply for a passport. They were preparing to move to America. Ecstasy! He considered himself an American; his father had brought him a canvas belt with a brass buckle, and he had glued a picture of an American flag on it. As he walked along the street in the neighborhood of Marassi, surveying the gray tenement buildings huddled on the hills beyond the Bisagno River, he walked on air. *Go ahead, stare at me*, he thought. *I'm not one of you, I'm an American, and soon I'll be away from here. I'll be in my country, the land of John Wayne and the Marines, Kennedy and skyscrapers.*

John F. Kennedy, his hero, smiled from photos, and during the Cuban Missile Crisis, the boy rushed down the stairs to buy the newspaper so he could read all the articles about the unfolding events, see the grainy black-and-white images of missiles on Soviet ships near Cuba. He liked the smell of the ink on the newspaper, liked how it felt as he held it in his hands. What a marvelous thing! He woke up wondering what had been going on in the world and as soon as he could, he'd run down the stairs and walk to the nearest newsstand, hand the man half hidden by stacks of papers and magazines the coins, then rush back home holding the paper, full of news of the world and the city where he lived, articles about books and movies, what the cinemas were showing.

The day finally arrived. June 19, 1963. His brother made several trips to take the baggage and all of them to the ship, and as the boy sat in the back of the Fiat 600, he glanced back at two old women dressed in black who sat on chairs outside their building's door. What was he thinking as the car drove down Corso Sardegna? He had lived all his life in Genova and the mountain village behind the city, with a few vacations in Orbetello, and now he was going to live in America! He had dreamed of this as far back as he could remember, and the dream was becoming true.

At the pier, people gathered and talked. Attractive

women in summer attire and dark glasses, men in light suits and flowery shirts. The boy had never seen such people except in the movies. They walked on the plank to board the *SS Constitution*, and his brother accompanied them to their cabin, a small room with four bunk beds. Noé sat on one of the lower bunks and talked to his parents, then turned to Sandrina and said, "Next time I see you, you'll be a woman." When it was time, Noé got up and left with tears in his eyes. They followed him and as he walked down to the pier, they stood at the ship's railing and waved. His aunt had said goodbye at the apartment and now stood on the pier, in a dress and sunglasses, holding a bouquet of carnations. How did she get there? Had Noé given her a ride? Why didn't she come to the cabin with his brother? The old man could not remember.

Eating meals in the dining room was like going to a restaurant every day. People dressed in suits and dresses for dinner and sat at round tables with white tablecloths. Each family had its own reserved table and the same waiter for the entire trip. Theirs was a very sad-looking man, and even though his sister tried to make him smile, he never did.

The *USS Constitution* was a luxurious ocean liner. President Truman and his wife had been passengers, as had Grace Kelly when she sailed to Monaco to wed Prince Rainier. Even in tourist class there was a cinema and a playroom, a bar, a swimming pool and a huge ballroom. As the days passed, he had long conversations with a slender young man who was the son of a diplomat from the Dominican Republic. As they talked about books and writers, the boy became aware of his own eloquence, of how easily thoughts flowed into words and danced out of his mouth. But the diplomat's son was in first class and he was in the tourist section, so after a while they lost track of each other. The other friend the boy made was Antonio Liburdi, who had boarded at Naples. Why did he still remember the name? Antonio was going to New Jersey, to work for some relatives, maybe in a restaurant. They met every day, went to the game room and played foosball, walked on deck and talked. Sandrina made friends with a girl her age and his parents began to talk to her parents. It was a family from Calabria.

In the middle of the Atlantic the ship encountered rough seas. He and his sister felt seasick and threw up the whole night in the cabin, while their parents went to the ballroom. How did the cabin look? Did he read during the trip? Did he fantasize about life in America? Did he long for Ornella? The briny scent of the sea, vast and restless, all around as far as he could see, the warmth of the sun and the cool breeze on his face and hair, the promise of the future in America sparked like electricity from his head to his feet.

One day they were told the *SS Independence*, the sister ship of the *Constitution*, was going to pass them on the way to Genova. As they watched on deck, the ship sailed by with blasts from the horn, a white trail behind it, a mirror reflection.

On June 29, at dawn, they approached New York. They were on deck with many others, including Antonio and the family from Calabria. The Statue of Liberty, gray, silent, seen so often in movies and photos, stood tall in the distance, and skyscrapers loomed ashore in the pale dawn, the scattered lighted windows like eyes opening to the new day. They all gazed speechless as if struck by an apparition. He glanced at Antonio, who stared at the sight in awe. They had arrived at the new world, after dreaming about it for so many years.

He said goodbye to Antonio. They promised to write to each other, then disappeared in the blur of disembarking and going through Customs. Some of the Italian families had brought cured meats, cheeses and other edibles, only to have them confiscated by officials, who no doubt were going to feast on them later.

6

THE NEW WORLD, 1963–1965

They rode by taxi to Don's apartment. His father's friend, the jovial tall, well-dressed man who came to dinner when the ship docked in Genova and left with tomato sauce on his white shirt, had told the boy's father they could stay at his place, since he was out of town. It was a long ride to Hoboken, New Jersey. In the small bachelor apartment, his mother tried to find something in the kitchen to make for lunch.

While in the apartment he wrote a letter to his friend Giulio, where he expressed the desire to be back in Italy. He had dreamed for years of being in America, and now that he had arrived, he felt like he wanted to go back. Why? Was it fear of the unknown? He sat in a chair and wrote, tired, his parents in a bad mood. His mother had found some spaghetti and that's what they ate, with some kind of tomato sauce she found in a plastic pouch. They stayed at the apartment for a few days while his father arranged for their trip to El Centro, California. At his mother's insistence that evening, or perhaps the following one, they had taken a bus to New York City. They walked into a drugstore to buy a Coke. It tasted so good, ice cold, on the hot and humid day. They walked around Central Park and midtown at night. In Times Square, they saw a huge billboard of a cigarette-smoking man; the smoke came out of his mouth and floated up in white clouds into the night sky.

At the end of their stay in New Jersey, they boarded a plane for Los Angeles. It was their first flight, but while his mother squirmed in fear, he was excited. From Los Angeles, they flew on a small turboprop to San Diego. He kept eyeing the young, sexy hostess as they approached the airport in late morning, on a clear July day. From the air, it looked like a city on the Riviera. His aunt Mary and uncle George were waiting and drove them to El Centro. He was impressed by their car, a big Chevrolet sedan. Sitting in the back with his sister and mother, he gazed out the window as the city slowly receded to give way to mountains and then the desert, until the car stopped behind a small bungalow. His heart sank. He had expected a big ranch house like the ones he used to see in the movies. He had to sleep in the same bed with his cousin Wayne. His other cousin, Carolyn, was a hairdresser, and she would give him a cut in her shop a few days later.

El Centro. A small desert town where in summer temperatures ranged from the 90s to the 120s. There wasn't much to do except watch TV or read. The boy was disappointed but took things in stride. Everything was new, and even though he was in a desert town, he was in America, the land of opportunity, the most powerful nation in the world, his country, rich and welcoming—with the youthful John Kennedy promising to lead him to a new frontier.

As the days passed, he met his other relatives—his aunt Hideko and uncle Caesar and their children, his cousins Steve, Eric and Pam. They lived fifteen miles away from El Centro, in Brawley, and the day they went to visit, Caesar was barbecuing in the front yard. Handsome, with a wide smile, he greeted them profusely, pointing to a bucket full of ice and sodas. Steve, sixteen, tall and slim, looked like a young Charles Bronson. Pam, fifteen, was trying to communicate with Sandrina, and Eric, thirteen, showed them his trumpet.

A few days later they drove to Santa Ana so they could meet his father's brother Joe, his wife and their children, Gary, Bobby, Marlo and Rosa. While the boy's father had fought with the US Army in Europe, Joe had been stationed in the Pacific Theatre and had served as a translator.

The boy took a liking to twelve-year-old Gary right away. Short and wiry, Gary was quiet, and even though they didn't speak to each other, there was a feeling of camaraderie between them. The family had rice and mackerel for dinner, then went for a walk on a pier.

Back in El Centro, it was hot. The boy had never experienced that kind of heat; it enveloped him like an electric blanket. He was overwhelmed by the changes, finding himself in a small town just a few miles away from the Mexican border, living in a small house with his new relatives, unable to speak or understand English.

One morning he went for a walk with his father. After a few blocks they were downtown, where they took Fifth Avenue and approached a one-story building. They passed by Blevins' Photography, and the next business's large window announced, in gold letters, "Ricardo Jimenez, Notary Public, Tax Services." He followed his father into the cool air-conditioned room. "Is the boss in?" his father asked the receptionist, who sat behind a desk typing. "He's in his office, go right in," she said as she pointed behind her. Down the hall, in a small room behind a desk, sat a distinguished-looking man in his early forties, who reminded the boy of the actor Anthony Quinn.

"Shiggy! My god!" he shouted as he got up. "You're back!"

"I got here a few weeks ago with my wife and kids. This is my son."

Ricardo turned to look at the boy and shook his hand. "Your father and I went to school together. Sit down, sit down."

His father and Ricardo talked for a long time, but the boy didn't understand what they said. He noticed on the left wall, right next to the desk, a bulletin board covered with holy cards, church announcements and photographs. As they were finally getting up to leave, Ricardo turned to the boy and said, "So you'll be going to Central High. It's a good school; you'll like it there." Before going back to his aunt's house his father took the boy to Main Street, just a street over, and at a small hamburger place called Mel's, they had two tall, frosted glasses of root beer.

His father needed to go back to New York for work—his ship, the *Exchester*, was going to sail soon. He had planned to leave them at his sister's house, but the boy's mother made it clear she wasn't going to live with her sister-in-law, so he rented a small house on Vine Street, in El Centro. The boy and his sister were going to have their own rooms, finally. Before leaving, his father enrolled him at Central High and on the first day, he walked to school in trepidation with his pocket Italian-English dictionary. He knew only about twenty words of English, so the counselor had suggested he take an ESL course, in addition to Latin, wood shop and another class.

On that first day of school, during lunch, he found the cafeteria intimidating, so he walked outside and ordered a hamburger at the window. When he got it, he unwrapped it and examined it—opened the bun and looked in alarm at the gray meat patty. It had a strange animal smell, and he threw it in the trash can and just ate the bun. From that day on, his mother made him olive loaf or avocado sandwiches and that's what he ate outside, sitting at a table.

His sister started the fifth grade at Harding Elementary School, which was just a block down from their house.

One Friday morning in November, he sat in Ms. McCracken's Latin class. A short, wiry woman who was married to the chemistry teacher, she made Latin interesting by talking about the exploits of the Ancient Romans and her visits to Italy. He sat at his desk, thinking about how after one more class he was going to have lunch, when an announcement came through the speaker that hung on the wall. President Kennedy had been shot. Later it was announced that he had died. In the early afternoon the boy sat in Mrs. Mina's ESL class feeling despondent, restless in his seat, not paying attention, so the teacher asked him if he was all right. After classes, as he walked across campus, he saw two girls walking on the green lawn. One was crying; the other girl had her arm around her. The boy's hero had died, and maybe with him, the dream.

That Sunday morning, he sat in the living room watching the news on the black-and-white TV. Lee Harvey Oswald was escorted out of a room by deputies wearing cowboy hats when he suddenly buckled over, and pandemonium ensued. The killer of the president was assassinated on national television by a nightclub owner. What was going on? A lone sniper in a nearby building killed the leader of the most powerful nation of the world. How could it have happened? The secret service, the FBI, local police—no one had thought of securing all the nearby buildings. Then he had watched Oswald getting shot in real time on TV. It seemed like one of the B movies he used to see at the Capital Theater.

Home from school, he ate a snack, then watched *Sea Hunt* and *Leave It to Beaver* on TV. Lloyd Bridges as Mike Nelson, the freelance scuba diver, made the boy yearn for the underwater world that for years he'd wanted to explore, and the Beaver lived in the mythical America he had dreamed about for so much of his life. Only many years later, he realized he would never have been accepted in that world.

What else did he remember of that time? Riding in a car while "I Wanna Hold Your Hand" played on the radio. It was evening, dark outside. He had never heard music like that.

Soon after they had settled in El Centro, in the house on Vine Street, he wrote a letter to Ornella. What had he written as a lonely fifteen-year-old in a new country with no friends? She replied, and he wrote a second letter. Ornella never answered it. He had probably declared his love for her. How pathetic.

What he hated most about school, besides the fear of having to speak in class if called upon by the teachers, was gym class. Having to go into a smelly locker room and changing, running around on the field and playing baseball or football, games alien to him, that he could not play as well as the others. Then forty-five minutes later, taking a communal shower, getting dressed and running to the next class. Every Friday, taking the stinking tee shirt and shorts from the locker home to be washed.

Then there was the agony of wood shop. He liked Mr. Hammond, the teacher, but had no interest in using tools and building a birdhouse or a picture frame. One day Mr. Hammond showed the class a 16-millimeter film on the consequences of smoking, and in one scene, the removal of a tumor from a man's lung was shown. That kept the boy from smoking for a couple of years. He got into a fight in wood shop one afternoon, but Mr. Hammond broke it up and never mentioned it later.

Early in the school year, he checked out from the library *The Murders in the Rue Morgue* by Edgar Allan Poe, his first English-language novel. He read it with the help of his trusted dictionary. He was determined to learn English as fast as he could. He liked the librarian, a serious-looking woman with glasses who helped him find books he was interested in.

The first time he heard Bob Dylan was during lunch one day, when someone drove him and a couple of other guys to his house to listen to a new album. As he sat in the living room listening to the music that came from the wooden stereo cabinet, the nasal voice accompanied by the guitar chords seemed like something from another planet. He didn't understand the words and sat in that living room without speaking, since he only knew a little English, and experienced the familiar feeling of being different, of not belonging.

When they had lived in Sella, in the mountains north of Genova, his brother Noé had brought home the motor of a record player and a speaker, placed a black 78 disc on the spindle and a lively polka suddenly burst in the room. His brother and his mother danced as he and Sandrina laughed. That was in 1955. Noé later built an elegant teak cabinet for the player and bought many 78 discs. His mother liked to listen to opera and would play Mario Lanza singing *"Vesti la Giubba"* over and over. Now that he was in America in the early 1960s, he was being introduced to quite different music.

His mother told his father that if he didn't come home, she would return to Italy, so he quit the merchant marine and came back, this time never to leave again. He had driven across the country with his friend Don, who stayed for a couple of days, then went back to New Jersey. The boy was glad to see

Don, who was always well dressed; he looked like a businessman instead of a machine operator on a ship.

His father applied for a position at the US Post Office and began working as a mailman. He bought a 1962 green Chevrolet sedan, and on Sunday mornings they began to go for picnics in Pine Valley, a small mountain community in East San Diego County, where it was cooler and they could spend a few hours away from El Centro. They would find a picnic table, spread blankets on the grass and relax. His mother read her Italian magazines and his father, the newspaper. The boy and his sister walked to the couple of nearby shops that sold snacks and trinkets or played with a ball. They stopped on the way back at a little store that sold olives, local honey, beef jerky and candy. They'd buy a jar of olives or some chocolates. It became a ritual, before plunging back into the desert, another week of school ahead, to stop at the little store flanked by boulders and oaks.

A couple of years later, his parents purchased a house in a newer part of town. His mother planted a palm tree on the side and bougainvillea in front of the living room window. In the large backyard, she planted succulents and cactus next to the fence and pomegranate trees by the sides. After so many years of living in apartments, except for the brief time at the House of the Fig in the mountains, she finally had a spacious home, but it wasn't on the Italian Riviera, it was in the desert, far away from her family. Her son Noé and her sister Avia sent letters and cards, which she eagerly awaited.

The boy had somehow survived his first year at Central. His English had improved, but he still spoke with a heavy accent and was self-conscious about it. During the summer he took a course in typing, and he learned how to type on new, state-of-the-art equipment: an electric IBM typewriter. With temperatures in the 110s, after the class he would go home to watch TV or read. He was now a sophomore and even though school was still a source of anxiety and stress, he liked English, history and science.

In the fall of 1964, on the field during gym class he met Frank, a junior, who lived just three houses down from his, on the corner of Brighton and Imperial Avenues. They started to talk about the pending presidential election and soon became friends. He went to Frank's house often to listen to records or discuss politics.

He also became friends with Gary W., whose father was a Choctaw Indian and mother was a schoolteacher. Gary W. had an anti-authoritarian bent, which he liked. They lived a few blocks apart and often walked around in the evening when it cooled down, talked and fantasized about the future. One day when Gary invited him to his house, his mother opened the front door and said, "I'm tired of seeing you with that bug-eyed Jap," then slammed the door. He was surprised by the woman's reaction, since she had seemed friendly at other times. *"I'm tired of seeing you with that bug-eyed Jap."* He still remembered those words more than fifty years later.

Wayne Johnson taught life science, which became the boy's favorite class. Mr. Johnson was a tall, slim man in his late thirties with a butch cut and a wide smile who was especially interested in botany and took the class on field trips. On one trip they went with a school bus to Palomar Mountain in North San Diego County, where they visited the 200-inch Hale Telescope. The boy was impressed by the big silver dome and inside, the telescope looked like something from a science fiction story. It had an aura of sacredness; it was a manifestation of human reason, of the quest for knowledge. In the gift shop he bought an illustrated booklet about the observatory, and he kept it for many years. Later, Mr. Johnson took them on a hike in a nearby park, and as they walked on the trail, he pointed out and discussed trees and plants.

The boy got an A in the class, and he liked it so much that the following semester he took biology with Mrs. Jensen. He fell in love with biology; he couldn't wait for the lab part of the class, when they could look at slides under the microscope. They went on a field trip once to take samples of water and specimens in a pond, and once back in class, he observed in awe the protozoa in the drop of water on the slide. Euglena, amoebas, paramecia with their cilia moving wildly, hydras. Afterward he took Biology 2 and decided to become a biologist. As a member of the Field Science Club, he also went to Painted Gorge, in the Imperial Valley desert. For the occasion, he went to Yellow Mart and bought a geologist's hammer, which he used to dig seashells that had been deposited in the gorge millions of years before, when the desert was underwater. He also took physical science, taught by Mr. Burnett, who was known around campus as the "one-eyed bastard," because of his eye patch. Mr. Burnett had lost an eye years earlier to an infection, and with his black patch he looked like a pirate. He had an area of black and white hair above his forehead like a lonely bush in the desert of the front of his head, the back covered by a thin layer of short salt-and-pepper hair. He drove around town in a red MG roadster, and often, if one walked by his classroom, he could be heard screaming, "You, knucklehead!" While he instilled fear in the beginning, he was a dedicated, fair teacher. The next biology course was biochemistry, which the boy failed miserably. He also failed algebra and trigonometry, and it dawned painfully on him that his dream of becoming a biologist was dashed.

THE OLD MAN got up from the chair. Cool air flowed through the partially open window in front of the desk, and Adam and Eve still walked out of Eden. The old man climbed on the stepladder and retrieved his 1965 yearbook from the top shelf. Due to an error he had gotten it late, so he'd collected no comments or signatures. It had a heavy textured cloth cover, with "La Solana" printed in big letters at the bottom. He sat back down, turned on the reading light and put on his eyeglasses. The photos began to pull at his memories.

The old school gymnasium had been torn down so a new one could be built, and on a two-page spread the old man gazed at the architect's idealized painting of what it would look like: a modern rectangular structure with a large porch, the school's name on the top left of the front wall and underneath, an idealized image of a Spartan head. It's evening; the sky is charcoal, but toward the west there are patches of light. Tall, slender eucalyptus trees flank the building. A big sedan is by the curb; families and couples walk on the paved path that leads to the box office window. Above it a lighted marquee announces, "High School Basketball Tonight 7:30." He stared at the illustration and wondered if the building still stood or if it had been torn down and replaced. It would be fifty-five years old now. It was just one of those drawings architectural firms produce, and yet the old man kept looking at it, as if in a trance. He wished he could have entered into the picture, walked down the sidewalk, smelled the warm, humid air, heard people talk and children laugh as he turned toward the box office window. Once inside he would have found a seat on a bench in the brightly lit gym, on the new polished wooden floor. Cheerleaders would have been warming up the crowd; amid the low roar of hundreds of people, his friend Henry would sit next to him, and they would talk and laugh. Henry had been one of his first friends. He had newly arrived from Mexico with his mother and lived a few blocks away. The old man could still see Henry in his mind's eye, black hair neatly combed, a sly smile and playful eyes. He excelled in math, studied hard and went on to major in engineering at Cal Poly. Was he still alive?

The boy was seventeen years old then, the future spread out in front of him; now he was an old man excavating the past. He knew what so many would have said: "Why waste so much time delving into the past? Stop it! Live in the now; there's still some future." Live in the now? With a raging pandemic that had already killed hundreds of thousands? He couldn't travel, couldn't go to art galleries, museums, plays, concerts or operas. And he was falling apart.

As the old man flipped pages, the senior class officers, students most likely to succeed, best personality, best looking, best dressed and most talented posed and smiled for the camera. They were all white and mostly sons and daughters of the wealthy and powerful in the community. Further on, in a photo of the Future Farmers of America, he recognized Frank, his friend who lived three houses down from his. Frank loved horticulture and art, and after high school he had transferred to Long Beach State University. After graduation he tried to work as an artist but did not like the art scene, so he taught art in high schools but eventually quit and started selling rocks and minerals. He lived mostly in his pickup truck and traveled to Utah, Arizona and other states to dig rocks and fossils he later polished and sold at fairs, swap meets and outdoor markets. The last time he had talked to Frank was thirty years earlier. "I'm going to Africa with a friend to search for minerals," Frank had said. Was he still alive? Should the old man try to find him on Facebook or Google? He closed the book and ran his fingers across the cover. Strange to think that when he first held the yearbook, he was seventeen.

Sandrina was now in middle school, and spent most of her free time reading. She walked to the library and lugged big piles of books home. Often she met Bonnie, her best friend, after school. They talked about books, movies and experimented briefly with a Ouija board. Now that they were teenagers with their own rooms, going to different schools, he and Sandrina didn't spend as much time together, but on many evenings, they still gathered with their parents to watch Bonanza, Rawhide, Combat, and other TV shows.

The boy had made it his most important mission to learn English as fast as possible. He read books with the help of the dictionary, even though it was slow going. In his junior year he joined a book club and read *Cry, the Beloved Country* and *Giants in the Earth*. He preferred science fiction, but these books exposed him to new ideas and themes, and, most importantly, helped him to learn English.

In the summer of 1966, besides working at Desert Seed Company, he helped Frank cut lawns, and with the money they made they took a week's vacation. They traveled by Greyhound to San Diego and walked to the corner of Laurel Street and Pacific Highway, where they waited with their suitcases for the bus to Mission Beach. There, they walked around searching for a rental, looking like a couple of country bumpkins, until a guy took pity on them and rented them his spare room. They spent their days at the beach, sunbathing, fighting the waves and walking on the boardwalk in the evening, when it was cool and breezy. They went to the movies and saw *Divorce Italian Style*, which was a revelation. Marcello Mastroianni played an impoverished Sicilian nobleman who no longer loves his wife and wants to have a relationship with his young cousin, Angela. Since divorce was illegal, he plotted to get rid of his wife so he could marry Angela. Watching the film took him back to his childhood in Italy, when he went to the movies two or three times a week and watched many black-and-white Italian films. The two movie houses in El Centro showed only popular Hollywood fare. That was the first time the young man had been to San Diego without his parents and it was exciting to be in the city he had admired from the plane three years earlier. He was a senior now, and Frank, a year ahead of him, looked forward to going to California State University at Long Beach. After that summer they would see each other only during Christmas vacations.

THE YOUNG MAN needed to have a letter notarized, so he went to see Ricardo Jimenez. As he waited in the front room, he picked up yesterday's *Imperial Valley Press* and looked at the movie section. *Hombre,* a new film starring Paul Newman, was playing at the Crest; maybe he could go that weekend. The receptionist typed furiously; on her desk, besides the typewriter, were in and out boxes stuffed with papers and a coffee mug. A long-stemmed rose stood proudly in a clear tall vase.

"Shiggy! Come on in," said Ricardo as he walked behind a couple who were leaving. He wore a white short-sleeved shirt and a pair of gray slacks. He smiled broadly as he shook the young man's hand. Ricardo eased himself into his black leather chair and put some papers in a folder as the young man sat facing the desk. The young man was amused by how Ricardo liked to call both him and his father Shiggy.

"I was listening to a sermon by Bishop Sheen before that couple came to see me." He pointed to the bulletin board on his right. Among other photos, including one of Ricardo in a Knights of Columbus uniform and some holy cards, was a large black-and-white photo of him dressed in a suit, beaming, next to the famous bishop, Fulton Sheen.

"I brought him to El Centro a few years ago. Nobody believed I could do it, but I wrote him a letter and he came to Imperial Valley," he said with a proud look on his face.

"The first time I saw you, you hadn't even started high school, and look at you now. You graduate next year; what's next?"

"I'm going to Imperial Valley College, but I'm not sure what I want to do."

"Education is the key. When my parents moved to the Valley, we lived in a shack on the outskirts of town and as a kid with bare feet, I'd sell tamales on street corners, but I wanted to learn, and I went to grammar school. Then, even though people wondered why I wanted to keep on going, I went to Central, graduated with your dad in 1940. I married Mae, my grammar school sweetheart, and joined the Navy. I liked numbers, studied accounting, and when I got discharged, I worked for the Internal Revenue Service for many years. In 1950 I opened my own business..." He looked at his bulletin board. "I wonder what I'd be doing if I'd listened to others and stopped going to school."

When the young man left the office and walked back to his car, he thought about what Ricardo had said. He had started from ground zero, but was a successful businessman, an outstanding member of the community. If he did it, why couldn't the young man do it, too?

THE YOUNG MAN had plans to attend the local community college the following year, and with the money he saved working during the summer at Desert Seed Company, he bought a 1955 Chevrolet Power Glide his father found in the want ads. He never drove it to the high school, since all he had to do was cross a street and walk a block to get there.

One day he felt sick and couldn't play baseball during gym class, so he found himself in the gymnasium with the rest of the students who had been excused. He began talking to a girl who had short brown hair and blue eyes. "I'm Roberta," she said. "I don't go out on the field because I have a heart murmur." She had an upturned nose and a charming smile. They began to see each other during lunch period, talked on the phone and went to the movies. Roberta was a Navy brat who had lived most her life on military bases. Her father had been a career master chief and her mother a member of the Women's Army Auxiliary Corps. Roberta's grandmother lived in a detached studio in the backyard, surrounded by shelves of *National Geographic* magazines. They were friendly and generous people, busy raising two little boys and a girl, Roberta's siblings.

On most weekdays he sat at a table outside the cafeteria with Roberta and Dawn, one of her girlfriends, and ate his olive loaf or avocado sandwich and apple, listening to the Beach Boys' "Good Vibrations" over and over, or Sonny and Cher's "I Got You Babe," the music squawking from the outdoor speaker; and on weekends he drove to her house, in the small town of Seeley, an eight-mile ride through fields of alfalfa and lettuce, seagulls flying low over the irrigated crops, Mount Signal on the left and Mexico beyond. With a few eucalyptus and cottonwood trees by the roadside, it was a relaxing drive away from parents and home. Robert, Roberta's father, usually sat in an easy chair smoking a cigarette, and Clara, her mother, in a muumuu and thick eyeglasses, busied herself in the kitchen while their two little boys and girl played in the living room.

When the young man told his mother that his girlfriend had been chosen the "Queen of the Seeley Christmas Parade," she insisted on going to see her, and so in the evening his father drove them to Seeley. They stood by the side of Main Street to watch, and when the float with Roberta approached, he pointed to the charming girl in a fancy dress and silver crown and said, "That's her." The young man's mother was silent for a few seconds, then said, "She's too beautiful for you!" A flash of anger passed through the young man. Why would his mother say that?

The old man put the book away. Strange how time had made it a historical document. The black-and-white photos included one of Roberta as a freshman, cars now considered classics, buildings no longer standing, the student body mostly white in a predominantly Latino area. He vaguely remembered going to pick up the annual yearbook in 1965. He had been seventeen years old, struggling with the language, socially inept, still thinking in his native tongue. Lyndon Johnson was president, Martin Luther King Jr. led civil rights demonstrations in Alabama, young men burned their draft cards on the steps of government offices, *The Sound of Music* was showing in theaters.

"What happened?" asked the seventeen-year-old boy. "From your time, I'm a memory you retrieve once in a while. But I lived. I thought, dreamed, hoped, desired. I followed the Gemini orbital flights, listened to 'Wooly Bully' by Sam the Sham and the Pharaohs and 'Help!' by the Beatles over and over as I lay on my bed, dreaming about the future. I didn't know what I dreamed about was my disappearance, the passing away of my world. You sit there in the chair an old man and try to find me in faded photos and school annuals, you search for something outside your mind that'll bring me back, but I'm gone. You could deny it, say 'no, he lives inside me, he's me,' but I am not you, and I'm gone, forever."

"No, that's not true," replied the old man. "I am you; it's just that time has passed, and I changed in many ways. A lot has happened, but I still think, dream, hope and desire. Your world is gone, but I forged another. Much of what you dreamed, hoped and desired I have accomplished. What I look for in old photos and school annuals is youth and the vivid, clear experience of your days, but you are not a memory I retrieve once in a while, you are me. So let's keep going—the journey is not yet over."

7

EL CENTRO, 1967–1970

When the young man graduated, he began his freshman year at Imperial Valley College, but things were not going well. His heavy accent made him feel different; in the classrooms he felt awkward; parking in the college's lot, he felt embarrassed driving such an old jalopy and ran over a concrete barrier. *I don't belong here*, he thought, so he dropped out.

After a few months, upon the recommendation of Roberta's father, he got a job as a firefighter at the Naval Air Facility in El Centro, where he worked three 24-hour shifts, then was off for four days.

In 1968 the young man celebrated his twentieth birthday. He had recently discovered Simon and Garfunkel after seeing *The Graduate* at the local theater. He bought their album *The Sounds of Silence* and played it over and over in his room. "And in the naked light I saw ten thousand people, maybe more, people talking without speaking, people hearing without listening, people writing songs that voices never shared...And the people bowed and prayed to the neon God they made..." At that time he had a record player on the bedside table, and he would lie on the bed and fall into the mood of the song, a cry of alienation that was also his. In that year, part of America's soul died with Martin Luther King Jr. and Robert Kennedy. President Johnson announced he was not going to run for a second term, more than half a million American troops were in Vietnam, more coffins arrived weekly and violent demonstrations convulsed the country. The naive views of America that had sustained him as he grew up in Italy began to crumble.

The 1955 Power Glide broke down, so he bought a used 1964 blue Chevrolet Bel Air. It had a V8 engine with a manual three gear shifter on the column. He bought a U.S. Divers' two-stage, two-hose regulator, twin air tanks and a spear gun and went diving with Pat Boone, his friend at the fire department. He had fulfilled his childhood dream of diving with scuba tanks, like Captain Nemo in Jules Verne's novel and Mike Nelson in *Sea Hunt*. Noé had sent the young man a wet suit, the pants were too small, but the jacket fit him. How often he had fantasized of scuba diving as he flipped through the pages of *Underwater World* as a boy! Pat Boone was going to Ensenada with his wife, and they invited him along. They stuffed Pat's old Chevrolet with gear and drove off. On the rough, curvy Mexican roads Pat drove like he was being chased by killers. The car screeched around the bends, and they had two blowouts. Pat must have been used to this, because he had two spare tires in the trunk. In Ensenada they camped on the beach, and the following day they hired a man to take them out on a boat. The young man almost caught a huge bass, but he only had the jacket of the wet suit, and at forty feet he was so cold he began to shiver. When he saw the fish he aimed the spear gun and pulled the trigger, but the cold caused his hand to shake and he missed. Later, he caught a moray eel near the surface and Pat's wife cooked it on an open fire. The sun almost at the horizon turned the sky into streaks of yellow and magenta, seagulls flew low and the warm air turned breezy. As they sat on beach chairs and ate the tender chunks of eel with tomatoes, onions and tortillas, he couldn't escape the thought that he had failed. He was the one with the compressed air spear gun; he had been face to face with the bass, but missed.

On TV in the lounge at the fire department, the young man watched the Democratic Convention in dismay. As he sat on a chair drinking a soda, he saw soldiers patrolling the streets, Chicago Police beating demonstrators and fires burning. "Yeah, crack their heads!" yelled some of his fellow firefighters as they watched in glee. This America was so different from the one he dreamed of as a boy growing up in Genova. That America was based on the movies and on the stories he heard from his mother and aunt. That America was not only vast, powerful and rich, but a just country founded on principles of equality, freedom and opportunity for all. A welcoming nation, confident and tolerant, where dreams could come true.

Growing up in Italy he was made to feel as if he didn't belong, but he had the dream of the new world to sustain him, the thought that he was not an Italian, but an American. As the ship approached New York Harbor, as he had laid eyes on the Statue of Liberty just beginning to be awakened by the dawn, he had felt trepidation but also an unconscious conviction that he had arrived home, at last. But five years later, even though he had learned English and graduated from high school, he still felt like an outsider. He spoke with an accent; his last name was still a source of curiosity and derision. And the way he looked was ambiguous. Mexicans spoke to him in Spanish; some people thought he was Polynesian or an Indian.

"You made it," his father told him. "You have a good job with the civil service; it pays well." Yes, as far as his father was concerned, all that remained for him to do was get married, eventually buy a house, and he would have been done. But the young man didn't like sitting in the crash and rescue truck for hours by the runway, as fighter pilots in F4 Phantoms practiced takeoffs and landings so they could go bomb Vietnam. Or the countless drills and the washing of trucks. The long, tedious hours in the barrack where he had to sleep with a bunch of mostly crude guys who on payday went to Mexicali to whore around, gamble and get drunk. Some of them came back four days later broke and begged to borrow some money.

What did the future hold? He didn't want to be a firefighter for the rest of his life. He registered again at the community college and took English, Introduction to Philosophy and other general education courses. The philosophy class was taught by Richard Hann, a thirty-year-old professor who had recently arrived from San Francisco. The topics captivated the young man: theories of human nature, free will and determinism, the existence of God, knowledge and opinion. He eagerly read the assignments, wrote papers and visited the professor often during office hours. Richard Hann sat with his boots propped on his desk, cleaning his fingernails with a Buck knife, and was always available to clarify ideas, give general advice or go over symbolic logic proofs on the small blackboard he had on the wall.

The young man got A's and B's on his first report card, which encouraged him to register for another semester, but the assistant fire chief had told him, "Being a firefighter is a full-time job. You'll need to study fire science and dedicate yourself completely to the profession—you can't do this and go to college full time. You must choose." The young man decided to quit his job and go to college. His father was so angry, he didn't talk to him for months.

Imperial Valley College, six miles northeast of El Centro, was a handful of squat buildings and a gymnasium surrounded by fields. A godforsaken place, some people would think, and yet there were inspiring and accomplished people teaching there, professors with degrees from Oxford, Columbia, Harvard, the University of California and San Francisco State. One of his favorite professors was Lloyd Farrar, who taught history. A jovial man in his forties, Lloyd had graduated from Oberlin and worked on a PhD at Columbia. He taught history at a private school for many years; then, tired of living in New York, he moved to California, where the only position he could find was in the Imperial Valley. Lloyd made history come alive in the classroom. He reenacted medieval battles, alternately pretending to be a knight or an infantryman. Always available to talk to students, he promptly graded and returned tests. Every morning the young man drove through alfalfa and fallow fields, a brown and green sea, already 90 degrees outside, toward a portal to exciting new worlds of philosophy, literature, science, anthropology and film as an art form.

Outside was a barren rural landscape with 110 to 120-degree heat and high humidity in summer, while inside, he read Plato and Descartes, Bertrand Russell and A. J. Ayer, Dante and Shakespeare, and watched films by Fellini, Antonioni and Bergman. Professor Robert Scott taught a course in film as an art form, and it became one of the young man's favorite courses. Professor Scott showed classic movies with a 16-milimeter projector, films the young man had never seen before, then talked about scripts, editing, cinematography, acting and directing. Now, when the young man saw films he had the tools to analyze them, to appreciate them even more. He especially liked Antonioni's *Red Desert*. In an industrial Italy, in the upper bourgeoisie, a woman feels out of place, alienated from the environment, from her husband and from herself. The young man could identify with that kind of estrangement, the feeling that one does not belong, and even more alienating, the pain of existing and the fear of not being.

Thomas Taylor taught creative writing. He was a

new professor who had moved to the Valley from San Francisco. He had long hair down to his shoulders and was married to an American Indian woman. He would come to class with a record player, play music and sit at his desk reading. When the young man asked him for the syllabus, the professor became irate. "This is a creative writing class," he said. "Write!" On April 22, 1970, the first Earth Day ever to be celebrated, Professor Taylor told the class he was going to walk through the fields from El Centro to the college, about three miles, and welcomed students to join him. A handful did, and as they walked through fields of alfalfa, Professor Taylor took a joint out of his pocket, lit it, took a drag and passed it around. Maybe it was a good way to celebrate Earth Day, thought the young man, as he took a few drags of the joint and walked on the tender green alfalfa. Bales of hay, stacked at least twenty feet high, stood in formation by the fields' sides, and in the cloudless sky a slim column of white smoke rose in the distance. It must have been at least 80 degrees, and he had begun to sweat. The young man had been puzzled by the unconventional teaching methods of Professor Taylor, but he grew to like him, and every year, on Earth Day, the old man remembered that day.

The young man joined the college newspaper as the editorial page editor and wrote long articles defending Angela Davis, arguing for the legalization of marijuana and prostitution and opposing the war in Vietnam. Community leaders—wealthy farm owners and law-and-order types—complained to the College Board, and ultimately the paper was shut down. He participated in student demonstrations against the war, usually just students with signs walking back and forth in front of the college administration building, but in the big one, Lloyd Farrar, the history professor, stood in front of the courthouse at the top of the stairs and delivered a fiery speech against the war. There must have been one hundred students listening to him, and all around, policemen and other law enforcement agents in civilian clothes took photos of everyone.

His cousin Gary, also a student at the college, became the newspaper's photographer. Gary's family had moved into a house on the same block as the young man, so they saw each other often. He and Gary befriended Mike, and through Mike, Larry, who worked at the local hospital as an orderly. They were all twenty years old or younger, basking in their youth, excited for the future. They'd meet at night, to talk for hours, drive around or gather at the trailer of one of Larry's friends, drink iced tea, and listen to records. Everybody loved Larry's iced tea. He'd boil water in a pan, put five Lipton tea bags in it to steep, pour it in a pitcher, then add cold water and sugar. When chilled, it tasted delicious.

They often wound up at Sambo's, drinking coffee for the wooden tokens that were "good for a 10-cent cup of coffee." The waitress that usually served them was "Flag," so nicknamed by them because she had a large American flag pin on her white uniform. She was a stout middle-aged woman who walked ponderously and never smiled. They gravitated toward a booth in the back, next to the large windows. Truck drivers sat at the counter, a few couples in the booths. It wasn't very crowded late at night, and he, Mike and

Gary talked about girls, classes and professors, plans and projects. Mike lived with a roommate at the Kaibab Apartments, on Highway 86, a sprawling complex a block in size. He drove a new Toyota Corolla and they often went for drives in the cool of night, humid air rushing in from the car's windows, with engine noise and the squeaking of tires on gravel. Aimless, they traveled dirt roads flanked by eucalyptus, surprised at times by a dog darting across the headlights' beams, or an owl flying up from a fence.

They talked about the war and the demonstrations, Humphrey and Nixon, the feminists protesting the Miss America Pageant. They wanted to see the new film by Kubrick, *2001: A Space Odyssey*, but it only played in San Diego, and they couldn't afford the gas or the ticket prices. They went to see *Planet of the Apes* at the Crest. After the show they went to Sambo's and talked about the movie. They had all been shocked by the last scene, at Charlton Heston falling on his knees at the sight of a huge bust buried in the sand, an arm holding a torch: the Statue of Liberty. It made an impression on the young man, who remembered seeing the statue as their ship approached New York: the symbol of acceptance and freedom, in the film a ruin buried in sand.

MIKE NEEDED A FORM NOTARIZED, so they went to see Ricardo Jimenez, who invited them to a weekend religious event at El Carmelo Retreat House in Redlands. "It's a beautiful place; there are interesting speakers, good food—you'll like it," he said. The young man and Mike drove to Mel's for a root beer. "Hell, we should go," said Mike. "We can do our homework there and they'll even feed us." So they found themselves in a room at the retreat house on a Friday night, their beds covered with books and notebooks. After a hearty dinner, they skipped a religious discussion and retired to their room to study. But after a couple of hours Mike wanted to go to town, so they drove to Redlands and wound up in a topless bar. The place was crowded, mostly with young and middle-aged men. It was loud, smelled of cigarettes and beer, and on a stage three women danced under bright lights. They smiled as they moved seductively, but the young man wondered what they were thinking as they danced. It was a job; maybe their feet hurt and they had mundane concerns on their minds: what they needed to buy at the grocery store, how they were going to pay for an expensive car repair. What did they think about men, seeing them drool night after night with eyes feasting on their bodies? The young men drank their beer, then returned to El Carmelo, went to their room and slept. The next day they ate and stayed mostly in their room studying, then that evening they left for home. The weekend had been a respite from the Imperial Valley, but they hadn't even tried to attend the religious functions, and they had probably disappointed Ricardo.

HE AND MIKE yearned to change the world, but how? Could it be done through political means? Capitalism, as Marx pointed out in *The Communist Manifesto*, had been a very productive economic phase, but it needed to be superseded if a more equitable, rational society was to be established. But capitalists owned the means of production and thereby controlled to a great extent the state and the institutions of civil society, including the means of mass communication, the justice system and education. The progressive vice-president Henry Wallace had been prevented from becoming the Democratic presidential nominee in 1944 by the capitalists, and the socialists and the communists had been destroyed, accused of being un-American, associated through the press with the Soviet Union. Could society be changed through violent revolution? No. The capitalists controlled the military, and there wasn't much support among the populace for a socialist movement. Could he and Mike join the Weather Underground? Could they blow up a building, burn something down? They dismissed such thoughts as unproductive, downright pathetic. And what if someone got hurt or killed? At times, in despair, they talked about dedicating their lives to the pursuit of knowledge and truth, living monastically, like Sarastro's brotherhood in *The Magic Flute*.

Larry had majored in English and Journalism at the community college in Yuma, Arizona, but when his father refused to help him with books and living expenses he quit. Bitterly, he moved out and began working as an orderly at the county hospital in El Centro. He found a place to stay at the mobile home of a friend and sought solace in literature and music. He talked passionately about writers and books, and the young man invited him over to see his library. Larry was excited at seeing all those volumes, and the young man gave him a copy of *Don Quixote*. That was the beginning of a long friendship.

Larry had hundreds of records and as the years passed, they became thousands. When the young man went to see him at the trailer, Larry would be ironing his clothes for that night's shift, and as they drank iced tea, Larry played records. "Have you ever heard Beethoven's *The Ruins of Athens*?" he would ask, "or Rachmaninoff's *Third Piano Concerto*?" "No," the young man answered, and so he'd relax on the sofa sipping the ice-cold sweet tea while listening to music he had never heard before.

HE PARKED in front of Thrifty and waited. It was almost six in the evening. After the afternoon class in the history of philosophy he had talked to Professor Hann for almost an hour about Baron d'Holbach's denial of free will. According to the eighteenth-century philosopher, to believe we act on the basis of choice is an illusion. Actions are the result of impulses derived from brain and environment. But could choices have causes, and still not be determined? His thinking about the problem was abruptly put to an end when he saw, in the side mirror, Roberta come out of the store. She wore her white uniform and walked briskly to his car. "Hard day?" he asked as she settled in the passenger's seat.

"Toward the end of the shift my feet hurt. I need new shoes."

"Want to get something to eat?"

"Nah, Dawn came by earlier; during my break we ate a bunch of French fries. By the way, she's having a party Saturday night—we're invited."

"I have a fifteen-page paper to write, and I haven't started yet."

"Because you spend all your time smoking dope with your friends."

"I'm taking seventeen units and I'm the editorial editor of the paper; I don't smoke dope that often."

"What do you want to go to college for? You had a good job and you quit... My dad's still mad."

"I don't want to be a fireman; you know that."

"And you keep writing that terrible crap, 'Free Angela Davis'! That communist. If my dad finds out, he'll blow up."

"So I shouldn't express my views for fear of offending your dad?"

"And you were in that demonstration against the war—it's shameful." She looked away and stared at the windshield. Her upturned nose increased her expression of disdain, and he felt his neck muscles contracting.

"All I hear from you is that I'm a criminal for smoking grass, a traitor for not supporting the war, that I shouldn't have quit my job. I'm fed up."

"I hate you," she said calmly as she stared out the window.

"I wish I had gone out on the field that morning during gym class. I wouldn't have met you."

"I wish you had gone out, too," she said. He couldn't wait to drop her off, never to see her again.

He put the car in reverse and sped out of the lot.

He took Main and turned on State Route 86, past fields, farmhouses, eucalyptus trees, the run-down building of the Knights of Columbus and the parachute training tower at the Naval Air Facility in the distance, painted with red and white squares that reminded him of the Purina logo, then Seeley. He stopped in front of her parents' house and Roberta got out and strode toward the front door, her head down.

He left and drove by Sunbeam Lake; he was going to take Ross Road, through the fields. The warm, humid air brought the lake's musty scent into the car's cabin. The sun had gone down; he turned on the headlights and tried to find something to listen to on the radio. The lake's surface was crimson and charcoal gray and a few ducks left silver trails as they leisurely moved toward the reeds by the bank. Often, he and Roberta would park at the lake at night to make out. She was his first girlfriend. In high school they had lunch together, talked about classes and teachers, listened to music in her room, but once they graduated, their lives diverged, and their differences revealed themselves like bruises. He felt a tinge of sadness, but also a sense of freedom, as if a heavy weight had been lifted from him.

Imperial Valley College was his home away from home. He spent most of his days there, taking classes, talking to professors and studying at the library, and on weekends he hung out with his friends and listened to music. He had practically forgotten about his girlfriend, but six months later, his mother told him Roberta was pregnant, and if he didn't want to marry her, she was going to give the baby up for adoption. The honorable thing to do, his mother said, was to marry Roberta. Getting married was the last thing on the young man's mind, but he didn't want to disappoint his mother and felt guilty at the thought of having the baby put up for adoption, so he agreed. He and Roberta met, looking guilty and repentant, and reconciled, "for the sake of the baby."

A few weeks after the hasty church ceremony, Roberta went into labor. When he saw the baby at the hospital the night she was born, the young man felt strangely detached. He was twenty-one years old, a sophomore in college. He didn't want to be married, didn't want to be a parent. The nurse had just come into the waiting room with the newborn in her arms, and the young man's father rushed to hold her. The young man's jaw tensed as he stood in the background.

His father had converted the garage into a room where the young man slept with his wife and baby daughter, whom they named Renée. A few months later they moved into a small house, and that's where he read Camus and Sartre, staying up until the early hours of the morning. Roberta still worked part time at Thrifty Drug Store and his mother took care of the baby for most of the day.

In 1970 he graduated with an Associate of Arts degree and transferred to San Diego State University. He and Roberta found an apartment in El Cajon; to supplement his financial aid package, she found a job as a secretary for Beneficial Finance Company. They left Renée with his mother in El Centro during the workweek. Every Friday, they drove to the Valley to spend the weekend there.

San Diego State University was a much bigger institution than Imperial Valley College, and parking was a problem. To get a decent parking place, he arrived at seven in the morning and took a nap in the car before his first class. In the beginning the young man felt out of place, but he liked the campus with its Spanish architecture, the grassy areas, flowers, shrubs and trees, and liked his courses, including a medieval history class taught by a Falstaffian professor who came to class wearing a monk's robe when he lectured on monasticism. He also looked forward to the Philosophy of Science course taught by Dr. Robert Filner, a young and shy professor, who would later become a congressman and then a disgraced mayor. But it was hard going financially and a long commute for Roberta, so they made plans to move back to the Valley. He transferred to the satellite campus of San Diego State University in Calexico, and Roberta found work at the Naval Air Facility coffee shop. When they rented a house a few blocks away from his parents, they could spend more time with their daughter. And so, in December of 1970, when the semester ended, they moved back to El Centro.

Calexico was a small desert town on the Mexican border; what kind of professors could be teaching there? As it turned out, interesting, scholarly ones and anti-establishment types. He befriended some of them and liked their classes.

James Harmon, who taught political science, was a progressive who had done his dissertation on political ideology and music. His office was lined with record albums. One night, the class over, Dr. Harmon turned up the volume of the stereo he had brought in so the students could listen to songs of political import, and the walls shook to the sound of Led Zeppelin. Dr. Harmon grinned happily.

Richard Hill, the sociology professor, delighted in writing long letters excoriating the university's president, and Dr. Polich made the diplomatic history of Europe come alive in long lectures. The old man felt a pang of nostalgia at the thought of sitting in class taking notes in Dr. Polich's night course, then during the break getting a cup of coffee from the vending machine. He'd select it with cream and sugar and grew to associate the taste with university courses, lectures and books. The smell of the freshly watered plants and trees in the humid air, the night smoothening the edges of building and trees, moths dancing around lampposts, the fifteen or so students stretching their legs, talking—all these things made him glad to be there. He liked the professors, and after a fifteen-minute drive he easily found a parking place.

THE YOUNG MAN sat on the floor in the living room, writing a term paper on the coffee table. He had scribbled a first draft on a writing pad, and now as he typed it, he made revisions. A couple of weeks earlier he had bought a cheap pipe at Marcot's Liquor Store, and the strong tobacco gave him a boost of energy. Renée was asleep at his mother's, where he'd had dinner earlier. He had followed his daughter around the living room as she pushed her walker wagon around. She squealed with delight as he made engine noises with his lips, and when she grew tired he sat on the sofa with her and read *Goodnight Moon*. Renee' sucked on her pacifier and looked at him as he read, until she closed her eyes. He picked her up and carried her to the bedroom. As he kissed her on the head, her soft tuft of hair tickled his nose. She smelled of milk and baby powder. He put her in the crib and covered her up with her pink blankie. During the day his mother babysat the baby and when Roberta worked late, they would leave her there. He was writing a paper on *The Greening of America*, a book by Charles Reich that Dr. Harmon had assigned. The book's author saw in the counter-cultural movement of the 1960s the groundwork for a new worldview, based on egalitarianism, personal freedom and an expansion of consciousness. Was a fundamental shift taking place in America? He wanted to talk about this possibility with Dr. Hill, who taught the History of Social Theory. As the young man relit the pipe, the front door opened. It was Roberta.

"You look bushed," he said.

"Sherry had to take her baby to the doctor, so I was the only waitress. After work I went to see her. Her husband is coming back to base Friday, and they're having a barbecue Saturday afternoon; we're invited."

"I don't think I can go."

"Every time one of my friends has a party or a get-together, that's what you say. You don't have classes on Saturday; you could go."

"I don't want to have anything to do with people at the base. They're all for the war."

"So you'd rather go smoke weed with your friends."

"You spend most of your time at that goddamn Navy base. Why don't you go pick up Renée after work and come home?"

She got up and went into the bedroom. She was fixated with the base, but then, she was born on one, had lived on one most of her life, as her parents traveled from one Navy facility to another.

The young man and Roberta began to live in different worlds, had mostly separate lives. He went to classes, read, studied and wrote papers, spent time with his cousin Gary and his friends Larry and Mike, while Roberta visited her friends at the Naval Air Facility.

The spring semester over, the young man went with Gary to San Diego for a couple of days to visit their cousin Eric, who was a student at San Diego State. Roberta encouraged him to go, and as Gary's VW took off, she stood in the driveway, waved and smiled. Two days later Gary dropped him off at the house, and the young man, glad to be back, was eager to see his daughter. But no one was home, and when he glanced at the closets, he noticed his wife's clothes were gone. He looked in the empty crib at his daughter's light blue footie pajama, picked it up and raised it to his face. It smelled like her, and tears filled his eyes. He called Roberta's parents' home to see if she was there, but her father told the young man that Roberta had run away with the baby to Hawaii with a Navy chief she had met at the Naval Air Facility; that was all he knew. She left no forwarding address, no telephone number. There was nothing he could do.

He was a university student, had no money to hire a lawyer and had to move back into his parents' house. Lying down on his single bed, he stared at the wall while listening to music on the stereo. Bob Dylan, Simon and Garfunkel, Joan Baez. He couldn't read; he felt as if his world had exploded, or at least, a part of it. He lost twenty pounds in a month.

8

EL CENTRO AND SAN DIEGO, 1970-1977

He spent most of the day lying on his bed, trying to read or listening to records. Roberta had been his first girlfriend, and he had married her out of guilt. She supported the Vietnam War, thought he was a degenerate because he occasionally smoked marijuana, and she had no interest in books. They had nothing in common except for their daughter Renée, who spent most of the day at his parents' house during the workweek.

But he loved his daughter. He had been a married man with a child, and now he was alone, back at his parents' house, feeling sad because his wife had left him. *Fool!* thought the old man, as he remembered that time. *You should have embraced your newly found freedom.*

He and his cousin Gary had planned to transfer to the University of California at San Diego and had to take some documents there, so one morning Gary pulled up in the driveway in his red VW bug. "I invited a girl I met to go with us," he said, "and she asked a friend to come along, we have to go to Calexico to pick them up." It took twenty minutes to drive the twelve miles to the house where the girls waited. An elfin blond girl introduced herself as Pinky, and her friend as Deborah. Deborah was seventeen and had just graduated from Calexico High School. With long, dark brown hair down to the small of her back, brown eyes and eyebrows that vaguely reminded him of Frida Kahlo, she seemed a wild creature.

After their business at the university, they stopped at a grocery store to get some chips and sodas for a picnic, then drove to the beach. "I must be really hungry—I could swear I smell roasted chicken," said Gary as he looked in the rearview mirror. Once at La Jolla Shores, as they sat down on a blanket, Deborah pulled out a roasted chicken out of her suede purse. They feasted on the chicken, surprised at how she had managed to stuff the bird in her small purse without being seen. Later in the evening, they dropped off the girls and drove back to El Centro.

A few days later the young man called Deborah, and they spoke on the phone for a long time. He couldn't stop thinking about her and one night, after their phone conversation, he jumped in his car and drove to her house. The twelve-mile ride seemed too long even at seventy miles per hour. He parked in the back of her house and jumped over the wooden fence. It was dark, but in the moonlight, he saw her waiting for him by the back door. They hugged and kissed, then she took him to her room, where they made love. "I dig you; I dig you!" she repeated.

One day Deborah borrowed her father's Facel

Vega and stopped in front of his house to pick him up. She looked out the driver's-side window, and with her long hair she had looked like a movie star. They had gone for a ride in the fast French car to Pine Valley. They had laid a blanket on the grass under a fir, had kissed and made out in the cold.

THE YOUNG MAN graduated from San Diego State University in the summer of 1972, thanks to Deborah, who convinced him to stick it out and finish the semester. He was having a hard time with a history course and was on the verge of dropping out. The young man had planned to work on a Master of Arts in philosophy but took a year off. He and Deborah rented a stand-alone studio in El Centro. This was the first time they had lived by themselves. He found work as a psychiatric technician for the newly created county mental health department and tried to write short stories with the guidance of a correspondence course, but as he sat at his diminutive desk with the Olivetti Lettera 22, staring at the blank sheet of paper in the roller, he didn't know what to write. He had a few story ideas, sent them in, and a few weeks later they came back with critical comments. The young man soon gave up on the course; it wasn't very helpful, and he felt depressed. What was he going to do? He wanted to get out of Imperial Valley, had made plans to do so in 1970, when he and his cousin Gary applied to UCSD. They had both been accepted, but the financial aid package offered was meager, and at the last minute the young man decided to continue at the Calexico branch of San Diego State. Tuition was much lower, and he could have lived at his parents' house and be near Deborah. However, he had abandoned his cousin and retreated to El Centro, the place they'd always talked of getting away from. Gary had succeeded, but the young man had not.

Now that he had his BA, he wanted to work on a graduate degree in philosophy, but how? Financial aid would not have been enough. He felt lethargic, fatigued, and became worried that he might be suffering from some dreadful disease, like leukemia. He drove to the emergency room because his heart was racing and he had trouble breathing. After running some tests, they gave him a Valium and sent him home. "You're having a panic attack," he was told. "There is nothing physically wrong with you." To be sure, he went to see another doctor, who told him the same thing. But the young man didn't feel well; he always feared that he was sick and didn't have long to live. *How can I read and write, if I may not be long on earth?* he thought.

After a while he began to feel better and the fear subsided, but he didn't like working at County Mental Health. He wanted to do more with his life than work with the mentally ill in that patch of desert he had been taken to nine years earlier by his father. Unlike Sandrina, who had moved to San Diego as soon as she celebrated her eighteenth birthday, he had remained in in El Centro.

His friend Mike had gotten married and worked for Philco Ford at the Navy base. They met periodically for coffee to talk about politics and their plans for the future. On a Tuesday afternoon they met at

Sambo's, where they sat in their usual booth, the big one at the end of the restaurant, next to the large, curved window.

"They already sell pumpkins at Safeway—how crazy is that?" said Mike with a scowl. "And it's 91 degrees outside. Colleen and I plan to move to West Covina in a few months. Her family lives there, and I can apply to the University of California at Riverside. But I need money, fucking money."

"Education should be a right, not a privilege. It burns me up how they talk about freedom and equality. Freedom for whom? For the rich to get richer and for the masses to be free to buy cars and refrigerators on credit," said the young man.

"There are more than 24 million Americans below the poverty line, and we're still killing people in Vietnam, Cambodia, Laos," said Mike as he waited for his mug of coffee to cool a bit.

"I wish I could do something about it, but what? Voting for McGovern isn't going to change much; besides, he won't win—we know that already. The capitalists will not allow it," said the young man.

"I might join the Communist Party—at least it's a real alternative," Mike replied. "They have a chapter in West Covina, and I also found out there is a member of the party in Imperial; I have his name." They had three coffee refills, then left, promising to keep in touch. The capitalist system was based on the profit motive, that was the name of the game—to maximize profits, to increase production and consumption, to flatten more hills and raze pristine land to make room for houses, malls, gas stations and highways. Population needed to increase in order to expand the consumer base. The more he thought about it, the more it made him sick. It was a mindless process, like digestion; there had to be a more balanced system, one that aspired to the democratization of the economic sphere. Perhaps he could join the Communist Party.

Hutch lived in Imperial, a town three miles from El Centro. The young man had phoned the old communist, who had invited him to his house. In his early seventies, tall, stooped, with black-rimmed glasses and thinning hair, Hutch warmly greeted the young man and they had a long conversation about politics.

Hutch had been active in progressive causes all his life, had been a member of the Industrial Workers of the World, and during the McCarthy era, like so many other members of the Communist Party, was forced to become self-employed. University professors, teachers and social workers suddenly became carpet salesmen, opened small restaurants, or found other ways to make a living. Hutch became a hog farmer.

ON HALLOWEEN DAY the young man and Deborah went to the courthouse to get married. They had told no one; they didn't want parents or relatives involved. Parents tended to encroach, influence, take over. They barely talked to each other on the way there because they'd just had a fight—who knows what about—and instead of a wedding celebration, in the evening the young man dragged his bride to visit Hutch, who'd recently had a heart bypass operation. When the newlyweds went to visit him at home, the hog farmer had looked depressed. "You know," he said, "in a way I wish I hadn't survived the operation. I feel different, as if I were someone else...I can't explain it." Deborah fell asleep on the sofa until it was time to leave.

In the following months, the young man met other members of the Communist Party and couldn't understand why they had been persecuted and considered national security threats. They were decent people who struggled to make a living in sales or small businesses, idealists who dreamed of a more equitable society. They worked long hours during the day and in the evening went home to their families, most free time occupied by mundane tasks. Lee owned a barbecue restaurant, William sold carpets, James worked in a mobile-home building outfit. They argued at times among themselves over trivial personal matters, like small loans that were not repaid or a used car that broke down soon after it was bought. The party had been a major force in the early 1940s, influential in trade unions and the culture, but it always remained aligned with the Soviet Union, never forged its own independent path, so it bled members, lost prestige and influence, and with the Red Scare of the 1950s, what remained was a small cadre of mostly old members, with practically no power in the social and political spheres. Disillusioned, the young man stopped going to meetings and resigned from the organization.

After working for several months at the county mental health facility, the young man quit. He wanted to get a Master of Arts and teach philosophy, so in the fall of 1973, he was back at San Diego State University.

He and Deborah moved into an apartment in the North Park area. He began to take philosophy courses and Deborah found work as an electronics assembler.

BESIDES COURSES in the history of philosophy and its branches, Western Marxism and existentialism, he took classes in Kant, Hegel and Heidegger. Listening to lectures, taking notes, writing papers, doing research in the library, reading, underlining, highlighting—he loved it all.

Dr. Andrew Feenberg, who had recently received his PhD at UCSD and had studied under Herbert Marcuse, chain-smoked Marlboros as he paced back and forth in front of the class, talking about critical theory and its development from Western Marxism. Tall and wiry, he had been studying at the Sorbonne when the 1968 student protests broke out in Paris.

Walter Koppelman, stocky and balding, smoked unfiltered Camels as he sat on the edge of his desk, trying to clarify the first part of Hegel's *Phenomenology of Spirit*.

Dr. Leon Rosenstein, with curly blond hair and rings that could have been worn by an ancient Greek nobleman, taught existentialism and Heidegger's *Being and Time*. He gave the young man the impression that the professor could have been Apollo, who, bored of life on Mount Olympus, had come to San Diego.

Dr. Eugene Troxell lived in the mountains and rode to the university in a heavy BMW motorcycle; he wore blue jeans embroidered with flowers creeping up the pant legs. He taught courses in the philosophy of language and Wittgenstein.

In his three years of graduate studies, the young man had many conversations with his professors, learning much not only about the subject matter they taught, but from their commitment to serious study, their love of careful analysis of the texts. He was inspired by seeing Dr. Troxell sit at the desk in his office, a heavy hardbound book on a wooden stand, carefully underlying with a ruler and pencil; and Dr. Rosenstein recounting that to study for his dissertation's oral defense, he had locked himself up in his room for several days, had food brought to him, and how, after days of study, something shifted in his consciousness and he had an experience of transcendence.

The young man liked the way Dr. Peter O'Reilly carefully enunciated words, the way he meticulously critiqued arguments and thought carefully before he spoke. A former priest, he was married to Nathalia, a poet and professor of literature. An unassuming man who lectured on medieval philosophy, he walked around carrying his leather briefcase, and always had time to sit on a bench and talk about Saint Thomas Aquinas or Saint Augustine.

Even the professors he didn't like for their personalities or teaching methods taught him important lessons about scholarship, the life of the mind, about the passion for understanding, the values of clarity and cogency. He had been excited about taking a course in metaphysics but became disappointed by Professor Jack McClurg's American pragmatist bent. When the young man wrote a paper tailored to appeal to the professor's views, McClurg had commented on the last page that he wasn't interested in agreement with his ideas, but in the arguments in support of the claims. Then there was the professor who taught the course in Kant's *Critique of Pure Reason*. The young man didn't like her, and during a class he noisily slammed the book and his notebook in his briefcase and left before the end of her lecture. She was a middle-aged woman with a severe appearance, but her passion for Kant's philosophy showed in the classroom and in her efforts to help students understand the German philosopher. She taught the young man something important, too. The old man had forgotten her name, but even forty-seven years later, he remembered her. She was long dead, but he wished he could tell her, "Thank you for having taught me to appreciate Immanuel Kant, and for having patiently helped me understand when I came to you in desperation. Much time has passed, but I still have the textbook we used on my bookshelf; I still remember you fondly."

At the university bookstore he bought a guide on traveling in Italy, and as he walked across the San Diego State campus, he felt pulled toward his original home. He yearned to be back there, but he was a student at State, married. In Italy students were much more politically conscious and active than in the United States; at San Diego State, only a few students were involved in progressive movements. There were small groups, like the Revolutionary Communist Party and the Democratic Socialists, but the young man didn't see how they could achieve anything; they seemed marginal.

"Looking for something in particular?" asked the balding man from behind the counter, glancing up from a newspaper.

"Just looking around," mumbled the young man, unable to take his eyes off the clerk's round face and granny glasses. Was the guy trying to look like Mao?

"Let me know if you need any help," said the clerk as he continued reading.

The bookstore, crammed with volumes, newspapers and journals on communist theory and revolutionary movements, was no B. Dalton or Pickwick, with the latest whodunits and cookbooks. On pine shelves, the works of Lenin and Mao in inexpensive editions imported from the Soviet Union and Red China radiated history and hope. The young man walked through the stacks, looking at books, posters and tapes. South American folk music began to blare from two cheap speakers hung on the wall as he picked up a newspaper entitled *Communist Revolution* and a nicely clothbound edition of Engels's *Anti-Dühring*. According to the paper's headlines, the United States was on the verge of collapse, and the American proletariat stood in the wings, waiting to take power. He strode over to the counter with book and newspaper.

"Do you think capitalism is collapsing?" he asked as he put Engels's book on the counter.

"The signs are all around," said the clerk, getting up from his stool. "Look at inflation. The social safety net is being dismantled, unemployment is increasing, as Marx predicted. The bourgeoisie is consolidating its power, but the working class is tired of exploitation."

The young man shifted his weight to his right leg. "I don't see workers becoming aware of their position in the system," he said, left thumb hooked in his jeans pocket, right hand clasping the newspaper at his side. "Capitalism is still powerful enough to keep people satisfied, and the jargon you use doesn't help. America is not Albania or China..."

"But the material conditions are there. It's up to us to unite and lead the workers toward revolution," said the clerk. "Haven't you read Lenin?"

"Yeah, but I just don't see it happening here," replied the young man in a tired voice as he paid and walked out with book and newspaper toward his white VW bug. He drove automatically, his mind trapped in the dungeon of his feelings.

As he drove up University Avenue, the tap-tap from the engine reminded him the valves needed adjusting; he couldn't afford to take the car to a mechanic, so he would have to try to do it himself. But that tap-tap also reminded him that he lived in an irrational society based on the profit motive—if you want mobility, you need money for car maintenance and repair, for insurance, for gasoline, and in order to get that cash you have to sell yourself on the labor market; you have to play the game. That tap-tap was the very spirit of capitalism mocking him through the engine's valves and clearances.

He had to finish reading two chapters for tomorrow's seminar, but his graduate program, his whole life, seemed far away and disconnected. What was the use of studying what Lukács wrote about class society? He glanced at the rows of middle-class houses with neatly trimmed lawns reflecting neatly trimmed lives. Predictable, from the womb to the grave. But wasn't that what his wife wanted? What had happened to the possibilities? Everything now seemed ironclad, impervious to alteration. How naive he had been, believing people would respond to the appeals of reason, that they would vote for their interests and a more equitable society. Reluctantly, he turned on 27th Street and returned home.

He came to a screeching stop in front of the house and slammed the door getting out. Tybalt was lying under the palm tree, his chin resting on the warm grass, and startled by the young man's sudden arrival, sat up in alarm. "Tybalt, you little revolutionary," he called, but the cat ran away.

Once in the house, he sat down on the sofa and tried to read. The new book felt good in his hands and the elegant interplay of ideas within reflected that world of intellectual pursuits he so admired. He turned the pages to see how long the chapter was, then he laid the volume on the coffee table, got up and went in the kitchen to pour himself another cup of coffee. It was three o'clock. Why did he always feel strange at this time of day? In the early afternoon the air changed; trees, buildings and cars seemed to shiver in a barely visible haze. He took a sip of coffee as Tybalt pushed through the cat door, stared at the young man for a few seconds, then began to nibble at the cat chow in the bowl by the refrigerator. The young man went back in the living room to drink his coffee.

Deborah had come home with the cat one Sunday

night in February. The car had pulled up in the driveway and he walked out to greet her. A half-moon shone from behind the palm tree, and he could see Deborah getting out of the car, holding a cardboard box.

"Look at what Granny gave me!" she said, setting the box on the driveway. A gray Manx kitten peeked out, meowing, big paws reaching over the top. "He's a wild cat Granny found in the backyard last week. Do you like him?"

"Looks kind of scrawny," he replied, frowning. And then, when they lay in bed—she listening to the radio, he reading a book—she propped herself on her elbow, turned toward him and said, "Let's call him Tybalt, like Juliet's cousin, okay?" They had gone to the Ken to see Zeffirelli's film version of *Romeo and Juliet*, and she had been impressed by it.

"That's a great name," he replied. He began to read again: "The essence of commodity-structure has often been pointed out. Its basis is that a relation between people takes on the character of a thing and thus acquires..." Ever since his undergraduate days and his discussions with his friend Mike, he had wanted to play a part in constructing a more rational, just society. He had even joined the Communist Party, a concrete sign of commitment to his ideas. He had been excited by having finally bridged theory and practice, only to find himself mired in a rigid, orthodox web of ossified rhetoric and organizational structures; and to top it off, nature and social conventions made their demands, and he had fallen in love and gotten married. He had quit his participation in political organizations, had pulled the anchor, so to speak, and now his ideals and convictions floated with no direction in a sea of domestic and academic responsibilities.

The following day, when the young man walked in, Deborah was in the kitchen, rummaging in the refrigerator. "Hey," he said, as he dropped onto the sofa. "How was work?"

"Not too bad," she replied, getting a chicken out.

"I did some research at the library this morning," he said. He continued watching her; in her jeans and shirt, viewed from the back, she looked frail. As she began to cut the chicken, Tybalt dashed through his little door and began to rub himself against Deborah's leg. "Mama has some goodies here for you," she cooed, as she bent down to pet the cat.

"What're you fixing?"

"Chicken adobo. A Filipino girl at work told me how to make it. Here, Tybalt," she said, throwing the chicken liver to the cat. Tybalt smelled the treat and walked back out. "That's weird," she said.

"Maybe he ate a mouse or two," the young man replied as he went in the living room and turned on the news. Tybalt still had a wild streak, he was a free spirit and didn't completely trust the world of human beings—a little like himself, he thought, or at least, like he would have liked to think of himself; he was after all imbedded in society, following social conventions.

After dinner he went in the bedroom and tried to finish his reading assignment. According to Lukács, only the proletariat, as a class conscious of how capitalism molds relationships and values, would be able to change reality though action. *You might as well wait for the second coming of Christ*, he thought as he went back into the living room. Deborah sat slouched on the sofa watching TV, Tybalt lying next to her asleep.

"What are you reading?" she asked him, handing him a lighted joint.

"A collection of essays by Lukács on Marxist theory. He wrote them in the early twenties," he replied, taking a hit and passing the joint back.

"What's it about?"

"It's an analysis of how capitalism molds relationships and values; a certain reality is created and objectified through ideology and institutions, and then it becomes accepted as the only reality...You're not really interested in this stuff, are you?"

She took a deep drag from the joint. "I don't understand it, that's all. Besides, what does it have to do with me? I spend eight hours a day sitting at a table, bent over circuit boards, then drive in traffic hoping the car won't break down."

"What it boils down to is that society doesn't have to be the way it is and people don't have to be the way they are; things could be different. The very material reality we live in, the way cities are planned, the workplace, it's all created by the people who have the power to shape them in ways that support their interests, their values."

"I don't like the way things are, but I can't see what I can do about it. When I come home from work, I'm tired. I just want to rest," she blurted out. "You're so worried about changing society that you don't enjoy life. I like to bake bread; I like to make dolls. Sometimes I like to get stoned. I like listening to Led

Zeppelin, watching movies. All you do is read those books and hate life."

He said nothing as his eyes anchored themselves on the TV screen. The atmosphere in the living room had become gelatin; it pinned him down on the sofa and began to ooze into his head, slowing down the movements of his thoughts. Deborah sat next to him, stoned, watching TV while he sat there, until the evening passed into night.

He remembered the night he and Mike went to Sambo's after classes four years earlier. They were sophomores at Imperial Valley College, and sitting in the back, next to the window, drinking coffee and smoking cigarettes, they had feverishly talked about how they could dedicate their lives to the pursuit of knowledge and to changing society. They scoffed at the drones that just went to work and had barbecues on weekends. Now Mike worked in West Covina as a short order cook at Denny's, married and expecting a child, and he, too, was married, struggling to do his homework and get decent grades. Deborah slowly got up and went in the bedroom. "I'm really sleepy—good night," she said.

The young man thought about her as she closed the door. A few years earlier she had graduated from high school, a young woman with her whole life ahead of her, and here she was, married to a student with politics and philosophy on his mind, while she spent all day in a sweatshop, putting together circuit boards. The commercials preannouncing the eleven o'clock news flickered into the living room with exhortations to buy anti-itch cream and denture adhesive, and the viscous stuff in the young man's head leaked out, leaving him calmer but fatigued. He glanced at the cat, still wild in a way, the little rebel, who got up, jumped down from the sofa and walked out through the cat door. "Bored with bourgeois comfort, are you, Tybalt?" he wondered. "I wish I could be like you." Then he watched the news and went to bed.

The following afternoon when the young man came back from his seminar, Deborah sat by the kitchen table, her eyes puffy and red. "What's going on? What happened?" he asked.

"When I got home, Tybalt lay down on the bed to take a nap, and then he came to me. He could barely stand on his legs. He lay next to me, and as I petted him, he died." Tears welled up in her eyes and flowed down her cheeks. He sat next to her and touched her shoulder.

"He must have caught distemper," she said. "We have to bury him."

They got up and went into the bedroom. Tybalt lay on his side, stiff, with open eyes. The young man bent down and picked him up; it surprised him to realize how small and light the little revolutionary was. He took him in the backyard and laid him on the grass. Deborah came out with a trowel, kneeled on the ground and began to dig in the little garden. A cool breeze passed through him. The droning of a small plane flying overhead and the laughter and yells of kids playing in the street reverberated in his head. He knelt, and with trembling hands put Tybalt in the hole and then covered him up with soil. Deborah, still crying, got up and went in the house, and he followed, head down. She went in the kitchen, and the young man put a Mozart violin concerto on and sat on the sofa. He had to read Lukács's essay "The Changing Function of Historical Materialism," but he didn't feel like it. What was the point?

THE GOLDEN BULL was a pipe and tobacco shop in San Diego's Old Town. As soon as the young man opened the door, lush aromas of tobacco reached him, and as he glanced toward the left, he was greeted by an impish-looking man with curly hair, a beard and thick glasses who smoked a pipe behind the counter. In the center of the tiny room was a black potbelly stove and a couple of chairs. On the counter were jars full of tobaccos, and on display under the glass top, pipes: Stanwells, Savinellis, Dunhills. The young man became friendly with Jeff, the owner, and began to buy pipes and tobacco there.

Larry, the young man's friend, came almost every Friday on the Greyhound bus to spend the weekend, and one day the young man went to the pipe shop with Larry, who bought a pipe, tobacco, a tamper and pipe cleaners. Deborah cooked mouthwatering dinners—green burritos, chicken adobo—and late at night, after she went to bed, he and Larry sat on the sofa, smoked their pipes and listened to Beethoven, Haydn and Rachmaninoff. His cousin Gary, who was going to UCSD, also came by to visit on Saturdays, as did Sandra A., a friend of Deborah's. They ate dinner, got stoned, talked and listened to music.

WHEN DEBORAH TOLD him she was pregnant, he felt unprepared to be a father again. He spent a lot of time on campus—the world where he attended classes, went to the library to read long articles on Nietzsche or Pasolini in Italian newspapers or the newest essays in philosophical journals, and talked to professors and other students. At home he had much reading to do, papers to write.

The sun unrelenting in a sapphire sky, he walked out of the campus library and went to the bookstore. He made his way through a stream of students, young women in shorts, tee shirts and flimsy blouses, their bodies tanned, blondes, brunettes—he could smell their scents, perfumes, body lotions. In front of the bookstore he sat on the steps, feeling slightly inebriated, sipped the coffee he'd bought from a vending machine and watched the girls go by. He felt happy to be alive. He was a student, wasn't ready to be a father and a provider. His wife wanted him to go with her to Lamaze classes, and he'd begrudgingly agreed.

July 12, 1975 was a hot, humid day. Deborah had gone into labor the previous evening. She had planned to have the delivery at home with the help of a midwife, but after several hours the midwife decided that Deborah should go to the hospital, and there she had a C-section. He was a father again, but this time his father wasn't there to take over; as a matter of fact, they did not tell their parents of the boy's birth until later. The young man had not forgotten when his daughter was born, how his father had rushed to pick up the newborn, while he, the father, looked from behind. This time the young man picked up his son, who they named Michael.

The days were sweltering, and there was no air-conditioning in the apartment. The little boy cried all the time, it seemed. It was not an easy summer. Then the semester began, but he was not doing well.

It was 4:46 a.m. He had finished a half pint of Cluny scotch. He'd had a good day, or yesterday, to be exact. He, Deborah, their infant son and Gary had gone to Julian, where they picked apples and had slices of apple pie; then on the way home they stopped at Lake Cuyamaca, where they rented a boat and rowed around the lake. In late October the weather began to cool down but the afternoons were still warm. Hawks and turkey vultures flew leisurely overhead and ducks left trails as they moved toward the shore. The pine forests and the Laguna Mountains in the distance reminded the young man of his childhood years spent in Sella. He and Gary shared the rowing, and Deborah sat holding Michael in a blanket. Gary, an avid fisherman, kept staring at the water, probably wishing he could have brought his fishing gear. "Who knows how many trouts I could've caught?" He mumbled. The young man could breathe freely in the pine perfumed air, his shoulders gently massaged by the breeze. So why did he stay up until the following morning, drinking scotch and listening to music? He kept thinking about his incompletes, his financial predicament, his daughter Renée. He wanted to be a philosophy professor, but something deep inside kept wanting to hide in the dark space behind the school and the wall. That day back in second grade, when he was turning the knob of the school door and heard the voices of his tormentors, he had slinked around the building to hide. Decades had passed, but that child inside him was afraid and still wanted to hide. His face was hot; his heart raced. The fourth movement of Beethoven's Ninth Symphony was on now, full of power, joy and love. He closed his eyes and let himself be lifted. "All creatures drink of joy at nature's breast…" Wasn't he a creature? Why couldn't he drink of joy?

IN THE SPRING semester of 1976 he took two courses, one in Buddhism and a graduate seminar in epistemology. He began working on an outline for his thesis but wasn't making progress. Michael was nine months old, growing into a handsome little boy. He loved his son, but he didn't have a job and was failing at his degree program. He went to see the psychiatrist at health services, where he was diagnosed with depression and prescribed antidepressants, which made him sleepy and groggy. He woke up around ten in the morning, had a couple of mugs of instant coffee and drove the 1968 VW bug to San Diego State. Deborah had quit her job after the baby was born. His financial aid wasn't enough, so now they were on welfare and receiving food stamps.

He smoked marijuana every day, and he had started taking Quaaludes to go to sleep, only to discover he liked them for their euphoric effect. He couldn't study at home, found it hard to concentrate sitting at his desk in the bedroom, so he went to the university library. The wooden stall isolated him from the world. It was quiet and cool, and he read the texts with a pencil and a short ruler, underlying important sentences, marking with a star or a checkmark paragraphs, sometimes writing short notes in the margins. Sartre's *The Transcendence of the Ego*, Heidegger's *Being and Time*, Gramsci's *Prison Notebooks*. Then, overtaken by drowsiness, he fell asleep with his head on a book. When his toddler son heard him come home from the university in the VW, he crawled to the screen door, raised himself up by holding on to the screen, and banged his rattle in anticipation. The young man couldn't wait to throw him up in the air, hearing squeals of delight as he caught him on the way down.

HE DROVE down Broadway and stopped in front of the Greyhound station. He got out to help Deborah exit the car with the baby and drove back home. After the huge fight they'd had the day before, she said she wanted to stay for a couple of days at her mother's house. It had been hot and humid, and the tension was heavy in the apartment. He could still hear some of her words: "You don't do anything, we never go anywhere, we don't have any money. I worked for years in that sweatshop while you had your head in your books, for what? What kind of life is this?"

Instead of taking the freeway, he decided to go straight up Broadway. He wanted to drive slowly, didn't want to get back too early. After all, he was going to be alone. What had happened to his plan? He had to finish the work for five courses and write a thesis. He should have completed it a year ago. What happened? He parked the car and walked in just as the phone was ringing. It was his cousin Gary, who said he had scored some cocaine and Acapulco Gold, so he was going to drop by in the evening. Gelsomina slept under the table. After Tybalt died they got another cat, a long-haired black and white one, which Deborah decided to call by the tragic character in Fellini's film *La Strada*. They had seen it at the Ken and had cried at the end of the movie. As the cat got up and went outside through the kitchen cat door, the young man put on an album by Tom Waits, filled one of his pipes with wine cavendish and sat on the sofa. The old beige carpet, the yellow plastic hippo his son lay on and with his legs pushed around, the bookcase brimming with books, the lamp on the right-side stand, the alcove window, the round table with the four chairs, the stereo, the barbell his mother had bought him when he was in high school, the poster of a stylized Hamlet looking at a white skull—why did those things hurt him? In their inertness, they absorbed what roiled inside him and reflected it back, painful truth mirrors.

There was a knock on the door. It was his cousin.

"This is really good shit," Gary said as he sat on the easy chair by the bookcase and began to roll a joint. With hair down to his shoulders and a mustache, he looked like he belonged in a rock-and-roll band. Gary took a deep drag and handed him the joint. Yes, it was smooth, not like the ten-dollar-a-lid Mexican shit that was mostly seeds and stems they usually got.

"I'm going to put some music on," said the young

man as he flipped through the records he had stacked on the carpet, next to the stereo. He had bought it at JCPenney a few years earlier, a Garrard turntable, a receiver and two bookshelf speakers. Certainly not audiophile quality, but it wasn't too bad. He had set it up on a stand he had put together with a couple of boards and bricks. He played *Rumours*, the latest album by Fleetwood Mac. "Don't stop thinking about tomorrow. Don't stop, it'll soon be here, it'll be better than before. Yesterday's gone, yesterday's gone." Tomorrow will be better than before? He had his doubts. Wasn't yesterday once today and tomorrow? Wouldn't tomorrow be yesterday the following day? Everything was going to shit. What did he have to look forward to? He sat on the sofa facing the stereo, as Gary, sitting on the chair by the bookcase, to his right, began to roll another joint. The lamp on the side table had magically turned the room into a rosy, gilded space where resentments, anxiety, fear, anger and disappointments dissipated. The deep cherry red of the lamp's body seemed like a living creature trembling at the music. He had spent so much time sitting on that sofa with Deborah, the baby and the cat, smoking his pipe and listening to music, reading, but soon they would have to move; the apartment had been purchased by a company that wanted to remodel it and sell it as a condo. The young man got up and went to get the bottle of Chivas Regal. "Scotch time," he said to his cousin as he handed him a glass half full of the gold-colored liquor. "Not bad, even though I usually have Jack Daniel's or Wild Turkey," Gary said. The young man put Jackson Browne on: "I've been aware of the time going by. They say, in the end, it's the wink of an eye. When the morning light comes streaming in, you'll get up and do it again, Amen." *If it's in the wink of an eye, why the fuck bother?* He wondered. He got up and went to get the bottle of Quaaludes. He popped one in his mouth and handed Gary one. "Here, let's feel no pain."

Gary's face brightened. "All right! Now you're talking!" They finished the second joint and took another Quaalude. The music became more luscious, clearer, three-dimensional, the lamp's glow warmer and deeper.

"So Deborah went to Calexico, huh?" asked Gary as he took a glass vial full of white powder out of his pocket. "Do you have a small mirror?" he asked, as he got up from the easy chair and stumbled toward the table. He seemed like a ship on rough seas trying to steer for the dock. He finally sat on a chair and put the vial and a short straw on the table. The young man somehow made it to the bathroom and came back with a small mirror. They snorted a couple of lines and felt revitalized. The young man put the latest album by Bob Marley on. "Don't worry about a thing, 'cause every little thing is gonna be alright"— the voice and the music, so loud and crisp, felt like living things swimming in the room. Amazing how great the JCPenney speakers sounded. Gary lit a Marlboro, handed it to the young man and lit another one for himself.

"Deborah wanted to spend a couple of days at her mom's house. Hell, I'm glad she went," said the young man as he sat on the sofa again. From deep inside, something dark threatened to enter, so he went in the bathroom to get two more Quaaludes. He handed one to Gary, and they popped them in their mouths and chased them with scotch. They did another two lines of coke and sat down again.

"Better not take any more Quaaludes unless we want to die," said the young man.

"I don't wanna die yet," replied Gary. "I kind of like my CETA job. You're a student, sit in classes, read books and write papers, your head in theories and ideas, then they hand you a piece of fucking paper and you're out, you need to make a living. Not the kind of job I had in mind, working for the water district, but I need the money."

"Yesterday's gone. Hell, I don't want to think about tomorrow," said the young man. He took a drag from the Marlboro and drank more Chivas. He liked it with ice and by now it was diluted. He got up, but trying to sit at the table knocked a chair down, tripped on it and fell on the floor. He felt nothing. He slowly got up and sat on another chair and stared at the bottle of scotch on the table.

"I think you might be looking for this," he heard Gary say, as a hand holding a glass appeared in front of him. "You dropped it when you fell. You need more coke."

After they snorted some more lines, he felt like he was going to be able to hang on to some level of consciousness. No pain; the record had stopped playing, but it didn't matter. Nothing mattered. There was the warm glow of the lamp, its dark red body trembling, trying to move—maybe it wanted to get nearer and tell him something. *I've been watching you for years*, it would say, *and you fucked up. You fucked it all up.* He turned his head away from the lamp. He poured some more scotch in his and Gary's glasses and took a swallow. He got up and stumbled toward the stereo. He couldn't seem to change records, so he played the same one again; then he made it to the sofa and sank into it. "Shut up!" he said to the lamp.

The following morning, around ten, the young man woke up. Where was he? He realized he was on the sofa and Gary was asleep on the easy chair. The sun was bright through the curtains, and he got up to go to the bathroom. Record albums were scattered all over the floor; two chairs were overturned; drinking glasses, potato chips and empty soda cans littered the carpet. Some books had fallen off a shelf; the ashtrays were overflowing with cigarette butts. *Yesterday is gone, tomorrow is here, but it's not better than before*, thought the young man. His head throbbed; his throat felt scratchy. He needed to drink some water and make coffee.

ONE DAY he woke up in a hospital bed. *Where the hell am I?* he wondered. He saw a man in a lab coat. "What am I doing here?" he asked. The man in the lab coat looked at him severely and replied, "You're in ICU. You overdosed on Quaaludes." His wife later told him she had gone out shopping with her mother, who was visiting, and when she came home, she found him sprawled on the bed, unresponsive. She had called the police, and he was taken to the emergency room. Once discharged from the hospital, he had to stay for seventy-two hours in a mental health unit.

Transported there in a van, he looked out the

window at buildings, people on the sidewalks and traffic, the sky still blue. The world was still out there, but he wasn't part of it anymore. The mental health unit was a hospital wing with locked doors. His stay began with a nurse asking him several questions as she filled out forms. "Why do you think you're here?"

"I took too many Quaaludes." He was assigned a bed in a room shared by three other patients, sat in the lounge drinking a cup of decaffeinated coffee and watched an old episode of *Bonanza* on TV. Why had he taken five quaaludes? They were three hundred milligrams apiece; he didn't think he wanted to kill himself. He had been angry; forces roiled in his head and chest and he had wanted to make them stop, had wanted to be unconscious, he remembered that much. In the evening, after a tray of bland hospital food, he was given his antidepressants, then lay in bed. The following days he had meetings with a doctor, talked with nurses, then was discharged.

Things began to spiral down from there. He hadn't made any progress in taking care of the incomplete courses and his thesis, and they had to move out of the apartment within thirty days. What was he going to do?

9

EL CENTRO, 1977–1980

He had decided to take courses again at the Calexico campus toward an elementary teaching credential. There was a need for elementary school teachers, and teaching kids sounded easier than dealing with adults. He and Deborah had moved to San Diego in 1973, and now, four years later, they were back in the desert, living in an apartment. It was a retreat, a capitulation. He had abandoned his dream of teaching philosophy; now he hoped to get a credential so he could teach elementary school kids. Michael was two years old. He had long brown hair down to his shoulders and loved to sit on the sofa and listen to him reading books.

How could the young man have allowed this to happen? He grew more despondent and depressed. His wife could not cope with his mood swings anymore and moved out with their son. He found himself back in his old room at his parents' house. He lay on the single bed and stared at the mahogany desk that stood in front of the window that overlooked the backyard. He remembered how in 1964, when his grandfather briefly lived with them, he would angrily pull the blind down when Mosaku, (that was his grandfather's name), happened to look in the window. When the young man met him, Mosaku was 77 years old, had suffered a stroke, and didn't speak much. He could still see Mosaku sitting on the edge of the bed, smoking a cigarette and reading the Japanese language newspaper he received from Los Angeles. Now the young man wished he could ask his grandfather many questions about his life. The young man's eyes moved to the bookcase on the left wall, so many of the books on the shelves were unread, just objects that had nothing to do with him now. What was he doing there? Had he just woken up? Were the past five years only a dream?

He had moved back to his parents' house when his first marriage fell apart, after he, Roberta and their daughter had relocated to El Centro from San Diego in 1970. And now, seven years later, after returning to El Centro with Deborah and Michael, he was back in his old room.

He wound up in a mental health unit again. "How is it here?" he had asked one of the patients. The guy had looked at him and replied, "It's hell." Disheveled men and women with blank eyes walked back and forth in front of the nurse's station or sat in the lounge staring at the TV. Lloyd had come to visit him on the second day. He wore jeans and a light blue shirt with rolled up sleeves, and as he smiled, a gold tooth like a jewel peeked from the left side of his mouth. "I brought you a couple of magazines and some chocolate bars," he said as he sat on the chair by the bed.

His green eyes shined behind glasses, radiating tranquility. He laid a copy of *Newsweek*, *The Atlantic* and *The Nation* on the side table with a Baby Ruth and a Hershey's. The young man had been staring at the ceiling, wondering if he was in hell or purgatory. Seeing his old professor lifted his spirits. They talked for a while, then Lloyd got up. "Don't give up, I have faith in you," he told the young man before he left.

There were long sessions with a psychiatrist, looking at ink blots, sitting, lying down, walking back and forth. He'd stand in front of the window and stare at the cars in the parking structure. It was the end of 1978. Fifteen years earlier he had arrived in his mythical promised land, the New York skyline at dawn his new Jerusalem, where he would prosper and find fulfillment. He was thirty now but had nothing. From the window, through the steel grating, he saw someone walk to a car and a couple of minutes later, the car left. Signs of a kind of life that eluded him. What would it have been like to have a good job, drive a newer car, have some kind of anchor or foothold in society?

Back home the young man lay on his bed for hours, listening to music or sleeping. He couldn't read —how could he when he was sinking under the waves, struggling to keep afloat?

He listened to Leonard Cohen's new album, *Recent Songs*. From the blue cover the singer stared at him with penetrating eyes, a black mane of hair framing his handsome face. The young man had first heard Cohen at Frank's house, and he bought every new album the singer released.

He remembered jumping over the back fence at

night and embracing Deborah for the first time. How sweet her lips tasted, her slender body quivering in his arms, making love on her bed. *I dig you; I dig you.* And now it was all over. What happened?

He had failed at the university, had failed at his plan to work toward a teaching credential, had failed at his marriage. He was back in his room at his parents' house. When Cohen's "The Window" played, a violin began achingly, then the sonorous singer's voice filled the room. "Why do you stand by the window abandoned to beauty and pride, the thorn of the night in your bosom, the spear of the age in your side...oh chosen love, oh frozen love, oh tangle of matter and ghost, oh darling of angels, demons and saints and the whole broken-hearted host, gentle this soul..." At the end, the young man rubbed tears from his eyes and played the song again.

He needed to get a job, but doing what? He began working in a convalescent hospital, on the night shift. He had to buy himself a white coat, and on the first night, after he punched the clock, the nurse had told him to follow her. She was a big African American woman with a friendly face who took him down the hall to the utility room. She showed him a cart with diapers and cleaning cloths stacked on the shelves and told him to get to work. Most of the patients were very old, some younger; there was even a young man who was dying of esophageal cancer.

Most of the residents stared at the wall or had their eyes closed when he changed them, but a bedridden old man would talk to him, asking him questions about the weather or how his day had been.

"How are you doing tonight, John?" the young

man asked him one night as he changed his diaper. The old man said nothing, but tears began to fill his eyes. "What's wrong?"

The old-timer rubbed his fading blue eyes, then said, "I remembered when I used to go fishing with my daddy. He'd take me in his pickup truck, and we'd stand by the stream as the sun came up, and I could see him, tall and smiling at me. Then he said, 'John, we're going to have trout for lunch today, and your mommy is gonna be proud.' And he was right, we caught six big ones, and my mother was so happy, she picked me up and kissed me...and now they're all gone, and I can never go back, never, never go back."

The young man was trying to think of something to say when the old patient closed his eyes and began to breathe deeply. He went to talk to the nurse, who came to look at the patient. She waved at the young man to follow her in the hall, then told him the old man was dying, that he was in Cheyne-Stokes respiration, and she asked him to sit there until he died. "There's no one to call. Many of these old people have relatives who live far away or don't care. Be careful about what you say, because hearing is the last sense to go."

She left, and he sat on the chair next to the bed and watched John for a couple of hours, until he stopped breathing. Then the nurse called the mortuary and two men came with a gurney to take him away. They were young, with bellies hanging over their belts; one had a crew cut and chewed gum. *So that's the way it ends*, the young man thought. *You languish in a convalescent home for a few years until one night you die and two tired, bored guys come to take your body away.*

Once John was taken away, the young man worked for a while longer, but a couple of hours before his shift ended he clocked out and left, never to return. He had seen dead people before: the young priest in Sella, when he stood behind his grandmother, who recited the rosary; the store owner in Sella who was laid on a table in the living room for a wake; the driver of a car at an intersection, lying on the road; but that was the first time he had witnessed someone actually die. It was a long, difficult process, like running a race.

The young man put kitchen knives in the trunk of the VW with the intent of driving to Boulder Creek and committing suicide. Deborah had lived in Boulder Creek when her parents worked at a coffee shop there, and she often spoke of it as an idyllic place. It was a ten-hour drive, and late at night, unable to keep his eyes open, he parked in a rest area and slept for a couple of hours. After more hours of driving he stopped at Santa Cruz for coffee, then continued to Boulder Creek. It was early morning as he drove on the mountain road, fog caressing the tops of pines and firs, cabins. Boulder Creek. Perhaps he hoped to find there the beauty Deborah often talked about; maybe something in that place would touch him, heal him. But he was tired and hungry, alone with himself. It was a serene place, with majestic redwoods brushed by low-hanging fog, thick ferns lining streams, crows cawing, the cold air rich with earthy scents—yes, an idyllic place, but indifferent to his pain. What was he going to do? Lie down by the side of the creek, slash his wrists and die as he gazed at trees and fog? No, he realized; he didn't want to kill himself. The knives in the trunk a silly ideation, he drove back to El Centro. The following day he returned the car to Deborah. Soon after, Betty, his mother-in-law, gave him an old VW hatchback to drive.

Lloyd, his former history professor at Imperial Valley College, had referred him for a mailroom job at a company in Santa Monica. "It would be an opportunity for you to get the hell out of the Valley, get a new start," he said over the phone. And so one early morning he drove the old, dented VW hatchback 240 miles to the interview. He had accepted the position, but on the day he was supposed to start he didn't show up. How was he going to find a place to live in Santa Monica, especially since he didn't have any money? How was he going to interact with people and learn new tasks? Why did he even go to the interview?

In 1979 he found a temporary job as a community worker in El Centro. The job involved interviewing people in their homes, assessing their needs and making referrals. Martha, the director, was a smart woman in her early forties who took a liking to the young man. They went on field work together sometimes, and she would buy him lunch. John, one of his fellow workers, loved beer. "Look at my Budweiser suit," he told the young man once, as he took a photo from his wallet, showing a smiling man in a jacket and pants covered with Budweiser logos, a can of beer in his hand. "It really is the breakfast of champions. I have a six-pack in the morning, before I come to work." The young man would sit at his desk smoking Gauloises cigarettes he'd buy at the Golden Bull, write reports and plan his appointments for the next day until it was time to go home. At times he and Martha went to Sambo's for coffee and talk. She was a single mother, a San Diego State graduate, and very active in community affairs.

Often, after work, he'd go see Larry at the trailer, have a glass of iced tea and listen to music, so he could spend some time away from his parents' house. His parents' house. The dark green carpet, the golden-colored sofa with side tables, his father's recliner next to it, the 25-inch TV cabinet in the corner. He'd open the front door and turn right, cross the living room and get in his room. He longed to have his own space, away from the judging eyes of his mother and father.

He finally found a detached studio in the back of a house and moved some of his stuff there, including the stereo and some records. But soon after, the EOC program ended, and his unemployment insurance claim was denied, so he could no longer pay the rent. Stranded in the desert of his dreams, he passed the time reading Engels's *Anti-Dühring*, the book he'd bought years earlier when he lived in San Diego with Deborah. When he tired of reading, he smoked Winstons and listened to music.

A couple of months earlier, he'd bought a .22-caliber rifle from an acquaintance so he could go to the countryside and shoot at cans. He had done that a couple of times and found it boring. Now, as he sat in the small living room of the studio he could no longer afford, estranged from his wife and son, trapped in the town he had so many times attempted to escape, his graduate program unfinished, he looked at the rifle propped in a corner and went to pick it up. He had put *Pyramid*, by Alan Parsons, on the record player, and he turned the volume up. "What goes up must come down, what must rise must fall..." He had failed, fucked up; he was thirty-one years old and had nothing, was alone. A surge of disgust and hate swelled up within him. *Fucking stupid bastard.* He inserted some rounds in the rifle as the song continued. "If all things must fall why build a miracle at all? If all things must pass even a pyramid won't last." *Fucking bastard. Well, take that, damn you!* He turned the rifle toward himself and pulled the trigger. A blast, and a sharp sensation in his shoulder. He dropped the weapon and walked out, got in his car, and drove to the emergency room.

"What happened?" the doctor asked.

"I was cleaning a rifle when it went off," he replied.

"You're lucky it just passed through. If it had hit a bone, it might have splintered; you could have died," said the doctor as the young man lay on a bed in the ER. But why were the police there? The rifle had been reported a year earlier as stolen, so he was charged with possession of stolen property and taken to county jail. And so, with his left arm in a sling, he found himself behind bars.

The place smelled like bleach, sweat and mildewed clothes. He was assigned a bunk in the dormitory, and with his arm in a sling, the pain radiating from his shoulder and back, he tried to sleep. There must have been twenty prisoners there. He drifted in and out of consciousness for a few hours until early in the morning they were awakened and marched to a dining hall, where he ate cereal and a piece of cold toast with jam and drank a cup of watered-down coffee. After mopping the dormitory's floor, he found a paperback by John Gardner, the American novelist, in the stack labeled "Westerns." Whoever catalogued the book must have been deceived by the title of the short story collection, *The King's Indian.*

Lying down on the top bunk reading the book, he found it hard to let go and give himself to the writing. What was going to happen to him? An underlying anxiety, angst, threatened to pull the ground from under him, and it took effort to read while fighting to keep hopelessness at bay. But he found the stories intriguing and well written, with philosophical allusions and crisp dialogue. Ten days passed, and in the end the charge was dismissed. His father came to pick him up and he found himself in his room again.

He had an appointment with a psychologist at County Mental Health, where in 1972 he had worked as a psych tech. After checking in at the front counter, as he sat in the waiting room he saw Bill, one of the psych techs he had worked with. "Haven't seen you in a while," Bill said, surprised.

"Psych techs wear suits and ties now?" replied the young man with a smile. Bill had been a manual laborer who lived in a small run down apartment with his wife and their infant son. He had been hired by the newly established county mental health program as a psych tech trainee, and here he was now, looking professional in a JCPenny suit.

"I'm the director; I have to dress the part," replied Bill. "Are you applying for the opening?"

"No, I have an appointment with Dr. Torres."

"Oh, okay, well, it was good seeing you again. You're in good hands with Dr. Torres," Bill said as he left. The young man was prescribed antidepressants again, which made his mouth so dry that he had to sip water throughout the day.

Lying in bed in his room at his parents' house, he stared at the ceiling and the walls. He had lain in that bed on and off since high school. He felt like a boxer who had been pummeled in the ring and was now on the floor. He needed to get up, keep fighting. Ever since he had read *Nausea* and *The Stranger*, ever since he had studied Sartre and Camus, he had considered himself an existentialist. He had been molded by genetics and environment, there were things he could not change (what Sartre called facticity), but there was still a break, a crack, in that mold, where he was free and had to accept responsibility for his actions. He had been "thrown in the world," as Heidegger said, in a particular time and place, in a context he had just found himself in, but in the face of death, he had to decide what was important to him and act accordingly.

Philosophy, the life of the mind, had been important; that was the reason he had gone to the university and had worked toward a Master of Arts. And his children were important. As he lay on the bed in his room, out of jail, his arm still in a sling, on antidepressants, unemployed, his wife no longer his wife, his daughter living with her mother in Virginia Beach, his son a little boy he could only see on weekends, his thoughts and emotions scrambled, he couldn't imagine himself in front of a class, teaching. He couldn't see himself in an interview. It took all of his energy to maintain himself as an ego, to get up in the morning and get dressed, to eat dinner at the table with his parents. He couldn't read. But if he was free, couldn't he decide to change? Couldn't he work his way out of the hole he was in?

He felt empty, yet at the same time too heavy to move. Lethargic, so tired, but he forced himself to go for walks, to put one foot in front of another, even if he felt like he could limply fall to the ground like a rag at any moment. "Not to act is to act, not to choose is to choose," Sartre had said. The young man wanted to act.

IN 1980 HE found a full-time job as an eligibility worker for the Welfare Department. Now he could afford to get his own place, and he rented one not too far from work. Due to extensive damage in 1979 when a 6.5 earthquake damaged the County Offices Building, the department had been temporarily housed on Main Street, across from Yellow Mart, where as a high school student he'd had his first part-time job, washing windows. It was in that store that he had bought the geologist's hammer with which he retrieved fossils from Painted Gorge, on the high school science club field trips.

He'd drive to work in the run-down VW at 7:30 a.m., looking through the dirty, cracked windshield at middle-class homes. Green lawns, picket fences, potted plants, signs of a kind of life that had always seemed other, alien. He had thought for many years that he didn't want that kind of bourgeois life, with its stability and ennui, but there was something appealing, comforting, about those picket fences and manicured front lawns. A few miles westward he would have been in the desert, but thanks to the Colorado River and irrigation, there was plenty of water in the Valley, not just for front lawns, but also for golf courses.

The car seat springs poked his back as he glanced at the gas gauge. It was on reserve, and he didn't get paid until next week. He parked the car, walked to the office, sat at his desk, studied the files, shuffled folders and forms and made phone calls. He poured coffee in a mug and drank it as the phone rang. Then it was time to see clients. Sometimes they sat in the waiting room for hours, and when he finally called on them they wanted to talk, tell him they needed an emergency medical card because there was blood in their stool, they needed an operation because they had cancer, and he listened, but his supervisor admonished him. "You're spending too much time talking to them. You only have five minutes per client; remember, you're not a social worker." When he wasn't interviewing clients, he had to verify their eligibility. Did they actually reside at the addresses they had listed? Had they worked at the places they had written down? Were they citizens? Lots of phone calls. Sometimes he drove to their homes to make sure they lived there, until it was five o'clock and he could leave.

He got along well with the workers in eligibility, and he especially liked Nancy, a woman in her thirties who liked to go dancing every week at the local nightclub. "My weekend starts on Thursday night and then on Sunday I sleep all day," she told him. She came to his apartment a few times to listen to music and talk. She had gone to Central Union and had lived with her family down the street in a house next to Gary's. With long hair parted in the middle and glasses, a smile on her face, she projected exuberance and sexiness. Bobbi, a social worker, was a jovial woman who had recently separated from her husband. She had a boy and two little girls. The young man and Bobbi would talk about the goings-on in the department and about music. "I like mellow jazz, mainly," she said. "Who? Leonard Cohen? No, I've never heard him. You should drop by my house with some of his music." So one afternoon he showed up at her door with some of his favorite albums and a bottle of wine. They sat on the sofa in the living room listening to Grover Washington Jr., Ronnie Laws and Leonard Cohen as they drank a glass of wine. Her two girls were playing on the floor with a doll. Vonnie shyly tapped him on the leg.

"Are you Chinese?" she asked.

"Well, I'm two things, Italian and Japanese," he replied.

"I'm two things, too!" she said and smiled.

He enjoyed Grover Washington Jr.' s "East River Drive" and Bobbi liked Leonard Cohen's "Famous Blue Raincoat." Back in his apartment, the young man felt less lonely. Talking to Nancy and Bobbi drew him away from the edge.

He was frustrated by not being able to spend more time with his clients, who were men and women in need of medical care, struggling to keep going, cleanly dressed in cheap clothes, some on the edge of death, like the 37-year-old man with yellow eyes and an extended belly, signs of advanced cirrhosis of the liver. He had to treat them as numbers, cases to be investigated with suspicion—but he was after all in eligibility, not social work. And once work was over, what did he have to look forward to?

He drove back home with the radio on whiskey music; that's what he called the sad country songs the only radio station in Imperial Valley often played. He glanced at the tired palm trees lining Adams Avenue. Outside, 110 degrees. In the apartment, trash smells, dirty dishes and an empty refrigerator. His children smiled from old photographs he had put on the wall in cheap frames bought at Thrifty. His daughter Renée lived with her mother in Virginia, and he hadn't seen her in years. He could visit his son Michael, usually on weekends. He turned on the TV: news, old movies. Why didn't he read? Why didn't he try to write? Tired after a day at the office, he became untethered from the world, and he sat in an easy chair in the living room wishing he could switch himself off, like a lamp or a television set.

10

SAN DIEGO, 1981–1982

He worked at the Welfare Department for a year, but it gnawed away at him: the five unfinished courses, the master's thesis he wanted to write, and that he had to move back to San Diego so he could meet periodically with his advisor and go to the campus library.

One afternoon, he changed the oil in his VW hatchback and gave it a tune-up, packed the books he needed, his trusted Olivetti Lettera 22 and some clothes, and left. His sister had invited him to stay at her studio apartment until he found a job. Sandrina lived in North Park and her place was detached, behind the main house. While he looked for employment he spent a lot of time in the studio, and Pie kept him company. She was a young Doberman-German shepherd mix, very disciplined and protective. When someone was eating she would go lie down on her bed, and if some stranger knocked on the door, she sounded ferocious.

He soon found work in nearby El Cajon, at a

shelter for battered women. Someone had to be there to do intakes at night in case clients came for help. He didn't like the hours because he could not sleep well during the day, but he needed the money, and it made his stay at his sister's easier, since when she came home from work he was gone.

As soon as he could afford it, he moved into the downstairs apartment of a small residential building in North Park, near University Avenue and 30th Street. In the upstairs unit lived Cathy, a single woman in her thirties who grew flowers and herbs in pots on the balcony. He contacted the philosophy department and began to work on his incompletes. Years had passed since he had taken the courses, so he had to reread hundreds of pages, write papers and take some oral exams, but after a few months of intense study he finally received grades for the courses he hadn't finished.

At the shelter, women showed up with bruises on their faces and would be given referrals and counseling during the three days they could stay. Most of them, chain-smoking cigarettes, unemployed with no education, went back to their boyfriends or husbands even before the three days were over. The shelter also housed some homeless couples and parolees. He befriended some of them, including a couple who spent their days at the nearby park, smoking cigarettes and drinking cheap booze. Jose, a heroin addict on probation, told him one day, "Yesterday at the park I hooked up with a hot chick; I had a hell of a good time. Not bad for a fat Mexican with a wooden leg." When the young man asked him what he wanted to do with his life, he replied, "I want to die with a needle in my arm."

The young man thought about Sartre. Those women who returned to their abusers; the transients who seemed content to spend the day at the park sipping cheap wine; Jose, who wanted to die with a needle in his arm, were they free? Could they have chosen different lives?

The young man began to write the thesis, mostly on weekends, sitting at the kitchen table, first in cursive, then after he made corrections and revisions, on the typewriter. Years earlier, when he took the course on Western Marxism, the young man had become interested in the writings of the Italian philosopher and political leader Antonio Gramsci. Mussolini sent Gramsci to prison for twenty years, but after eleven years, Gramsci died. He wrote almost three thousand pages of notes while in jail, and they were published in a definitive edition in four hardbound books in 1975. How can society be changed into a more equitable, rational form? That had been on the young man's mind since his Imperial Valley College days, when he and Mike talked about dedicating themselves to the cause.

Gramsci understood revolution as a process of hegemony, a multifaceted notion exemplified in terms of consensus achieved through people's education in new values and a new worldview. Worldviews are not simply abstract constructions, but are embodied in concrete institutions. How can a more progressive worldview become the leading one? This was one of the fundamental questions addressed by the great Italian philosopher, and in his thesis the young man wanted to elucidate Gramsci's theory.

One day he received a call from work. The supervisor said that their funding had declined and staff had to be reduced, so he was let go. Now he lived on unemployment, the highlight of the day his afternoon walk to the newsstand to buy the *New York Times* and read it at Winchell's while eating a doughnut and drinking a mug of stale coffee. As he dragged himself out of the apartment, fresh air and sunlight, and the squeals of children playing in the nearby schoolyard, reminded him that outside of his place a world existed.

He crossed the street and soon was on the corner of University Avenue and 30th Street. At the newsstand he saluted the clerk, who always sat behind the counter. "Here's the Bolshevik," the clerk greeted the young man with a grin. "What are you conniving now?"

The young man smiled. "Don't worry, when we take over you can keep your newsstand. That's not the kind of private property that needs to be abolished." The man behind the counter, short and portly, food stains on his shirt, owned the newsstand with his brother, who looked like Rodney Dangerfield, always with a cigar stuck in his mouth.

At Winchell's, as he perused the paper while sipping the bitter, flat coffee, in the obituaries he saw a photo of John Gardner, the author of *The King's Indian*, the book he had read in the county jail. "John Gardner, 49; Novelist and Poet" had died in a motorcycle accident. The young man had read other books by Gardner and liked the author's style, his craft, the way he created characters and settings, the dialogue. He had looked forward to many more novels by Gardner. John Gardner, long hair down to his shoulders, smoking his pipe, professor of creative writing and prolific writer, represented for him love of literature and passion for creating worlds through words; when the young man found himself in jail with his arm in a sling, the book he found in the prison's "library" was a lifesaver thrown at him as he drifted in despair. The stories he read, the style and philosophical allusions, had lifted him up. And now, the writer that had given him hope and affirmation was dead.

It was late afternoon, and as he turned right on Wightman Street he saw his neighbor Cathy on the balcony, watering her plants. A recovering addict who had moved away from the East Coast, Cathy was a warmhearted, generous woman who jogged, gardened and meditated. He said hi as he looked up, then opened the door to his apartment. He went in the kitchen, drank some water and sat in the easy chair, the only piece of furniture in the living room. In the wall niche he had the philosophy books he needed for his thesis. He glanced at them, then closed his eyes.

Soon my unemployment benefits will run out and I won't be able to pay the rent. The thought poisoned every moment of the day, and even during sleep, it haunted him. He was searching the want ads in the paper every day, driving downtown to the employment office, going to job interviews where he was told he was either under- or overqualified.

Anxiety, like the constant erosion of cliffs by waves, threatened his foundations. How could he read philosophy books when he didn't know how he was going to pay the rent? The doctor had refused to refill his prescription for Quaaludes, but scotch could blunt the pain of erosion, even if for a short while, and he needed relief. He didn't have enough money to buy a bottle, but he searched for change in the closet and drawers and found an additional three dollars, so he went to get half a pint. Back from the liquor store, as he was getting out of the car he dropped the bag, and the bottle shattered on the street. The cracking sound of glass and the smell of scotch in his head, he closed the car door in disbelief. Just an accident, but it felt like a sign, as if the universe was mocking him or trying to tell him something.

He sat in the chair in the living room listening to the noise of a lawnmower across the street. He stared at his books in the wall niche. The future a blank screen, the present a still life of loneliness, there was only the past in which to find some respite. And so he found himself driving by the places where he used to live when he was married. He'd drive slowly down Louisiana or 27th Street, motioning to motorists behind him to pass, and then lean forward and turn his head sideways, hoping to catch a glimpse of Deborah sitting on the front doorstep watching their son waddling around chasing the cat, or himself taking out the trash.

He wanted to appear more self-assured; it would help him in job interviews. He had read about method acting; couldn't he learn to act more confidently? He drove down University Avenue in the evening, heading toward Hillcrest. Past the bridge, the senior citizen apartment towers loomed on the right, and as he passed a bus, clouds of exhaust fumes enveloped his dented old hatchback. On Sixth Avenue by Balboa Park, a group of derelicts sat on the grass under a tree and smoked cigarettes. He had sat under that tree years earlier with his wife, infant son, and Larry, who had come to visit them from El Centro. KIFM played a piece by Ronnie Laws and in the distance, the lights of downtown beckoned. He was going to Seaport Village.

After parking, he walked along the boardwalk. How often had he been there with his parents, his daughter, with Deborah and his son? He saw the massive shadows of two aircraft carriers in the distance. Realms in which thousands of human beings were integrated in social structures with missions and goals. Couples sat close together on the low wall, talking and laughing. He walked into the Upstart Crow Bookstore and Coffee House and ordered a cappuccino. The aroma of coffee was in the air and recorded classical music played. He had been there so many times, with his parents, friends and his wife.

He asked a clerk if he could suggest a book on acting. "Oh, are you an actor?" the clerk had asked with interest, and he replied, "No, I'm just curious." The clerk looked at him with a hint of disappointment. "Well, Uta Hagen's *Respect for Acting* is a good one," he said, went to pick it up and handed it to the young man. Perhaps he could teach himself how to act and speak more authoritatively. He browsed the books on the shelves while listening to piped-in folk music, finished his coffee and left.

A couple sat on the low wall and kissed. The

musty water leisurely lapped behind them, and the yellow glow of the lamps illuminated his way. As he walked, he gazed at the twin towers of the InterContinental Hotel and at the skyscrapers, looming dark shapes sprinkled with lights, and for a few very long seconds, he had a feeling of unreality. What if he wasn't able to come back to that everyday sense of being alive in a world with others? Luckily, as he glanced at the waxing moon, he was back into himself. He started walking toward the parking lot and heard music from the merry-go-round.

He bought a ticket and climbed on a white horse, the taste of coffee still lingering in his mouth, in his hand the book he hoped could change him. Bright lights, laughter from the children riding those frozen dreams, the smell of cotton candy in the breeze. The carousel, shabby in sunlight, became enchanting at night. Young couples and grandparents stood around and smiled at their children and grandchildren, just as his mother watched him so many years ago on merry-go-rounds in Genova, just as he watched his daughter and then his son ride their white horses. There was no one he knew watching him ride his stillborn dream. It was just as well.

WHAT THE HELL am I doing? thought the old man as he pushed the chair forward and took a drink of water from the hydro flask he kept on the side table. He rubbed his face with his hand and ran his fingers through his hair. Was he a masochist? Hell, he didn't want to remember that. There were times he wished he could edit his memories—not delete them, just put the ones he didn't like in a folder labeled "Archived" so he could retrieve them if he ever wanted to. He wished he could go back in time and tell himself, "Get your act together, stop fucking around. Finish your thesis, get a teaching job. Even if you can't find a full-time one, you could teach enough courses as a part-timer to scrape out a living. At least you would have been true to your vocation."

It was almost seven the next morning when the old man woke up, feeling groggy, glad to be alive. As he walked to the bathroom, a dull pain like a giant hand grabbed him by the lower back, trying to pull him down. He went downstairs to brew a pot of coffee, then back to bed to read the papers on the iPad. He sipped the Brazilian brew and scanned the headlines, read a few articles and savored the comics. After an hour he got up, took a long shower, got dressed and made the bed. His wife had gone for a walk with one of her girlfriends. It was too early to have breakfast, so he sat on a chair in the living room and pondered his options for the day. He could go for a walk, write, read all day, watch movies, listen to music, go for a drive or call a friend.

But instead he sat there, feeling out of joint. Was Macbeth right? Was life "a tale told by an idiot, full of sound and fury, signifying nothing"? Here was the world—eight billion naked apes infesting the planet, global capitalism the dominant mode of economic and social organization, the most powerful nation led by a spiteful, crude billionaire and his enablers, many of them racist and misogynist haters and hypocrites who, supported by the corporate-controlled media, incited the masses.

And then there was the cancel culture, identity politics, the language police, political correctness—you could not make a joke or say anything for fear someone was going to be offended and attack you on social media. All someone had to do was utter the wrong word, even if done in an appropriate context, and the consequences could be ostracism, the loss of a career. You'd better be careful how you were going to dress for a Halloween party—you might be accused of cultural appropriation or racism. The new inquisitors delighted in changing the language in famous works of fiction; they scoured the background of people living and dead and at the least whiff of what might be racism, relished canceling them. Free speech was dead. How could people have become so fragile, so easily offended, so easily hurt? So intolerant and mean? They needed trigger warnings; they needed "safe places." *Idiots. There are no safe places.*

And what about the deforestation of the Amazon, pollution, run-amok building developments, an unjust penal system, increasing inequality and climate change? But no, that was not all; now there was a pandemic to worry about. Did he whine too much? The world had been going to hell since it started. There had always been disasters and pandemics; life was short, full of disappointments and suffering, except for the privileged few, the ones who'd won the lottery of genetics and environment and were young, attractive, smart and rich. But even to them, the days of suffering would come.

AFTER A DAY when more than three thousand infections were reported and sixty-three people died of Covid-19 in San Diego, the old man sat in his chair with a small clothbound volume in his hands. Under an embossed image of a flower basket, the title read, *One Hundred and One Famous Poems*. He opened it and saw he had written the date on the flyleaf: September 3, 1966. He vaguely remembered having bought the book, probably at the El Centro Office Supplies Store on Main Street. He flipped through the pages. They had yellowed a little, and before he closed the book, he put his nose in its gutter and sniffed—no matter how much he tried to name the scent he couldn't, just a faint mustiness of more than fifty years. He had just finished his sophomore year at Central High when he got it. As he held the small volume, he closed his eyes and tried to go back in time. His heart began to beat faster; the walls moved closer. He didn't want *to just remember,* he wanted to go back to that day, to walk in and buy that book as he took a deep breath and glanced at the new Royal and Olivetti typewriters on the shelves, but he was trapped in the future. He put the book down and ran his hand through his thinning hair. Lately, looking at his books on the shelves or stacked on the floor, he found volumes from long ago, books that survived all the moves he had made, like the *Webster's New Collegiate Dictionary* he bought brand new at Office Supplies in 1972, now without the dust jacket, the blue cloth binding frayed, the gold lettering faded, the pages yellowed. Or the paperback copy of *October Light*, the novel by John Gardner he had recently reread. He got up to retrieve it from the top of a stack and sat down again. It was more than forty years old now, the paper cover had detached from the spine at the bottom and some of the pages were loose. John Gardner. The old man returned to the time he lived in North Park and read the writer's obituary, and he was back in 1982.

CATHY, his upstairs neighbor, was running in place in her living room, and in anger, the young man took his broom and hit the ceiling several times with it, until there was silence. She would have stopped after a few minutes; why did he have to bang on the ceiling? His unemployment benefits had run out and he couldn't find a job. The rent was due. How was he going to buy food, keep his car running? Larry was making a decent living as a respiratory therapist; maybe he could do the same. But he needed a license. He'd applied and had been accepted into the respiratory therapy program at Grossmont College, in El Cajon, but had to wait a semester. He could move back to his parents' house and take two courses required by the program at Imperial Valley College.

He had lived in the North Park apartment for a year. He was taking a shower. Some of the wall tiles had come off, and the bathtub was chipped and stained. The hot water felt soothing on his neck and shoulders. As he looked out the dirty window at the green shrubs and a patch of blue sky, a realization flashed inside him—*I am living my life, here, right now*. It surprised him; it was a shock. He had always assumed he was *preparing* to live, that only after years as a student, after earning degrees and certificates, after finding a successful career and a meaningful long-lasting relationship, he would truly *live*. No, he realized, *this* is my life; I am living it *now*. It frightened him, jolted him. The hot water on his back, the green shrubs, the sky, the dilapidated bathroom, and he, divorced, unemployed, getting older, his master's program still unfinished. He took a deep breath, sighed and smiled. He was living his life.

11

EL CENTRO AND SAN DIEGO, 1983–1985

He found himself back in his room at his parents' house in El Centro. As he lay on his old bed, the new GE plastic alarm clock his mother had bought him on top of the headboard, he felt enveloped again in a safe cocoon. The constant anxiety of not being able to pay the rent for his apartment was gone, but it was another defeat. How many times had he lain on that bed and planned to leave his parents' house and that desert town, to go and create a life for himself? And how many times had he found himself back in that room?

How awkward to be back in the spring of 1982 at the community college he had graduated from in 1970. He had planned to get his master's in 1975 and start teaching, but he was back there taking undergraduate courses so he could become a medical technician. Many of his old professors were still there. What did they think, seeing him back after so many years? At least they had the tact not to ask him what he was doing there. He took microbiology and chemistry, two required courses for the program.

He liked microbiology, and in the lab, had two partners that he became friends with. One was a petite blonde his age. He liked her and finally found the courage to ask her out. They soon began dating. "I did a background check on you and you're okay," she told him over a glass of wine at her place. She worked as a dispatcher for the Highway Patrol but wanted to become a nurse. Pam was a divorcee, politically conservative and religious. She had a framed photo of Barbara Bush on a wall in her bedroom and had dragged him to her church one Sunday. The sex was good, even though he didn't like Barbara Bush staring from the wall. Pam drove a new Nissan 370, was a heavy smoker and loved horses.

He found a room for rent in an older couple's house in El Cajon and moved in, a month before the respiratory therapy program at Grossmont College started. He continued to see Pam for a while, but then she also moved, and they lost touch. He wondered if she ever became a nurse.

He had to finish his thesis; time was running out. He received grades for the incomplete courses and had more than half of the thesis done. *If you don't finish it now, you never will*, he told himself. He pounded away at the typewriter in his rented room during the September heat, an oscillating fan on the desk still leaving him drenched in sweat.

As he drove the old, dented VW hatchback in the early morning to Grossmont College, he felt awkward. Most of the students in the program were younger.

The first-semester courses weren't demanding, so he had time to meet with his graduate committee members and polish the thesis, *Gramsci's Concept of Hegemony,* which was approved in November of 1983. He was granted the Master of Arts in philosophy. He had finally achieved his educational goal, but he had given up on his dream to teach. Positions were rare and when an opening came up, experience was required. And he couldn't see himself in front of a class.

He concentrated on the courses at Grossmont. He studied pulmonary pharmacology, anatomy and physiology, principles of respiratory therapy, ventilators and blood gases, and began field work in hospitals. For the Associate of Science degree he was required to take physical education courses, which resulted in his becoming the most physically fit he had ever been. He learned to play racquetball and began to lift weights again.

Donna, one of the students, pushed him to go jogging, and with her prodding and encouragement, he began to jog and then swim from La Jolla Cove to the Shores, three-quarters of a mile. With a mask, fins and snorkel he could rest halfway to the Shores, and his heart opened at the sight of schools of fish, leopard sharks and undulating seaweed and as they approached the sandy Shores, skates. From there they jogged back to the Cove barefoot on the sidewalks. They went to Mount Laguna and ran uphill on trails for miles. Donna was ten years older than he was, but much more physically fit. With her help, he became slim and healthier. He weighed 165 pounds, with little body fat. Edwin, Donna's husband, worked at San Diego State and jogged to work and back every day. He also became an inspiration for the young man. Edwin was older but could run ten miles without signs of fatigue.

When the young man came home one day he found a letter from Sandrina. She had returned to Italy in 1984. After working as a pottery maker for many years, she had traveled to Central America and lived in India for a year. Following an unsuccessful business venture she decided to return to Italy, study at the University for Foreigners in Perugia and become a teacher. But before going to Perugia she went to visit Noé. In the letter she wrote that he didn't look healthy, his sciatic nerve caused him a lot of pain, and Bruna, his wife, gave him injections. The young man wished he could go visit his brother, but it wasn't possible. He was busy with classes, clinicals and a part-time job in the respiratory therapy equipment room at Sharp Hospital.

As the months rolled on, the thirty students in the program became more or less familiar with each other. He went jogging at times with Jack, there was a Hawaiian student he went to see *The Terminator* with at the Cinerama in Grossmont Center, and then there was Dorothea. They'd go places in her pickup truck, books, empty Styrofoam coffee cups and racquet balls on the floor, her stethoscope hanging from the rearview mirror. She had a 24-foot sailboat and took him sailing around the bay. When the sails caught the wind they flew in salty spray, sandwiched between sea and sky. Then one day she told the young man she could no longer see him because her feelings for him were more than friendship, and since those feelings were not reciprocated, she could not deal with the pain. It wasn't easy for men and women to just be friends, it seemed. He was disappointed, because he liked spending time with Dorothea. But he did well in the program, even received an award for having written a winning paper on new treatments for asthma in children, and he received the Associate of Science degree in respiratory therapy in June 1985.

That summer, his parents moved to Italy while he remained in San Diego. They went to visit Noé, who found them an apartment in Sella. His mother wrote that Noé's pain was getting worse, so he was taken to the hospital in Genova.

The young man rented a house, bought a new car and worked full time as a respiratory therapist for a home medical supply company. He felt relieved that his parents had left; finally he would be on his own. He drove to Bayview Medical, worked in the office for a few hours, then spent most of the day out seeing patients. On weekends he drove to El Centro to visit his son. They usually had a burger and fries at Carl's Junior or Burger King, then went to the movies. Michael was three years old when the young man and Deborah separated, and even though he visited his son often, read him books and brought him toys, the close bond they had once shared had loosened.

THE OLD MAN surfaced from the ocean of memory and took a deep breath. It seemed to him as he was reclining in his chair that almost everything he had done had been a mistake. "You should write a book by the title *How Not to Live Your Life*," Larry's friend Kay had told him one day. Maybe she had been right. The old man felt like drinking a scotch but dismissed the thought as soon as it entered his mind. Alcohol would cause his heart to race, acid reflux to worsen, his stomach to burn; he would not be able to fall asleep and would not feel that great in the morning. And forget about smoking marijuana. It would irritate his throat and bronchi, give him the munchies and put him in a bad frame of mind. Sometimes he wished he could take something that would render him unconscious or make him not care about anything. Maybe opium could do that, but he had no intention of trying it. He had enough problems as it was; he didn't need to become an addict. He turned his head toward the books on religion that were on the shelves to his right: Taoism, Confucianism, Buddhism, Christianity, Islam.

He picked up a holy card he kept on a shelf. It was a photo of Edith Stein in the garment of a nun. She had studied phenomenology under Husserl, had converted to Catholicism and took the religious name of Sister Teresa Benedicta of the Cross. On the back of the card was a short excerpt from her book *Paths to Interior Silence*. It said in part, "And when night comes, and you look back over the day and see how fragmentary everything has been, and how much you planned that has gone undone, and all the reasons you have to be embarrassed and ashamed: just take everything exactly as it is, put it in God's hands and leave it with him. Then you will be able to rest in him—really rest—and start the next day as a new life." The old man wondered how a highly intelligent woman who studied philosophy could have become so religious. He gazed at her face, especially at her eyes, which seemed to really see him. He wished that God existed and felt a desire to pray to God the Father, Jesus, Mary and the saints, but that wish hit the wall of critical thinking and burst.

He felt again the pain of claustrophobia, of being trapped in a box with no hope of escape. In the box was ignorance. *What is the universe? Why is there life? Does God exist, is there anything transcendent?* And in the box was also irreversibility: himself as an old man, condemned to decrepitude and death.

IT WAS the fall of 1985. One day, after visiting his son in El Centro, the middle-aged man stopped to see his friend Larry. A tall woman with short blond hair sat on the sofa, drinking tea. Her name was Penelope, and the man felt an immediate attraction. Larry had put on a record by the Little River Band, and they relaxed, talked and listened to the songs, including "Cool Change" and "Lonesome Loser."

Penelope was an elementary school teacher with three teenage children, a dog and a cat. He called her one day and after a long talk, he invited her to come see him on a Saturday. They went to Old Town for lunch and got tipsy on New England iced teas, went to see *Eraserhead* at the Guild in Hillcrest and browsed in the Blue Door Bookstore. She hadn't liked the film. That was the first David Lynch film he had seen, and he was puzzled, challenged and impressed by it.

They often drove to the Menghini Winery near Julian, where they would buy a bottle of white cabernet and had picnics with sourdough bread, salami and cheese. The winery was a simple barnlike room with a wooden counter and some bottles on it for tastings. On the left side stood tall wine tanks, fermenters and other equipment. Mr. Menghini, a slim, friendly man, said the grapes came from the Escondido area and he made the wine in Julian.

The young man and Penelope went to movies often and listened to music. She was especially fond of Jimmy Buffett, and they would sit on the sofa with a glass of wine and listen to cassette tapes of his songs, including "Jolly Mon Sing," "Who's the Blonde Stranger?" and "Changes in Latitudes, Changes in Attitudes." The young man had never heard of Jimmy Buffett; it was different from the music he usually listened to, but he liked the cheery, light sound.

He began to tire of driving around every day visiting patients and doing assessments. On the freeway on the way home after work, caught in the rush hour gridlock, he thought of the patients he visited, many in their sixties and seventies, suffering from chronic obstructive pulmonary disease, living alone in run-down hotel rooms, senior apartment buildings or mobile homes, eating out of cans, tethered to an oxygen tank or a concentrator. Some were wealthy, residing in fancy apartments in Coronado or downtown, or in homes overlooking the ocean in La Jolla. He dreamed about them, men and women who had lived vibrant lives, now reduced to smoldering things soon to become cold. Some of his patients were young, like the teenage boy who was dying of cancer on a hospital bed in his parents' living room, or the boy who had fallen off the bed of a pickup truck and become paralyzed, living out his days in a house for the disabled. In a squalid room, now connected to a ventilator, what was the child feeling? Even after work, the young man couldn't stop thinking about those people, and anger and sadness kept eating slowly at him. Was his problem weak ego boundaries? No, he didn't want to work at this nexus of human interaction; he wanted to work with people who were young and healthy, beginning their lives, going to school.

He decided to finish the education courses leading to a credential and teach at the high school level. At least there was a demand for high school teachers. He and his supervisor came to an agreement: he could have Tuesdays and Thursdays off if he worked during the weekends. And so, beginning in January of 1986, he drove 120 miles to Calexico and back twice a week. He would have had to wait a year for admission to the school of education at the main campus, and he didn't want to wait.

On the first of February, his mother called to tell him his brother had died. Noé had been diagnosed with metastatic cancer and had been allowed to go home for Christmas but had gotten worse, and he died on the twenty-third of January at the hospital. The young man had hardly ever written to his brother; he had always assumed he would see him again. But now his brother was no more. His funeral was held in Sella on January 24, 1986. Noé, who had been the most important father figure the boy had, growing up in Genova; the brother who gave him gifts, took him to the movies, brought him everywhere on his motorcycle, was gone, and the young man could no longer hug him, talk to him, tell his brother how much he loved him. It was too late; it was irreversible.

12

EL CENTRO, 1986–1988

After completing the required courses and passing an exam, the now middle-aged man received a secondary emergency credential and accepted a position teaching English at Calexico High School. He resigned from his therapist job and moved into an apartment in El Centro. He was back in the desert, but that's where Penelope lived, and he was closer to his son, so he could see him more often.

At the high school, he was given mostly the classes with difficult students. He had problems maintaining discipline, and when he sent a troublemaker to the office he would be sent back within the hour. He took some solace in his Introduction to Literature course. He assigned short stories, epic poetry and novels, and had students keep a journal and write poems, film reviews and short stories. One of the books they read was *Grendel*, by John Gardner —the story of Beowulf, told from the monster's point of view. Uncanny how life works; if he hadn't wound up in county jail years earlier, he wouldn't have known who John Gardner was, and his students wouldn't have read *Grendel*. Most of the kids did the assignments, and toward the end of the school year, he had assembled some of their poems, drawings and short stories into a magazine entitled *The Encinas Avenue Journal, 1987*. Penelope helped him with some of the illustrations, and he made copies for the whole class. When he handed them out to the students, they were surprised and proud to see their work in a magazine.

He and Penelope got along well. On weekends they'd drive to San Diego, where they shopped and went to the movies, or to Julian for a picnic, or they just hung out together, watching a movie on TV or listening to music.

It was the summer of 1987. He had survived his first year of high school teaching. At the end of the school year one of his colleagues had given his students several F's, and the principal told him he needed to change those F's to C's or he would not be back in the fall.

He and Penelope decided to go on vacation to Italy, and he wanted to stay for five weeks. His twelve-year-old son Michael was also going, to the irritation of Penelope, who thought they would be going alone. He hadn't seen Italy since 1963, and a part of him was afraid to go back—afraid that his memories of Italy would be corrupted, altered by the new. Twenty-four years had passed since he had been in the land of his birth. He had left a boy, and now he was going back a middle-aged man. In the Italy inside him he was still full of dreams about America, his brother was alive and everyone was younger, Italy unravaged by the economic boom.

THEY ARRIVED at Fiumicino Airport on Monday, July 6. They took the bus from the airport to Stazione Termini, Rome's main railway station, and he had his first glimpses of Rome: the heavy traffic, the Colosseum in the distance, monuments, palazzi, crowds on sidewalks. It was only ten in the morning, but it was already getting warm. The bus's open windows let in a mixture of breezy air and exhaust fumes.

He was born in Rome but saw it now for the first time. They stayed in a *pensione* near the train station, rested, then went out to dinner, and at a newsstand he bought three newspapers and *The Name of the Rose* by Umberto Eco. He could speak in his native language again; he felt at home and a stranger at the same time.

The next morning they took the train to Orbetello, then a bus to Albinia, the small Tuscan town his parents had moved to from Sella after Noe's death. All this involved painful waits in long lines in hot, humid weather. The bus stopped almost in front of his parents' street, and as they walked to the apartment building dragging their suitcases, he saw his mother watching from the third-story balcony. He hadn't seen her in two years and was glad to see her smiling and waving.

What followed was a reunion with his uncle Libero, who lived a few blocks away. He remembered Libero as a wiry young man; now he had a belly and thinning graying hair. They met his uncle's wife and boys, had dinner at their apartment and long talks, reminiscing and laughter, but Penelope felt out of place. She didn't speak Italian and probably thought, *What am I doing here? I could be at home with my kids and my dog, visiting my mom and dad, who are not getting any younger, but I'm stuck in this place with these strange people.*

It was five thirty in the morning. He had been awake since four. He sat on the balcony, smelling freshly baked bread, and watched the swallows chase each other and screech over the rooftops. It was cool, and as the sun started to rise, trees and red-tiled roofs began to assume their colors.

Albinia, a town near Orbetello, in the Maremma region of Tuscany, was crowded with tourists. Within walking distance to the shore and to numerous camping sites in the thick pine groves lining the Silver Coast, it was a popular destination, especially for German campers. The young man, Penelope and his son often went to the beach. They walked by the side of the road for a mile and turned in a roundabout that led, on the left, to a country lane lined with tall stone pines. On either sides were campgrounds and at the end, a bar and the beach. The bar occupied the ground floor of a small, modern two-story building and had a large terrace with a roof that gave shade to several tables and chairs. They passed the time sunbathing, reading, frolicking in the water and playing ball. At times the young man's parents also came, and before leaving they would all sit at a table on the bar's terrace. An old waiter cleaned the tables, took orders and brought drinks. Of medium height, stocky, wearing a shirt with long folded sleeves, the waiter smiled and chatted with customers, and after he came to their table he greeted the young man's parents, talked to them for a while, then left. "He's the owner of the bar," said the middle-aged man's father. "His son works behind the counter, and his wife usually stays home. They live in an apartment across the street from us."

IN 1954, Libero, nineteen years old, taciturn, unemployed, had shown up at the House of the Fig in Sella with his little suitcase, and the boy had jumped up and down, would not leave him alone, cajoled his young uncle into playing guns with him. They had no toy guns, so they used their index fingers. After several weeks in Sella, Libero left, and the boy didn't see him until years later, when he appeared at their apartment in Genova and drove them to Orbetello in his used Opel. And now, at fifty-two, hair balding, heavier, Libero drove his new Alfa Romeo to Porto Santo Stefano. It was a balmy evening, and he was taking the middle-aged man and Penelope for a ride. They drove on one of the spits of land that connected the Monte Argentario peninsula to the mainland; then, as the car turned around a bend, down in the distance the seaside town sprang from the darkness, lights reflecting golden and red on the water, fishing boats and yachts docked at the tiny harbor. Scents of hay, deep green foliage and briny water entered through the open car window. The middle-aged man's mother was born in that seaside town in 1914, in her grandparents' farmhouse. On the slope of the mountain, they had vineyards and olive trees; now the small village had become a destination for tourists and the rich. After parking the car, Libero bought ice cream cones, and they sat at a table by the water looking at the fancy yachts docked where half a century earlier fishermen kept their boats. On the way back, Libero drove through Orbetello and passed by the *cantoniera*. "I grew up in that house, as did your mom, Avia, Gaetano and Angelo. When my mother died the house was put for sale by the city. We didn't have the money, and it slipped away from us," Libero said, and he pointed toward the small two story building barely visible in the moonlight. The middle-aged man saw himself as a boy walking on the abandoned train rails as his grandmother picked tomatoes in the vegetable garden with his sister.

THE OLD MAN sat up in the chair and took a drink of water. He remembered certain events, particular scenes of that trip, but most days were erased; it was as if he were watching a film with missing parts, corrupted frames, scratches and burns. His parents didn't have a car yet, so they traveled by train to visit his sister in Perugia. They had to get off at one station and board another train. He learned to hate traveling by train in the summer—the heat and humidity, the crowds, the rush, having to stand up because no seats were available.

The middle-aged man's sister lived in an apartment in the historical center, and from her window a sea of red roofs, hills and campaniles extended to the horizon. He was fascinated by Perugia: the Duomo, Fontana Maggiore, the walks to the Carducci Gardens, the medieval alleyways flanked by boutiques and intriguing shops, the stone floors, the smells of baked goods and cured meats. The surreal night of the Umbria Jazz Festival when Corso Vannucci became a human river in danger of overflowing, the sides lined with tables and blankets, young people selling trinkets, the lights, the music. It was past midnight, but as bright as daytime.

In the morning they all went to Assisi by train—his parents, he and Penelope, his son, and his sister. It was a hazy day, but when they arrived at the station, he could see the town perched on the mountain. A bus took them to a huge parking lot below the Basilica di San Francesco. They admired Giotto's frescoes on the walls of the church, then had a picnic in a nearby park. In the afternoon they went to see other churches—one had the remains of Saint Clare; another one, unadorned, struck him by its simplicity and evocative nature. On the way back they wandered through the Church of Santa Maria degli Angeli, where the Porziuncola, the small chapel where the first followers of Saint Francis met, was under a dome, looking like a butterfly trapped in a jar. Exhausted, they walked back to the train station to return to Perugia.

The next day his parents boarded the train back to Albinia with his son, but he and Penelope took a bus to Florence. They arrived by nine thirty in the morning and went to the Duomo, where they climbed all the way to the top, more than 460 steps. Could the old man do it nowadays? Maybe if he tried on a rainy winter's day, when not many tourists were there, so he could have taken his time and rested along the way. But it was probably closed now. No way to keep six feet of social distance in that narrow stone staircase. At the top they had a grand view of the city. Innumerable palazzi, basilicas, cupolas, medieval towers, campanili, green hills, villas, trees. What he read in history books and saw in movies and photographs came to life all around him, and he felt inebriated. It was as if the city was telling him, "You're finally here, we have waited for you!" Afterward, they spent three hours in the Uffizi Gallery, thrilled by the works of Michelangelo, Leonardo, Botticelli, Dürer, Raphael and many, many other artists. This was the first time he had been face to face with such paintings and he felt awed, *I wish I could live here*, he thought, *and everyday partake of all this history and art.* At five, they took the bus back to Perugia. They eventually made it back to Albinia, where after a few days of rest on the beach, they boarded a train for Genova.

After six hours in the crowded, sweltering compartment, the middle-aged man was covered in sweat and his back hurt. His father had his eyes closed, probably trying to sleep and his mother sat next to him, reading a magazine. They arrived at Stazione Brignole in the afternoon. Walking out of the station he stepped into his past. He saw the Torre San Vincenzo, a skyscraper built in the sixties. Noé had worked on it, so long ago. The middle-aged man looked at the building and felt close to his brother. *Fucking time.* He took a deep breath and looked around; it was four o'clock, and he smelled focaccia just out of the bakeries' ovens. He remembered walking there as a child, and his mother buying him and his sister hot, fragrant slices. He recognized the park in front; the air still smelled the same, a faint mixture of exhaust fumes, pine trees and the sea. They left their baggage at the bus station in Piazza della Vittoria, where with his mother and sister took the bus when they lived in Sella. They had to wait for Fabrizio, his nephew, to get off work, so they walked up Via Venti Settembre. They passed the theater where as a boy he had seen *The Ten Commandments*. They entered the Oriental Market, where Penelope took photos of a calico cat sitting on a fish counter licking its paw. As a boy, his mother shopped there on the days they came here from Sella. Then they made their way to Piazza de Ferrari, where as a child he walked on the low wall surrounding the fountain, holding on to his mother's or father's hand.

His nephew picked them up at six thirty at the bus station, and luckily, they all fit in the station wagon, their bags in the trunk. On the way to Davagna, the small village adjacent to Sella, where his nephew lived, they passed through Corso Sardegna, where he had lived with his mother, brother and sister in the early 1960s. When they left Italy in 1963 his nephew was one year old; now he was twenty-five and married to Elena, a charming blond young woman from Bassano del Grappa, a city in the Veneto region. As the middle-aged man sat in the back, squeezed next to Penelope and his mother, he saw the Church of Holy Faith, and up ahead the building they had lived in. For a moment, he expected to see the two old women dressed in black sitting outside the apartment building, as they were in 1963 when his brother drove them to the dock.

They rode through the mountains on the narrow road and gazing out the car's window, he saw himself holding on to his brother as the Ducati sped through the trees. When they arrived, Bruna was waiting for them. There were hugs and kisses on the cheeks. His brother's house was a villa with a downstairs apartment, where his nephew and wife lived. His brother had sent them photos of the house as he built it in his spare time with the help of his wife and her parents. He could discern Noé's craft in the high ceilings, ornate moldings, marble floors and fireplace. Objects spoke eloquently of him: the free-hand pipe he had sent his brother years before, now cradled in a shell ashtray on the coffee table, Noé's teeth marks on the black bit; the championship award from the Provincial Motorcycle Union hanging above the mantel; the teak cabinet his brother had built back in 1962. That night he saw fireflies. He hadn't seen them since he left Italy as a boy and seeing them again, green-yellow pulsating lights slowly moving through bushes and trees, brought him back to his childhood.

He woke up the next morning to church bells. Light shone through the wooden slats of the window coverings. After coffee and breakfast, they went with Bruna and Fabrizio to the cemetery to visit his brother's tomb and leave flowers. The trail led steeply downward, skirting terraced fields of recently cut grass, wild cherry, hazelnut, nectarine and chestnut trees. Yellow and white daisies, ivy, nettles, wild wheat and blackberry bushes seemed to welcome him. Behind them were jade-green highlands, and in front, far away, the highway skirting the hazy mountains that as a child had seemed like a white string on the folds of a blanket.

The small cemetery, protected by old stone walls, had an intimate feeling. In front of his brother's tomb his mother began to cry, and he had to force himself to keep his tears inside. The last time he had seen Noé was the day in 1963 when he had stayed in the cabin with him for a while, until all visitors were asked to leave the ship.

He had many memories of his brother: the gifts he gave him for Christmas and birthdays; the drives on the motorcycle; the day Noé took him to get a haircut and then told the barber to shave his head because it was summer; the rainy day Noé brought him to visit their mother at the hospital in Genova. He had pleaded with his brother to take him to the movies, so afterward they had gone to see *The Bridge over the River Kwai* and sat in loge, so his brother could smoke. Now his brother's remains lay behind a marble slab and an electric candle glowed next to his photograph. They arranged the flowers in a vase, and he was struck by how life went on in that garden of tombs: bees buzzed over flowers, the trees' leaves outside the walls moved gently, so green, in the breeze.

He had found himself up there with his mother, sister and brother in 1953, tall green peaks with small villages: Davagna, Sella, Moranego, where people woke up early to hike mountains and cut wood, take their oxen out to labor in the fields, tend their trees and postage-stamp vineyards. No TV, no telephones, no radios, just church bells marking the hours, sun and moon, wind and trees. Now the oxen stalls had been converted into garages, satellite dishes sprang from roofs, and many of the houses had been bought by city people who used them as vacation homes.

Bruna took him to see "the House of the Fig Tree," which now seemed much smaller. The windows' wooden green shutters looked the same, as did the cement terrace on which as a child he would lie down on, propping himself on his forearms, and gaze at the mountains, but the fig tree was gone.

He regretted the decision to stay five weeks in Italy because Penelope felt trapped. She had cried one night as they tried to sleep on the sofa bed in his parents' apartment, fighting humidity and mosquitoes. And his son, having to sleep on a cot in his grandparents' bedroom, forced to suffer in the heat on trains and buses, grew despondent. Luckily, the day of departure neared.

After another day at the beach, they went to Orbetello to visit his uncle Gaetano and Lilia, his wife, at the piece of land they owned near the Feniglia beach. Gaetano had been very active in the Communist Party, had held an administrative post in the town, but in the early eighties he gave up on politics and like the famous Roman emperor Diocletian, spent the rest of his life tending his vegetable garden, vineyard and trees.

The middle-aged man had someone else to visit before they returned. Avia and her husband, Angelo, had moved from Genova and had lived for many years in Alassio, a picturesque town on the Riviera, but after retirement they moved to Foiano della Chiana, a town eighteen miles from Arezzo. Libero gave him, Penelope and Michael a ride.

The last time he had seen his aunt she had waved from the pier in Genova, and he had been fifteen; now she was standing in front of him, her face wrinkled, doughier, but her hair still black and her eyes sparkly. Angelo, with receding wavy white hair and a thin white mustache, looked like a distinguished English gentleman, a comparison the man would not have liked, because during the Second World War he had been a prisoner in an English camp in Africa. They shared a great dinner, much talk, a long walk around the town, then goodbyes around 7 p.m. before the drive back to Albinia.

The vacation had come to an end. They spent the last day in Rome, then took the painful flight back, with long delays and connections.

BACK IN HIS APARTMENT, 115 degrees outside, he sat on the sofa, the droning of the air conditioner a reminder he was back in the desert. A couple of days earlier he had been in Tuscany, yesterday in Rome, and now he was back in El Centro. He rested his head on the sofa and closed his eyes. He felt heavy, drained, sick. He wanted to go to the newsstand and buy a copy of *La Repubblica*, stop by the bar, order a Campari and drink it at a table outside as he watched swallows weave arcs above rooftops and heard them screech. He wanted to take the train to Siena, Florence and Rome, walk in places that gave him a sense of history and art, loose himself in museums and hide in ancient churches.

The school year started, and as the weeks passed, he became fed up with the kids who talked in class, with the ones who refused to stay at their desks and threw books on the floor; he'd send them to the principal's office and a half hour later they'd be back. According to the administration, discipline was the responsibility of the teacher, and if a teacher had problems with students, it meant the teacher was weak. There were students who did no work and deserved F's but had to be given C's.

Did he want to spend the rest of his life in the Imperial Valley, teaching at the high school? In the middle of the second year, he resigned. He wanted to go back to Italy. A few weeks of vacation had not been enough; those few weeks had given him a thirst for exploring the architecture and art, the culture of the land from which he had sprung and on which he had lived the first fifteen years of his life. All he had experienced growing up had been parts of Genova, those mountain villages north of the city, and Orbetello in Tuscany.

He sat on the sofa in his living room, drinking a cup of tea. He was an English teacher, had a girlfriend, friends, a new car, a comfortable apartment and the toys everyone wanted: a computer (which Penelope had given him), a stereo, a TV and a VHS player, but he couldn't sleep, couldn't relax. Everything appeared devoid of any possible connection to him. It was six in the evening; he had to get out of those four walls, go for a ride, see a friend. He drove down the alley behind the apartment complex, trying to avoid the potholes and broken glass. The sun, an orange disc partially hidden by a eucalyptus, was about to disappear. In the distance he saw cars and trucks pass by on the interstate, then a yapping made him turn his head—a white Chihuahua ran to the gate of a backyard. He drove north on Imperial Avenue. In twilight everything became soft, the desert sky no longer assertively blue but pensive with reddish clouds, pale yellow stripes and pink hues.

He turned on Brighton Avenue and saw the house his parents bought when they arrived from Genova, thirty years earlier. He slowed down and stopped a moment to look at the one-story house with the green front yard. When his father retired, his parents sold the house and after a year in San Diego, moved back to Italy. It was strange to think that other people now lived there, someone else slept in his room. The palm trees his mother planted had grown tall, but the red bougainvillea in front of the living room window was gone. That house had been his mother's consolation. She missed Noé, her older son, her sister Avia, and Gaetano and Libero, her brothers. When her mother died, she couldn't go to the funeral, so she mourned alone. She never learned English well, so it was hard for her to interact with others outside the home. And El Centro was certainly not Genova, with its markets and harbor, its fountains, gardens and sea. She planted trees, tended the vegetable garden, made ravioli and tagliatelle, chicken *alla cacciatora*, tripe in tomato sauce, baccalà and minestrone. She read the Italian magazines she subscribed to and wrote many letters to Noé, her sister and brothers. The middle-aged man drove on. He wanted to see his friend Larry.

"Are you out of your mind?" Larry said as he gave the middle-aged man a glass of iced tea, put a record on and sat on the sofa.

"I want to experience more of Italy. One year, then I'll be back."

Larry scratched his graying beard and looked at him. "And Penelope? And Michael?"

"Penelope's life is here—her parents, children, house, career. And Michael..."

"One year is a long time. And then what will you do?" Vivaldi's music sparkled in the air like fireflies. The middle-aged man couldn't think of anything to say.

"There's the ocean in San Diego, La Jolla Cove, the Ocean Beach Pier, the Ken and Unicorn theaters, the Mithras bookstore," Larry said. "You have Penelope, Michael lives a few minutes away, you had a full-time teaching job. What is wrong with you?"

"I don't know," the middle-aged man replied. "Remember all the dreams we had? We were going to move to San Francisco, you were going back to college to study literature, I was going to teach philosophy. So many plans..." There was silence for a while, except for a kid riding a Hot Wheel trike on the sidewalk outside. "We went to the park to read Camus's *A Happy Death*. We were twenty-four, remember?" Larry stared in his tea and nodded.

"You think life will ever be better than that time?"

"No," he replied, then he looked at the middle-aged man. "That was fifteen years ago; we were young."

"I'm leaving in June."

Larry took another sip of tea. "You're crazy," he said.

Maybe I am crazy, thought the middle-aged man on the way back to his apartment, *but I hate the high school job. Academic excellence, what a joke, when almost no one is given an F or a D. There's little discipline, not much respect for teachers. Penelope's life is here, in the Valley, but I want to leave. Renée is married, lives in Virginia...Michael is fourteen years old; I see him once a week. We had a strong bond, but now it seems like he has only time for his friends. We seldom talk. I've been trying to make him understand why I want to go to Italy. I wonder if he cares.*

When he told Penelope he had quit his job and planned to move back to Italy for a year, her world crashed. The old man couldn't remember the first time he told her and what her reaction had been. Maybe he had repressed it, buried it deep, but he recollected an instance when they talked about it sitting in the car. "I thought you loved me, that we were building a future together," she said. They had planned to buy a cabin in the mountains, but now she was going to be alone. He kept telling her it was going to be just for a year, that he wanted to go back to Italy to experience more of the culture, but at the same time he wondered what the hell was wrong with him. Did he really want to return to El Centro after a year? And what did he plan to do in Italy to support himself? What kind of job was he going to get? Did he actually expect Penelope to patiently wait? Maybe in the back of his mind he had mistaken her for Homer's Penelope, but she wasn't, and he was no Odysseus.

THE MIDDLE-AGED MAN sat at the desk in front of the class. He had turned off the lights because he was showing *The Stone Boy*, a film starring Robert Duvall, about a family's struggles to cope with the death of a child in a hunting accident. They had read the short story earlier, and now he was showing them the movie adaptation. Someone was making a noise by tapping a pencil on the desk, but most of the students were quiet. He felt tired; ever since he'd tendered his resignation he hadn't slept well. Once he moved, he would be thousands of miles away from Penelope and his son. Could he find work in the land of his birth? Due to a bureaucratic glitch, he didn't have Italian citizenship, which limited his job possibilities. What else could he do? These questions tormented him day and night.

He had planned to go to Italy soon after he resigned from the teaching position, in January of 1988, but he needed more money, so he asked Penelope if he could live at her house while he worked at the hospital in Brawley for a few months, and she agreed.

On the first day of work, he showed up in the afternoon for a training shift. As he was talking to the supervisor, a call came from the emergency room and they responded. An ambulance had just brought a young woman who had been riding an ATV in the sand dunes when it flipped and landed on her. All-terrain vehicles were the 700-pound motorcycles with four fat tires that people liked to ride up and down sand dunes. The woman was unresponsive and he began to do CPR. She must have been in her early twenties. She did not respond to the doctors' emergency procedures and was declared dead. "Keep on doing CPR," he was ordered. "Her family agreed to donate her corneas, so keep her body oxygenated." He kept doing chest compressions as sweat dripped down his face, until someone came to remove her eyes. He took the ambu bags that were used to the Respiratory Therapy Department, and when he returned to the ER, the young woman's eyes were looking at him from a glass jar.

They gave him the night shift, and since he couldn't sleep during the day, he was drowsy most of the time. Luckily most of the work involved routine procedures: doing aerosol treatments, chest physical therapy, taking EKGs. But he had to respond to code blues and ER calls. Young men with stab wounds or head traumas came in; older men with heart attacks or abdominal aneurysms.

Weekends and holidays were hectic at the hospital, since people came in droves from Los Angeles County to ride their ATVs on the nearby Glamis sand dunes. Beer and riding all-terrain vehicles kept the ER busy.

One night surgery called. They needed a piece of equipment and as he brought it in, he saw on the operating table a patient he had seen daily in the ICU. He was a fifty-year-old Mexican American man who read the Bible every day. Now he lay on the table under the bright reflector, two surgeons bent over his open abdomen. The room smelled like raw meat, and the man seemed just a carcass. The patient survived the operation but died a few hours later.

As the middle-aged man left the hospital in the early morning, cars in the parking lot, the sky, trees and chirping birds seemed like flimsy props, designed to provide him with an illusion of tranquil stability. *You're just an organism going through its life cycle. Don't give yourself so much importance. You're just a tick in the infinite tick-tock of time. Just a beat in the never-ending pulsation of quantum fluctuations; it doesn't mean anything. You are caught in it, embedded. There is no escape, no way out except in death, which will come soon enough. Then it will be as if you had never been. You can't fight it. Go have breakfast. Jack off. Go watch TV or go buy yourself something. Go talk to a friend. Forget about it.* As he drove to Penelope's house, he couldn't stop thinking about the man he had seen in the ICU for days, reduced to a carcass, the smell of an open body, men in white with gleaming instruments bent over the red exposed organs. In an instant, what he had thought for so long had been proven to him: the soul, subjectivity, philosophy, art, science and love are only ephemeral manifestations of fragile human bodies informed by thousands of years of history, language and culture.

ONE MORNING he looked at Penelope as she sat at the vanity putting on makeup. He lay in bed, the cat kneading his chest waiting for her canned food, the news on the radio not really news. He held his favorite mug, the terra-cotta one from Assisi. They drank the coffee they'd bought in Santa Barbara, strong and sweet. The sun shone through the tree's branches outside the window and brightened Penelope's face. He noticed her tired blue eyes, graying hair, her wrinkled pale skin and drooping mouth. Did he love her? If he did, would he want to leave her?

"I BOUGHT A CABIN THIS MORNING," Penelope said as she walked into the living room. He felt a tinge of regret and sadness. They were supposed to buy it together, so they could escape the heat of the Valley during weekends and summers, and eventually live in it after retirement. He felt left out. Maybe he shouldn't have quit his job at the high school, shouldn't have entertained the crazy idea to move to Italy.

"So you bought it...where?" he asked as he put the book he was reading down on the sofa. She sat next to him. "In Live Oak Springs—you know where it is, off Old Highway 80, near Boulevard."

"You really did it."

"It's small, but it's next to a hill, secluded."

"I'd like to see it," he replied, and so they went. After an hour's drive, they turned right from the highway, past a restaurant and a grocery store, then up a dirt road, and in the back, near a hill, was the cabin, guarded by giant oaks. The only sounds the cawing of crows and the breeze rustling the trees' branches.

After she showed him the unfurnished interior, they stood in the small living room. She opened the window and a cool breeze came in. He caressed her hair, drew her close and kissed her. She felt warm; he could feel her heart beat. They sank to the dusty wooden floor.

THE MIDDLE-AGED MAN bought a toy poodle, which he planned to take to Italy to his mother. The puppy liked to run in the bedroom, jump on the bed and greet him and Penelope by licking their faces. The middle-aged man bought a small carrier and planned to take the puppy with him on the plane, but one day the puppy could not be found, and he, Penelope and her son Ronnie looked everywhere, to no avail. Then the puppy's body was discovered under the plastic cover of the swimming pool. The middle-aged man went in the bedroom and began to cry uncontrollably, his face contorted and his eyes blurry. The puppy was life, innocent and exuberant life new to the world, and it had been snuffed out. A sad event, but not uncommon. These things happened. But to the middle-aged man, it was another sign that he lived in a world beyond good and evil. A world conjured by mindless mechanical processes, by algorithms. Behind the veil was a monster.

The time of departure grew near. The middle-aged man found another puppy, a light brown toy poodle, and at the vet's office procured a couple of tranquilizers to give the dog during the flight. He gave his car to his ex-wife; she was going to take over the payments and buy it. On the day of departure, Penelope gave him a ride to the airport. What did they talk about on the four-hour drive? The old man couldn't remember. Penelope had accompanied the middle-aged man to the gate, and when it was time to board, they hugged. "I'll be back," he told her, then she turned around and left with tears in her eyes.

13

ITALY, 1988; EL CENTRO, 1989

The dog carrier easily fit under the front seat, and the puppy slept most of the trip. A couple of times the middle-aged man took him out of the carrier onto his lap and gave him some water. Once at the airport in Rome, the middle-aged man exited without any trouble and when he met his parents, he gave his mother the carrier with the little poodle. She smiled, surprised.

After several weeks at his parents' apartment, making phone calls to private schools and the US Consulate, he realized he couldn't find work. But what did he expect? What had he fantasized? Experience more of the culture? He needed a job before he could think of history, art and architecture, but what could he do? He decided to go back. In the States his education, his degrees and credentials, were recognized, at least he could make a living, but hadn't he known that before he left?

His aunt Avia was ill, so he traveled with his parents to Foiano della Chiana, and on the day of her operation, the middle-aged man, with his parents and Angelo, went to the hospital and waited a long time for the surgeon to finally come talk to them. The operation had been a success and the patient was recovering well.

One morning he was left alone in his aunt's apartment and took advantage of the opportunity by calling Penelope. "I'm coming back," he told her, expecting her to be happy at the news. Instead, after a long silence, she told him their relationship was over. His heart beat faster. He wanted to be in front of her, to hold her, implore her, but she was more than six thousand miles away. "Everybody has been happier since you left," she said. If she had really loved him, would she have given him a second chance? If he had really loved her, would he have left? *Everyone has been happier since you left.* He couldn't stop hearing those words. He hadn't realized his presence at Penelope's house had made her children unhappy, but then, he had been moody, was probably irritating. Richard, her oldest son, was a serious young man who was going to a trade school; Ronnie, a rambunctious fourteen-year-old, was smart and a little wild; and Renée, a high school senior, was a charming young woman full of dreams. How uncanny that his daughter's name was also Renée. The middle-aged man had thought he got along well with them, felt sorry that he had been a source of tension.

What did he do those couple of months he spent in Italy? He must have gone for walks in Albinia by the bird preserve, crossed the bridge over the Albegna River, walked down the road flanked by pines to the beach. He must have called Penelope again and asked her if she could pick him up at LAX, because she was waiting for him the evening he arrived.

During the four-hour drive she didn't say much. She told him the air conditioner had been turned off since she and the kids were staying at the cabin in Live Oaks Springs. He had hoped to use her spare car, but her kids were using it now. "You can stay here for a few days, but then you'll have to leave," she said as she pulled in the driveway. He took his two suitcases from the trunk, and she drove off to her cabin in the mountains.

Jet-lagged, in that desert town again, he was back in Penelope's house but as persona non grata. Late at night it was still hot and there was no air-conditioning. He walked to the liquor store to buy some scotch, got drunk and made a rambling call to his supervisor hoping to get his job back, but the position had already been filled.

He bought an old Ford Pinto station wagon from his ex-father-in-law, Deborah's father, who wanted fifteen hundred dollars for the car and told him he could pay it off at one hundred per month. "Come over for dinner tonight and you can pick it up," he said over the phone. At the time Frank lived in El Centro, in a house not far away. As the middle-aged man walked that evening, he remembered the first time he had seen Frank. It was in December of 1970, soon after he met Deborah. *"I dig you; I dig you."* Her room was painted blue, a Janis Joplin poster on the wall. He remembered the story Frank told him about how he met Deborah's mother.

After a stint in the Marines Frank moved to Imperial Valley, still recuperating from a wound he suffered in a firefight in Korea. In El Centro to see a movie, as Frank walked in front of the Aztec Theater, he noticed a gorgeous girl with raven black hair sitting in the ticket cage, eating a hamburger. He began talking to her, and she was embarrassed because she was chewing and couldn't talk, but getting red in the face and swallowing her food, she managed to reply, "Hi, my name is Betty." She was 17, he 19. They began to see each other and two years later, in 1952, they married. Frank and Betty had a daughter, Deborah, a son, Richard, and another girl, Liz. After twenty years they divorced, Frank married a younger woman and had three more children, but recently his second wife left him, and now he lived in El Centro.

"We're going to have spaghetti and salad," Frank said as he let the middle-aged man in. After the dinner and wine, Frank gave him the keys to the old white Pinto station wagon, and his transportation problem was solved.

He found a respiratory therapy job in Yuma, but wanted to live in El Centro, because he still hoped to reconcile with Penelope. He moved into an apartment at the Aurora Arms, near Fourth Street, where twenty years earlier his history professor Lloyd Farrar had lived. He used to visit him with his cousin Gary and listen to the professor talk about world affairs and politics, the soft yellow light from the table lamps scattering on the multicolored backs of the thousands of books covering the living room's walls. That was the apartment building where Larry had also lived for many years before he moved across town, and the middle-aged man remembered the day he went to see him and had met Penelope. A two-story complex with a swimming pool in the middle, it had appeared luxurious two decades ago, but the place had become shabby, the palm trees sickly, the pool empty, the paint flaking.

The apartment was upstairs, furnished with a small table and chairs, a bed and an old sofa. He retrieved a few boxes of books he had stored at a friend's house and with boards and bricks, made a bookcase in the living room.

He would sit on the sofa and stare at the books. What were those things? What did they have to do with him? Just a year earlier he had been an English teacher, had a girlfriend and a new car, and now he was alone, drove an old Ford Pinto station wagon he still had to pay for, and had a respiratory therapy job sixty-five miles away. He was determined to win Penelope back, but Penelope had already found someone else. He spent Christmas day of 1988 alone, mostly lying on the bed, staring at the palm branches rustling outside the window, surrounded by white walls. Veils of smoke rose from his cigarette as he waited for the telephone to ring. He imagined himself picking up the receiver and hearing Penelope's voice: "Hey, come over, we're having dinner soon." But the phone, next to him on the unmade bed, had taken a vow of silence, and he stared at the patterns on the walls and at the dirty clothes and tired Reebok shoes in the open closet facing him. He and Penelope had flown one summer across the ocean to the land of his birth, she had been a prisoner of his past and had cried one night, but one day in Florence, after wearing out their Reeboks in the Uffizi Gallery, she had smiled and bought him lunch.

The year ended and 1989 arrived. He didn't have the personality for hospital work—didn't like the military chain of command with nurses as sergeants and doctors as commanding officers; the smells, the sights of sick and dying people. The witty old man who had had an operation and every day looked more and more lethargic, unresponsive. Organic brain syndrome, he read in the chart. The young, bearded man who was airlifted to the ER. The doctor had taken an arterial blood sample, looked at the syringe and almost smiling had said, "Look at it, cherry red." Normal blood is dark, but with carbon dioxide bonded to the hemoglobin, it became bright red. The young man had locked himself in the garage and killed himself by carbon monoxide poisoning. As he looked at the young man's muscular frame, at his face, he felt angry at him. Such a waste of life.

After the three twelve-hour shifts, he had four days off, when he could rest, do things, but a deep, gnawing pain wouldn't leave him alone. As a nine-year-old boy, when the doctor had made a house call to excise the abscess in his buttock without anesthetic, when his mother and aunt held him down on the bed as the doctor began to cut, he had yelled at the top of his lungs, "Jesus, Jesus! Help me!" No one was holding and consoling him now as his decisions and actions cut deep, and so he began to seek refuge in the old beliefs.

The Book Nook was the only bookstore in Imperial Valley. When he first discovered it, years earlier, it was a small, narrow shop that sold only used books, then a couple bought it and expanded it to include the empty store next door. They began selling new books and teaching supplies, and as one walked through the aisles, ancient typewriters, framed photos of the Valley from the early 1900s and old mechanical toys, like punctuation marks in sentences, separated book genres. "Granny" was the cornerstone of the place, a middle-aged woman with a wide smile who made you feel at home. Her husband mostly worked in the back. Pat worked behind the counter. A slim woman in her late thirties with short, sandy hair, Pat was a practicing Catholic who enjoyed going on long motorcycle rides with her husband whenever they could.

He liked talking to Pat, and one day she told him about a new book they had just received, an illustrated tome based on interviews Joseph Campbell gave Bill Moyers. It was about mythology, and she thought he would find it interesting, so he bought it.

"I'm thinking of going back to the Church," he told her as he wrote a check for the book.

"You should go see Father Bob—he's the priest in Holtville. Alan, my husband, helps him with Sunday mass at times. He's a cool priest—you'd like him," she said, and so he made an appointment.

Holtville, a town of four thousand best known for its annual carrot festival, was only ten miles away. That was the town where his father found the Chevy for fifty dollars. Back in 1967, they had driven to a gas station and looked at the car, a twelve-year-old Power Glide with faded beige paint, in dire need of work.

That was the town his philosophy professor had lived in with his wife and two Irish wolfhounds. Driving on Evan Hewes Highway, green and sandy fields on either side, he thought of how his mother used to drag him and his sister to church on Sundays, and how the marble, candles and statues frightened him. Outside was life; inside, death. Outside, the air roamed free; inside it stagnated, heavy with scents of wax, incense and people. He remembered the catechism he had to study, how the eye of God in a triangle watched him sternly from the cover illustration. First communion and confirmation, the times he found some solace in reciting a colored-glass bead rosary in a newly constructed church, one of those "modern" ones quickly built to serve the apartment buildings that sprang up during the economic boom. The fear and guilt that would not leave him alone, that cut his spirit with small, sharp knives. Then the doubts and the liberation at the thought that there was no cosmic eye watching his every act, reading his every thought and desire.

As he parked in front of the church and walked into the sacristy office, he was a drowning man desperate to hold on to something. The priest, more or less his age, sat at a desk in jeans and a short-sleeved shirt. They talked, and then Father Bob gave him a paperback copy of the Bible and some other literature to read. "If you're serious about coming back to the Church you must refresh your knowledge of Catholic doctrine. Come back next week and we'll talk more." He attended mass and then left with the paperback Bible the priest had given him.

Back in his apartment he sat at the small green

desk Anita, his ex-wife's grandmother, had given him. The mahogany desk he received as a gift from her years earlier had somehow been lost in all the moves he made. Anita, now frail and old, had been an elegant and attractive woman. At one time she had been the madam of the most renowned house of prostitution in Imperial Valley, then she met someone special. Joe was in the U.S. Air Force and had been stationed in the Philippines during the war, where he worked on airplanes as a mechanic. Out of the service and back home, he met Anita, who charged him for her services until they fell in love. The end of the war heralded a new beginning, and she could envision a new life with Joe. She left her profession and they opened a second hand store in Calexico. Anita, as well as Deborah's mother, Betty, had always been good to him, even after he and Deborah split up. It was at Anita's warehouse that most of his books were stored.

He placed the *New American Bible* on the desk and opened it. He had read much of it before and heard many passages in church. He had always found the Old Testament disagreeable; the gospels were more interesting, but as he forced himself to read, he felt nothing. He closed his eyes and prayed, but he couldn't escape the thought that he was just uttering words to himself in his head.

The old man thought about his desire to reconnect with the Church. Had he been like Cypher, the character who wants to be reinserted in the Matrix because he would rather live in a comforting illusion than in a painful reality? Once religion's veil of maya drops off, once the symbols and images of God, Christ, angels and saints disappear, aren't we left with the "desert of the real"? What does life become then, but a repeating of nights and days, routine following routine, until old age, disease and death erase all? Sure, he could put a positive spin to it, as humanists are wont to do, finding in a world devoid of divinity not only liberation but happiness, but he couldn't. A kind of liberation, yes; happiness, no.

The more he reasoned, the less sense the whole thing made, so he stopped. Maybe thinking could only lead to a certain point, and no further. Beyond that point, another path must be found. A plunge into oneself, a connection with the transcendent. He was reminded of William James's *Varieties of Religious Experience*. In the book, James says the essence of religion is in experience, not in dogmas or rituals. Feeling is the deeper sense of religion. He remembered the course he had taken in medieval history, the lectures on Western monasticism, Peter Abelard, Saint Bernard. Maybe that was the path to follow to go beyond reason.

He went back to the Book Nook and ordered more works on religion, including one on Saint Catherine of Genoa and *A Life of Prayer* by Saint Teresa of Avila. The saints intrigued him. Catherine was the daughter of a powerful Genoese family. At an early age she dedicated her life to God, and she spent her life serving the sick and the poor.

Saint Teresa, a Spanish nun, wrote much about prayer, and her whole life was devoted to seeking unity with God. She professed that our love must be untouched by sensuality, not affected by the passions; that is, it must be spiritual. Intrigued by these saints, he bought a book by Saint Catherine of Siena, *The*

Dialogue of Divine Providence, a 300-page volume in which she wrote about God as being the first sweet truth, that God is truth and love and our goal on earth is to seek to approach God, who has given us a bridge in his son for us to travel on. She was active in the Church's political events of the time and was called to Rome by the Pope. She died at thirty-three and was declared a Doctor of the Church. The only other woman so declared in the history of the Church was Saint Teresa of Avila.

What attracted him to those women was their passionate dedication, their purity of heart. They lived their beliefs, and their actions and writings overflowed with radical love and fervor. He found it hard to read their works in which God spoke to them in prosaic ways, the writings full of scriptural quotations, but he liked reading about their lives, and he enjoyed gazing at the book covers, which featured watercolor portraits by the artist Joseph Trepiccione. Catherine of Genoa looked at him in a questioning, musing way, while Catherine of Siena, holding a branch of red lilies, gazed inward.

On Ash Wednesday he decided to go to mass. He parked the 1974 Pinto a block away and walked to Our Lady of Guadalupe. It was six thirty in the evening and it was cool. He found a spot in a pew, and soon after, the church filled up, with many standing in the back. It was a long service, with bright lights, candles, incense, the long readings and homily. He felt the warmth of hundreds of yearning bodies surrounding him, holding hands for Our Father and shaking hands during the sign of peace, followed by the holy communion, the line to the eucharistic minister who anointed his forehead with ashes. "From ashes you came to ashes you shall return," she said. Devotion, desperation and need were embodied in those sweating men and women of all ages who crowded around him, and he felt a part of them, he was them, and they were him.

His hopes of getting back together with Penelope waned. She had moved on; he was no longer part of her life. Let go from his job in Yuma, he could not afford the rent, so he moved into Larry's apartment. He began to teach an English course to adults for the Calexico School District. All the students were Mexican Americans, mostly single women on welfare. What followed were parties at his students' houses, lots of beer and tequila, a couple of affairs and trying to dance the cumbia while drunk in Mexicali.

He opened his mailbox at the post office and found a letter from the University of Siena. It was a job bulletin informing him of open positions for teachers of English. Was this a sign that he had been granted a grace? Was it a rope he could grab hold of and escape from El Centro?

He didn't belong in Centro, but then again, where did he belong? Did he ever feel at home anywhere? He wanted to leave, but what about his son? Michael lived with his mother in Calexico, just a few miles away. He visited him on weekends, took him to Carl's Junior or Burger King, then to the movies, played ball with him in the park. If he left for Italy, he would not be able to see or spend time with his son. On the other hand, if he remained, what was he going to do?

He had made several charts with columns of pros and cons, but nothing helped. He was always left with pain. When did the pain begin? Hadn't he dreamed for years of coming to America, the promised land, the country his father had fought for? The land of the free, the just, the brave? His dream had become reality, and now he longed to be back in Italy; he longed to leave.

He saved money until he had enough for a ticket to Rome, quit the part-time teaching job, gave up his car, stored his belongings at a friend's house and flew back to Italy.

14

ITALY, 1989–1990

A couple of days later, after he'd recovered from jet lag, he took the train to Siena and found the university, but when he inquired about the position he'd applied for, he was told by the clerk that he didn't get it. In the following weeks he called several private schools, to no avail. He tried to find a job as a translator, but he lacked the required certification and experience.

In October his sister Sandrina married, so with his parents, he went to the wedding in Perugia. She looked radiant in a pink dress, kneeling in front of the altar next to Giuliano, a local businessman. The middle-aged man and his parents stayed for the mass and the reception, then took the train back to Albinia.

What were his options? Could he find a menial job working for cash, under the table? He might make enough money to rent a room in a run-down part of a city and survive on spaghetti and jarred sauce. But was that the life he wanted?

What was wrong with him? Was he really that

stupid? Why did he move to Italy before making sure he had been offered the teaching position? Was it just an excuse to leave El Centro and his life there? Hadn't he done the same thing the year before?

He was going to return. Back in the States he had a chance of finding a decent job. He called the travel agent in El Centro but was told he had to wait until March for the one-way ticket, so he was stranded at his parents' place.

The middle-aged man spent the days huddled in the cold apartment, getting up early so he could make the sofa bed and get dressed before his parents came into the living room/kitchen. He went to sit on the balcony and looked at the top of the church campanile, at apartment buildings and trees, then down at the street, watching people walking or driving by.

The two-story house directly in front belonged to Franco, the town veterinarian. He had his office on the ground floor, his apartment upstairs. A tall man in his early forties, he had lived in Florida for a while and had married an American woman with whom he had a daughter. His wife didn't like living in Italy, so she had divorced him and returned to the States. His daughter, who was nine or ten, lived with him part of the year. Sometimes, on his walks he'd see Franco watering plants in the side yard, and they greeted each other and exchanged a few words. Franco's mother lived in a villa up the street and when the middle-aged man went to the newsstand or the store early in the morning, he often saw her on the sidewalk, and she would stop briefly to talk. "How's your mother? I see her every day sitting on the balcony.

She must be happy you've come to visit. And how long are you staying?" Tall and slim, with blondish hair and fancy sunglasses, she had an air of elegance about her.

The middle-aged man went with his father in the mornings shopping, or visiting his father's friend, who had a TV repair shop across the street, in the building next to Franco's. He bought *La Repubblica* and read it on the balcony, then after lunch he went for a long walk. At times it rained for days, and while his parents watched TV, he went in their room and read.

Alberto Sordi, one of his favorite actors, was going to be in a televised miniseries of *The Betrothed*, so in November he read the renowned work by Alessandro Manzoni. One of Italy's most cherished books, it probably would have been required reading if he had gone to high school there. While his parents sat on the sofa watching TV, he lay down on their bed and read.

A historical novel taking place in the early nineteenth century in Northern Italy, the love story of a couple who desperately want to marry, it was a sprawling saga of murderous, corrupt noblemen, thugs, cowardly and courageous priests, conniving nuns and common people going about their shenanigans until the bubonic plague arrives in Milan and brings out the worst in most people and the best in some.

He could hear the rain outside and the muffled noise of the TV in the living room as he lay with head propped on a couple of pillows and lost himself in the narrative. Would he have liked it if he had read it as a sixteen-year-old in school? Probably not; he was into science fiction then. He tried to push it far away from his mind, the thought that he was forty-one years old, unemployed, staying with his aged parents, waiting to return to the place from which he had tried so hard to escape.

THE OLD MAN opened his eyes and was back in the study. Thirty years had passed since he had read Manzoni's novel. He turned to look at the shelves that held the Italian books. There it was. The pages had yellowed, but the paperback was still in decent shape. After a few minutes he found what he was looking for, the chapters on the plague in Milan.

A doctor had informed the department of sanitation of many cases of the plague in the region, but after an attempt at investigating, the department concluded the deaths were caused by evil emanations. Further investigations in the countryside showed that indeed the plague was real. Recommendations were made to keep travelers from entering the city, but the government sabotaged the efforts by ordering public holidays to celebrate the birth of the king. Travelers were a source of income the authorities relied on.

In the towns, whoever mentioned the plague was ridiculed, attacked, treated with contempt. The rich, the nobility and the merchants denied the disease existed, even as the sick and the dying increased in number.

Crowds began to attack physicians and blamed them for fomenting fear. As the outbreak continued to decimate the towns and to attack not only the poor and the common but the notables and wealthy as well, the plague could no longer be denied. Now scapegoats were needed, and conspiracy theories flourished. The rumor spread that the scourge was brought by foreigners: they were the plague spreaders, who with evil intent brought contagious powders into the towns and rubbed them on walls, doors and church benches.

The plague Manzoni mentioned in his 1827 novel actually took place in Northern Italy in the 1600s. It seemed to the old man that the same events were unfolding around him. As medical experts began to warn that a dangerous virus was beginning to cause infection and death in the country, the rulers (Trump and his party) and many businessmen kept denying the threat and accusing the authorities of fearmongering. As the experts advised the use of masks, social distancing and other safety measures, the "king," Trump in this case, ordered huge rallies to take place, where he derided the wearing of masks. Like in the plague described in Manzoni's book, doctors and medical experts were blamed, attacked and threatened with death. Anthony Fauci, scientist, immunologist and physician, was demonized by politicians, right-wing pundits and anti-vaccine proponents. And when the pandemic could no longer be denied, Asians and other foreigners began to be physically attacked and, in some cases, murdered. On Facebook, according to one conspiracy theory, Chinese foreign students were sent to the United States with vials containing the virus. Their mission: spread Covid-19 in order to bring down the United States of America. Asians were the plague spreaders, as well as Mexicans and other immigrants. The old man wondered if perhaps Freud had been right after all. In *Civilization and Its Discontents*, he says that human beings are instinctually aggressive, so "...their neighbor is to them not only a possible helper or a sexual object, but also a temptation to them to ...seize his possessions, to humiliate him, to cause him pain, to torture and to kill him." Wasn't this demonstrated daily all over the world? Hiding behind the veils of religion and patriotism, wrapping themselves in flags and robes, human beings eagerly attacked those with whom they disagreed. On social media, on the streets and on battlefields, they discharged their aggressiveness with glee.

He ran his fingers across the cover of the paperback, which had been printed with a photo of the two protagonists from the miniseries, and was transported back to 1989, when he had read *The Betrothed* and watched the televised version with his parents. The old man closed his eyes and was back in Albinia, in 1989.

ALMOST MIDNIGHT, and he was trying to fall asleep in his parents' living room. As he lay there under the covers, listening to the ticking of the plastic clock on the wall, he thought about his mother. He was surprised at how much she had aged in a year. Her face looked different. She was much slower, her memory poorer. When they had lived in Genova so many years ago, she was young and he a child. Where did the young mother go? That child?

He remembered when as a seven-year-old he'd talk his uncle Libero into playing guns when he came to visit them in Sella. After years of odd jobs and periods of unemployment, his uncle had gone to Germany as a factory worker, where he had stayed for many years. When he returned to his hometown, he bought a truck and began working for the Nobel Explosives Company. To get the middle-aged man out of the apartment, his uncle took him on trips. "You can keep me company and I'll show you Italy," he said. And so once or twice a week he'd go with Libero, who chain-smoked cigarettes as he drove his Mercedes truck.

THEY WENT TO TORINO, but all the young man saw was a warehouse on the periphery. After unloading the explosives, they stopped at an Autogrill for lunch, then drove back to Albinia.

He had a bad taste in his mouth—too many cigarettes and coffees. It was December 6, mid-afternoon. He leaned left and right as the truck snaked between hills smooth as women's breasts, the color of pale skin, sand and emeralds. Libero lit up a cigarette, gave him one and said, "*Fuma!*" The middle-aged man lit up and inhaled. Through the dirty window—it had rained in Torino—gray farmhouses passed by, houses with red-tiled roofs and green wooden shutters, vegetable gardens, stacked wood, black sheep grazing near the road.

His uncle, looking like a diminutive sumo wrestler bent over the steering wheel, glanced at him, stubby black cigarette holder protruding from his lips, and said, "So my American nephew likes Italy, eh?" A golden hill appeared, a single pine on top, against luminous white sky. "*L'Italia e' bella*," the middle-aged man had replied, staring at a red tractor in an alfalfa field, at a double row of cypresses leading from the road to a white farmhouse on a hill half hidden by pines. Leaning on the steering wheel, his uncle said, "Yes, Italy is beautiful, but America is America!" Bare poplars extended branches upward, betraying empty nests of hay, twigs and mud. The middle-aged man turned his head toward the trees and held on with his eyes to those bare branches and empty nests. His uncle looked at him with his old hound face and said, "*E sí*, you don't believe in the witches." What did Libero mean? When asked, his uncle looked at him and repeated, "You don't believe in the witches!"

The sky darkened, and brown leaves swirled in the wind and fell like snowflakes. On the left side of the road, he noticed an old stone house with a sign that said "*Antichità*." He saw himself driving so many times from Pine Valley to El Centro with a woman he loved, or his son, or a friend, and seeing an antiques store on the left side of the road. He'd been reading so many books on mysticism and Zen, the holy moment and how we should look at the world always as if for the first time, but everything reminded him of everything else, and his thoughts followed flocks of birds through the mauve sky.

∽

HE WAS AT HIS PARENTS' tiny apartment. A kitchen/living room, a bedroom and a bath. *Why are you here? What are you doing here?* he kept asking himself.

At five in the afternoon, colors withdrew from buildings and trees as the sky struggled to keep some gold before the night stole it. In three days it would be Christmas 1989. The middle-aged man accompanied his parents to Perugia, to spend it with his sister. They traveled on buses and trains, through crowded stations, trying to find empty seats, carrying bags and backpacks. Strings of lights and decorations lined the streets and people hurried in the cold, getting ready for a redemption that wouldn't come except in the excitement of their children as they opened presents, in big family dinners celebrated with panettone and prosecco.

The first Christmas he remembered, he had been awakened by his mother. "Wake up, wake up! Look what baby Jesus brought you," she said, pointing to a stuffed woman's nylon on the bed, next to him. He rubbed his eyes and thrusting his hand in the stocking retrieved little bundles wrapped in colored paper. He smiled at the sight of tin toy cars and candy, but the last small bundle wrapped in newspaper revealed a few chunks of coal. "Oh, you must have been bad sometimes!" she said, smiling. He was three years old and had never forgotten that Christmas morning.

He had first been in Perugia in July of 1987 with Penelope and his son, then in July of 1988, and just two months earlier, in October of 1989, for his sister's wedding. And now, here he was, having somehow believed (what madness!) he was going to teach English at the University of Siena. Why hadn't he called from El Centro to find out?

No, you were not offered a position, the young clerk had said, and his dream of teaching and living in Siena popped like a bubble. He had walked out the office feeling hollow, floated down the marble stairs, out into the street, wondering what he was going to do. Then came his sister's wedding and now Christmas. He shivered in his tweed jacket and the Reebok tennis shoes left his feet cold. Overweight, his face puffy, he felt superfluous, something in the way, like Sartre's character Roquentin in *Nausea*.

"Why don't you come with me to Giuliano's store? I'm going to assemble gift baskets; people will pick them up tomorrow," his sister said. In the back of her husband's store, Sandrina placed chocolates, candy, nuts, local salami and small jars in baskets that she wrapped in cellophane. The middle-aged man sat on a stool, watching his sister, the free spirit who traveled to Mexico and Central America, lived in India, worked as a pot maker in Ocean Beach during the 1970s, and having grown tired of life in America, decided to move back to Italy. "I think you'll like this tape," Sandrina said as she turned on the player. Soft piano notes floated, then a sonorous voice came out of the speakers. "Here, I also got one for you." She handed him a cassette, *La Vita Mia* by Amedeo Minghi. He looked at the description on the back: twelve songs by one of Italy's most popular singers. The music and the songs plunged him into a sea of nostalgia. He wished he could relive those winter days when they lived in Sella and his mother took him and his sister to Genova, and traditional Christmas music spilled out of churches.

He smiled and talked, ate and drank, he was spending the holidays with family, but a voice, a voice that did not speak but made itself heard, kept reminding him he had no career or job, that he had betrayed his vocation. He had been called from childhood to wonder, to probe the ultimate questions. As he read about Plato and Aristotle in the weekly issues of the encyclopedia, hadn't he aspired to know more about them? As he gazed at the mountains in Sella and the sea in Genova, hadn't he wondered what they were, besides names colors and shapes? What was he and why did he exist? Was there really a God? And then, at the college, as he listened to Professor Hann explain Plato's theory of the forms, hadn't he heard the call of philosophy? *That is what I want to do*, he had thought. And then, when it came time to answer the call, he'd retreated.

Two days after Christmas, he went to Assisi with his father. Wearing pleated olive-green chinos, white tennis shoes and his only jacket, he had glanced at his reflection in a shop's window but had rapidly turned away from the tired, sad face. He and his father climbed the stairs to the Upper Basilica of Saint Francis and stepped into beauty, into time magically stilled in stone and glass, given form by artists and craftsmen centuries earlier. Under vaulted ceilings of gold stars on malachite blue, they walked on a stone floor decorated with geometric designs as from the upper walls, tall, slender Gothic stained-glass windows enriched the light. They stopped to admire the frescoes of Giotto on the lower walls, depicting major events in the life of Saint Francis. In Giotto's naturalistic style, in resplendent colors, Francis is in front of his father in the public square renouncing worldly goods; he is preaching to the birds, driving out the devils at Arezzo. The middle-aged man's breathing slowed and deepened. Climbing Assisi's cobblestone streets, soaking in the pale light reflected by the simple walls of the Church of San Pietro, the tension inside him decreased. As he stood by a wall and gazed out at the Umbrian countryside extending below for miles, watching flocks of birds flying over green fields, undulating hills, small villages like those in nativity scenes, he closed his eyes and felt a moment's peace.

The end of the year approached. The middle-aged man and his parents left Perugia in the early morning, and another long train ride took them to Foiano della Chiana, the town in the Abruzzi region where his aunt Avia and her husband Angelo lived. After a long stay in the hospital, Avia was told she had pleurisy and sent home, but she had cancer. It was routine for patients not to be told the truth about their diagnoses; only close relatives were. Did she know or suspect it? The old man didn't remember; the passage of more than thirty years made events blurry, fragmented. If he could go back in time he would talk more with her, buy her something nice, share memories, tell her how much she had meant to him. He had been fifteen when he left for America, and when he next hugged her, when he was on vacation in 1987, twenty-four years had passed. It pained the middle-aged man that his aunt knew he was unemployed, floundering.

He took a bus to Arezzo, the city where according

to legend, Saint Francis drove out the devils. The eighties finally over, would the nineties be more perspicuous? Offer hope? As he walked on the cobblestone streets surrounded by medieval towers and walls, he wondered what he would discover. He turned a corner and saw a church with a simple facade. The ancient stones, gray, white, brown and rust, reminded him of his old tweed jacket. He stepped inside and entered a cool, dark space, with a wooden ceiling and cream-colored walls. Chapels stood on the left side of the nave, and he passed statues and frescoes as he walked toward the altar, where a huge wooden crucifix hung from the ceiling. As he looked up at the major chapel behind the altar at the vaults, he entered a dream.

On three levels of the side walls, frescoes by Piero della Francesca, which he later discovered were called *The Legend of the True Cross*, greeted him. Based on medieval stories, after Adam was buried, a tree grew from his grave, and wood from it was used to make the cross on which Christ was crucified. The middle-aged man stayed there a long time, feeding coins in the boxes that would turn on the lights for a minute or two. The first fresco showed Adam as a dying old man with a long white beard seated against a tree, surrounded by his children. The middle-aged man had never thought of the death of Adam; he had always seen him as a young man, as depicted by Michelangelo in the Sistine Chapel. After exile from Eden, Adam entered into time, impermanence, the death spiral, and there he was, an emaciated dying old man. Had it been worth it? Eating of the fruit of good and evil? These thoughts swirled in the middle-aged man as he walked out of the basilica to explore more of the city, until it was time to catch the bus back to his aunt's house.

He spent only a few hours in Arezzo; there was so much to see, to study, to experience, but there wasn't enough time. *Fucking time.* He had to pay for it in so many ways, even for those few minutes to turn on the lights to see the frescoes. As he walked up the stairs to his aunt's apartment, he thought of the tall, slim woman with long hair that brought him little toy cars, at how happy he had felt when she came to visit them in Sella. Now she was an old woman dying of cancer. Angelo, who in youth had looked like Clark Gable, hopped around with crutches, because they had amputated one of his legs. There was no elevator in the building where they lived, so he would slowly hop down the stairs to go play cards with his friends at a nearby bar.

BACK AT HIS PARENTS' house he mailed the check for the plane ticket to the travel agent, who had said that by early March he would be able to return. He was stuck in Albinia for two more months. He didn't have money to travel, except for a few day trips. He resumed his long walks and kept his uncle company on the truck rides. "I'll show you Italy," Libero had said. In a way he did. His uncle would lift a hand from the truck's steering wheel, point in the distance and say, "See that city, over there? That's Venice." Or from another freeway, he'd point to his right and he'd say, "Look! That's Pisa, see the leaning tower?" The famous campanile was so far away that it looked like the eraser of a pencil stuck in dirt. He rode in the truck to Bolzano, at the very north, and to Reggio, at the southernmost tip of Calabria.

On one trip to the south, the middle-aged man had seen from a highway bridge, way below, what seemed like an endless green valley, and a bare-chested man behind a plow pulled by a horse. Had there been a crack in time? Had he glimpsed a few moments of the past?

Libero knew where the good places to eat were, and they had particularly good lunches, with fresh pasta, seafood, bread and light wine. They talked for hours about everything, and he grew to like his uncle even more.

ONE MONDAY in February the middle-aged man decided to go to Siena for the day, and early in the morning, he took the local train. Five months earlier, when he had gone to see about the teaching position, he had seen Siena for the first time and he yearned to be there again, to go visit Saint Catherine's city.

As the train gained speed, through the glass, the other line's rails whipped and lashed on the ground like snakes caught in the fangs of a dog. Alone in the vibrating coach, he smelled naphtha and grease. Charcoal fields, a hint of pale road and steep hills materialized as the sky whitened and bled behind medieval towers and walls so high above time. The train stopped at towns with strange names, like Tala-mone, Montepescali, Sticciano and Roccastrada, all preannounced by two-story farmhouses, red-shingled roofs, green shutters and vegetable gardens full of cauliflowers and artichokes. A group of men gathered around a fire smoked cigarettes and talked in a brown cornfield.

The conductor, so official in gray polyester, checked his ticket and left. He glanced at the front page of *La Repubblica* and put it away. Saint Catherine, young and bold, refused to marry as her parents wanted her to and locked herself up in her room for days, praying. It was in part because of her that he was on that local train.

Suddenly a curve, a whistle, a slashing sound, darkness, a popping in the ears, then out of the tunnel into the blinding sun. A sun gone mad, running through poplars and pines, chasing dark jade streams, a gorge; dancing above grapevines' naked limbs crucified on wires, laughing at a white pig grazing under an oak; throwing silver dust at haystacks and frosty bushes; skating on snow on a fence; sparkling on rusty rails. Then it hid behind hills. What was he doing on that train? He was no longer young; he was forty-one years old and sleeping on the sofa in his parents' apartment. What must his relatives have thought? He had gone to America as a fifteen-year-old boy and almost thirty years later he had no career, no family, no home. Truly he found himself in a dark wood, like Dante at the beginning of the *Inferno*.

The train stopped. University students climbed on and talking and laughing, entered his compartment. A fat woman in a black overcoat waddled past the window with her mouth open, from which escaped little vapor clouds. Her face red and puffy, sparse chunks of black hair on her pink scalp, carrying two bags, she hurried to get on. A whistle, and the train began to move again. He wiped holes on the sweating glass and saw blue-and-white signs announce "Siena." The train, whistling and screeching, slowed down and stopped in front of the crowded station.

Instead of taking the bus to the center of town like he had a few months earlier when he went to the university hoping to get a teaching assignment, he decided to walk. It was up a steep hill, but he enjoyed the climb after the two hours in the train. Once at the top, he roamed up and down medieval alleys, pounding grooved cobblestones under a distant sun. Shirts and sheets under windows waved, flags of another Palio. Past the fountain of Fontebranda he saw Saint Catherine's house. Red geraniums, fragrant stigmata, dripped on the terraces where she once stood. He turned at the corner and climbed amid the aroma of freshly baked bread, the flutter of pigeons, children's voices. He approached San Domenico's church, guarded by cypresses. He climbed five marble steps, then two more, and was on reddish stone floor. Sunlight pierced double lancet windows, paled on fading frescoes; on the left side, red and yellow lilies bowed on slender stems in front of a gesso *Madonna with Child*. Embarrassed by her pink gown, blue robe and electric halo, she looked away. A chubby middle-aged nun sat on a bench and prayed a plastic rosary in front of the gold box holding Catherine's head.

Light burdened by smoke and petitions, reflected by stained-glass saints, transmuted by Il Sodoma's frescoes, reached upward only to be trapped under the wooden ceiling. By Catherine's chapel, votive candles warmed her ecstasies, her flowing white veils, her blood oozing from open hands. The middle-aged man put three coins in the offertory and lit a candle. The glow, the heat, the scent of wax was her embrace. He walked softly to the Cappella delle Volte and stood in front of her portrait. "Caterina, can you hear me?" He bent down and caressed the rough marble floor, where she had paced and prayed centuries earlier. What could he tell her? How could she hear him? She died in 1380. He wanted to believe, needed to, but could not. There was reason, science, logic. *Please, Caterina, help me!*

He wandered into the third chapel to the left of the main altar. There he found a Christ crucified on a bare white wall. Where was his cross? The face looked down, half hidden in penumbra, frozen in a scream, the brown toes eaten by the leprosy of time. A Gothic window's oblique reflection left his body cold. Poor wooden Christ never born for resurrection! In the cold chapel, between wood and stone, what did time mean? He stood there and imagined he was back in the fourteenth century. He stilled his mind and closed his eyes. What did time mean in that moment? It didn't exist as a subjective experience, but it made itself present in the sound of footsteps, and he opened his eyes to see tourists approaching. Slowly, he left the basilica and made his way to the bus stop so he could get down to the train station.

The compartment was almost empty. He sat by the window and stared at the scenery unfolding outside: fields, hills, trees, houses, vegetable gardens. The comforting vibrations of the train, the lulling music of wheels on tracks and the faint scent of machine oil acted as an anesthetic. He wished he could sit there forever.

Back in Albinia, he sat on the sofa with his parents watching the news, old American movies dubbed in Italian or stupid variety shows on their twenty-inch tube TV, bundled up in his jacket, hands in pockets.

In late afternoon the window's light in his parents' room retreated, the bedside lamp's weak glow turned the wallpaper into rust and he could no longer read, so he joined his mother and father in the living room and watched whatever was on TV until they went to bed. Only then could he open up the sofa bed, lie down and read. He went through Fleur Jaeggy's *Sweet Days of Discipline*; *Across the Line*, a short book by Jünger and Heidegger; and *A Simple Story* by Leonardo Sciascia. Jaeggy was a Swiss writer, and in the short novel she describes life in a boarding school, a girl's infatuation with an older student and the relationships among the girls and the staff. The middle-aged man wasn't sure why he liked the book. What did he care about the feelings of a bunch of schoolgirls in Switzerland in the early 1950s? But in little more than one hundred pages, the author created an intricate world full of unforgettable characters. In a terse writing style, she brought to life their emotions.

The Jünger-Heidegger book was a small paperback, but not easy to understand. Lying down on the sofa bed, as the rain fell outside, under the blanket, he tried to make sense of it. The small volume contained an essay by Ernst Jünger, written for his friend Martin Heidegger on the occasion of the latter's sixtieth birthday, and Heidegger's reply.

Nihilism was the theme. For Dostoevsky, the view

that everything is devoid of meaning is shown through the alienation of troubled characters, while for Nietzsche, nihilism is the breakdown of traditional Western values, which are basically the values of Judeo-Christianity and the Enlightenment. Jünger marks that breakdown as a "zero point, a line," which he thinks can be superseded through art and poetry, while Heidegger is not so sure. It was a short book, fewer than two hundred pages, but very dense, encapsulating the life work of the two philosophers. Raindrops splashed on the balcony and the French window, and the lamp gave out some warmth as he lay in the sofa bed under the covers. In his twenties he had harbored nihilistic feelings and ideas; now, he thought that even though human life had no "objective" meaning or purpose, it was up to each individual to create his or her own meaning.

After the philosophy book he read Sciascia's novella, a murder mystery involving the mafia, the police and the government. It reminded the middle-aged man of the dark history in Italy of the mafia's control of social and political institutions, of the corruption that had always pervaded Italian society.

IT WAS late morning when the train stopped at Stazione Termini, in the city of his birth. After days of rainy weather, stuck in the little apartment, he felt like a prisoner. He needed to get out for a day.

Rome was his face reflected in a puddle. Streets choked by cars, trucks and scooters, monuments eaten by smog and acid rain; heroin addicts, priests, transvestites, workers, pickpockets, nuns, beggars, elegant people—they gave the city life in an endless Fellini parade. He stayed in a cheap *pensione* by the train station, not far from the place he had stayed two years earlier with Penelope and his son.

Every corner hid a surprise. One morning as he walked along Via Ludovisi he came upon a small piazza. An obelisk stood in the center; Egyptian hieroglyphics carved on its surfaces contrasted with the metal cross crowning the top. He crossed the square and stood at a low wall that overlooked a flight of steps and a larger square. He gazed at the white clouds that earlier had hidden the sun and threatened rain but had broken up to reveal patches of blue. A German photographer was shooting a series of photos of two men modeling suits as some *carabinieri* and tourists looked on, amused. He crossed the square again and climbed the steps of a sixteenth-century church. Inside, the walls offered colorful frescoes. One on the left wall, near the entrance, captured his attention. Mary stood on the sun being eclipsed by the moon, and with her hands upward, an expression of humility on her face, received God into her womb. Only later did he discover that the church was Santa Trinità dei Monti, and the square below the famous Piazza di Spagna.

He wandered in the shadowy space inside the Pantheon, with the sky entering through the oculus and resting on the dome walls. He saw *The Martyrdom of Saint Matthew* by Caravaggio in the Church of San Luigi dei Francesi, full of light and darkness, violence and wonder; inhaled the aroma of fresh bread in a hole-in-a-wall bakery.

He was born in this city, but he had been only a year old when his parents moved to Genova. He walked along the Tevere, hands in pockets, the collar of his tweed jacket up around the ears. He watched pieces of aquamarine sky, clouds stolen from paintings, plane trees straining to remain green, reflected in the rippling river, so dark, as if it had seen too much.

He crossed Ponte Cavour and walked in front of the Palace of Justice, a gigantic gray building resembling a prison. By Castel Sant'Angelo he bought a sandwich and a Pepsi from a street vendor, sat on a bench and had lunch. Pigeons suddenly landed at his feet and waited for crumbs. He gazed at the castle's battlement walls and imagined it in older times: soldiers armed with crossbows looking through the merlons, prisoners languishing in the dungeons. Almost everywhere he turned he saw sediments of history. What a difference from California, where cities were slabs of concrete adorned with plastic, their monuments and basilicas mega department stores, business towers and shopping malls. San Diego was about 150 years old, Rome almost three thousand. There was a density to the feeling of time in Italy, a richness, a ripeness that made even going down a sidewalk or wandering in the countryside an experience he didn't have back in the States.

An old man impeccably dressed in a brown suit walked by with the help of a cane; a young American woman in jeans sat on a bench and changed her infant's diapers. He threw a piece of bread to the pigeons and got up. He walked along Via della Conciliazione and crossed Piazza San Pietro. The Egyptian obelisk towered in the center, carved by an ancient civilization and brought to a new land by another civilization now ancient, taken again by a new civilization now becoming ancient.

He climbed the steps and entered through Saint Peter's Basilica into another world, cool, dark marble informed by the divine. He walked down the nave and gazed at Saint Peter's dome. When he was a boy, he imagined the eye of God staring at him from above, an eye in a golden triangle, as depicted on the cover of the catechism he had to study for first communion. Now he looked into God's eye as Michelangelo gave it form. As he sat in a pew in front of Bernini's *Chair of Saint Peter*, above it, the holy spirit came down in the form of a dove. He closed his eyes. He had been a teacher, had been in a relationship with a woman who loved him, had had friends, a new car, a comfortable apartment. Now he had nothing. But didn't he have the Basilica of Saint Peter's and all the treasures it held? He had Rome. He closed his eyes and rested in that feeling of belonging. Raphael, Michelangelo and Bernini had worked on the Basilica; ninety popes were buried in its tombs, including Saint Peter, the first bishop of Rome. He took deep breaths, emptied himself of images, thoughts and feelings, and rested in a place beyond time, but then he heard footsteps, distant voices. He opened his eyes again, got up and walked around until on the way out he came to *La Pietà*. He stood in front of the glass and couldn't take his eyes off Michelangelo's sculpture. How could a man have created this out of stone? Mary's face infinite acceptance and sadness, Jesus's right hand. He stood and gazed for a long time, then left.

He sat on the parapet at Villa Borghese and gazed at Piazza del Popolo below. The setting sun on pink and peach-colored palazzi, the umbrella-shaped stone pines, the campaniles and gray domes. The city of his birth. Why couldn't he carve a life here? But how? What could he do?

The following morning he took the train to Orbetello. Two old women behind him talked about their vegetable gardens and chickens as he watched pines, bare locust trees and farmhouses roll past the window. It was almost noon when the train arrived. He caught a bus and in fifteen minutes was in Albinia.

ON A COLD MONDAY, he went with his uncle on another truck trip. "You want to see Trieste?" Libero had asked. How could he not? The city of scirocco winds, rain and fog, aromatic coffees, cathedrals and castles, the city of Italo Svevo, Umberto Saba, James Joyce, Eugenio Montale, Rilke? After a long drive, the truck stopped at a depot somewhere in the boondocks, and after unloading, Libero drove back home. All the middle-aged man had seen of Trieste was a gray smudge in the distance.

ON A TRAIN AGAIN, this time with his father on the way to Pisa. They walked around the city, climbed up the leaning tower, and as he stood on top, next to the huge green bells, he gazed out at the sea of red roofs and campaniles and felt a wave of longing, yearning, melancholia. There was so much history and art, so much life he could not grasp, hold on to, because he was just a tourist, passing through; he was a flat stone skipping on the surface not just of history and culture, but of that special *feeling of things* the residents would have formed after years of walking on the streets, breathing the air and dreaming their dreams. It was the same feeling he had in Genova, Rome, Florence, Perugia, Siena, or even the small towns, like Orbetello or Assisi. Many of the inhabitants of those cities probably found them stultifying, boring and oppressive places; they probably dreamed of living far away, perhaps in America or Argentina.

HIS FATHER HAD BEFRIENDED a couple who owned and operated a TV installation and repair shop across the street. Silvana took care of the VHS rental service and Mario repaired TVs and VCRs and installed equipment and antennas in homes. The middle-aged man liked them, and almost daily would go in the store with his father to talk to them. Mario had invited him to go on some of the installation jobs so he could get out of his parents' house, and he enjoyed riding around and seeing the expensive villas that Mario worked in.

When he didn't go on truck drives with his uncle or accompany Mario, he went on five-mile walks. After lunch, around two o'clock, he put on his jacket and gloves and left the apartment. He turned right on Via Fattori and passed the bus stop and soccer field, ran across Via Aurelia, then took the dirt pathway that flanked the wild bird oasis, turned on the Strada Provinciale della Giannella and crossed the canal that ran into the Albegna River. On the right side, beyond a field, loomed the fortress constructed in the late 1400s by the Republic of Siena, and soon after, he passed the entrance to the road that led to the bar and the Albinia beach, but he kept walking straight for miles, pines and villas on the right side, fields, trees and the occasional restaurant on the left.

Toward the end of February, he noticed the first signs of spring: the sun broke through clouds and stayed longer, the fields became greener, birds' chirping increased. The air, even though still cool, had lost its sharpness, and he'd often see a group of bicycle riders in their colorful racing clothes coming the other way. What did they think of him, an odd-looking man walking along the road?

He tried to lose himself in the scents of pines and sea, in the cool air, in the weak sun's warmth. He turned on one of the paths leading to the beach and walked near the waves, the sand almost black near the water, the equipment rental shacks boarded up, lumps of seaweed crawling with iridescent flies. The sky was brooding with thunderheads, a translucent vault under which he was alone. He often picked up seashells scattered on the sand: striped conches, miters (which true to their name looked like the hats worn by bishops), harps, cockles, scallops, wandering tritons and sundials, and once in a while a pale sand dollar or sea urchin shell surprised him. The remains of living creatures, in exuberant shapes and variegated colors, were like little works of art the sea had left for him. He stuffed his pockets with them as he dreamed of owning one of the villas nestled among the pines, so that after his long walks he could go home, put the seashells on the mantelpiece, get the fireplace going, sit in front of it with a good book and read for a couple of hours, then take a nap. But he had no home, just some clothes and a few books.

He had received the return ticket, his time of departure drew near, but he didn't have any money. The middle-aged man was keeping his uncle Libero company on another truck ride. They had gone to Bolzano, in the north. They had arrived early in the morning; it was cold and he could see his breath. The old guard gave them coffee with grappa, and since they were short-handed, the middle-aged man helped unload the truck. He picked up the heavy sacks, threw them on his right shoulder and carried them in the warehouse. He remembered when as a junior in high school while working for the seed company in the summer he had unloaded a truck; that time the sacks were full of onion seeds, not explosives. On the way back, after they stopped to buy some sandwiches, Libero looked at him and said that he had a moving job the following day, but, he explained, "I usually go with Enzo, a helper; we take the small truck. Why don't you take my place? You'll get paid, and I'll have the day off." The middle-aged man needed money, so he agreed.

The job involved helping to carry sofas, credenzas, tables, chairs, a refrigerator and washer and dryer up five flights of stairs to an apartment, from one end of

Rome to another. As he rode in the passenger seat of the truck on the way to get another load of furniture, fountains and palazzi, churches and monuments passed by the windshield and Rome, the eternal city, was as far away as a dream, a postcard. It had become a backdrop for him as a furniture mover. And yet, he felt at the same time a part of the city. He wasn't a ghostly tourist admiring fountains and palazzi. The man he was helping was a young, friendly guy, and toward the end of the job, in late evening, as they carried a white leather sofa into the new apartment, the young man said to the residents, "This guy is an American professor," and they had looked at him in amusement.

Whatever he was, he had nothing now, and was working in a sort of delirium. He had woken up that morning with a bad sore throat due to chain smoking on his uncle's truck, had felt sick, but had pushed himself out of bed and forced himself to go do the job.

Yes, he had nothing now, but as he held the end of a sofa and walked into a high-ceilinged room under the eyes of the owners, he felt a strange feeling of lightness. He remembered the lyrics from one of his favorite Kris Kristofferson songs, "Freedom is just another word for nothing left to lose." His inflamed throat on fire, in a trance, climbing five flights of stairs carrying sofas and tables, riding in the truck back and forth through traffic, past statues and fountains, he felt strangely free. With the money he earned and the five hundred dollars his father had given him, he had eight hundred dollars.

The day before his departure, he went for a walk with his parents and had a last Campari at the bar overlooking the beach. The owner came to talk to them. "So, you're going back? We'll see you next year, *buona fortuna!*"

Then the following day the goodbyes, and the middle-aged man was on a plane back to San Diego.

15

SAN DIEGO, 1990

The old man sat up in the chair and glanced at the dog sleeping by the bookcase. Berry's back heaved almost imperceptibly up and down. If only he could sleep as peacefully. He got up and went to bed. His life appeared to him as a series of circles, compulsions to repeat. And why did he replay those memories if they caused him distress? But weren't those memories his life? He thought about the day he helped moving furniture. If he had really wanted to, couldn't he have stayed in Rome? He could have found a cheap room for rent on the outskirts, in one of those foreboding apartment buildings he saw whenever the train approached the city. He could have worked doing odd jobs. But he didn't have the purity of heart to accept poverty to live in Rome. He lay in bed, pulled the cover over himself, closed his eyes and traveled back to his life's story.

∼

It was the third of March, almost midnight; the plane was about to land. From the window, as if wrenched from the darkness by yellowish light, he could see Balboa Park, the white tower of the Museum of Man, the Cabrillo Bridge over the 163 highway. By the time he checked in at the Travelodge near the airport, it was two thirty in the morning. He slept fitfully for a few hours. The following day a friend picked him up and drove him to El Centro, where he checked in at one of the hotels on Adams Avenue. In 1963, when he had arrived as a fifteen-year-old boy, those hotels had looked plush and elegant, but now, twenty-seven years later, they were shabby places frequented mostly by seasonal workers. Why did he keep winding up in that desert town? He had a couple of friends there, his son and the memories of so many years, growing up, high school and college, girlfriends and wives, children. And yet he had tried so many times to leave, to get away.

He hadn't seen his son in six months. The following day he borrowed Larry's car and went to pick up Michael, took him to Carl's Junior for a burger and then to the movies. He sat in the theater next to his son, munching popcorn, watching *The Hunt for Red October*. How strange to have been in Rome yesterday and in El Centro today, the good feeling of being with his son corrupted by the anxiety of having no apartment, no job, no transportation. *What am I going to do?* he wondered, as he took a sip of Pepsi and watched Sean Connery command a Russian submarine.

After a couple of days at the hotel, he stayed at Larry's apartment for a week while he applied for substitute teacher positions at school districts in the Valley. Larry was fed up with him staying at his place; he needed to move out. He and Larry had been close friends until 1978; after that, they had drifted apart, and Larry had befriended people who were heavily into speed. Larry had the night shift at the hospital, and before leaving for work he snorted crystal meth.

"You know, that shit's going to fuck you up," the middle-aged man told him one night.

Larry stood at the kitchen counter, dressed in his white Lee's jeans and a long-sleeved shirt. He took a vial half full of white powder, raised it in front of the middle-aged man and said, angrily, "See this? This is the only thing that makes me go to work!" On his days off, two or three of Larry's friends from the hospital dropped by and they snorted meth, smoked marijuana and listened to music until two or three in the morning. The middle-aged man needed to get out of there.

He rented a room in the house of a teacher he had worked with when he taught English at Calexico High School, and with the help of his former philosophy professor at Imperial Valley College, bought an old Chevrolet from the college automotive department. The Impala was a project car the students had worked on, and he got it for 350 dollars.

He began to substitute teach but had to wait a whole month for his first check. He had just enough money left for gas, so he went to a church and asked if he could do any work for food. The pastor gave him a voucher for twenty dollars redeemable at Vons, and he bought bread, lunch meat, peanut butter, bananas and apples. For lunch and dinner, he took four slices of bread and four slices of bologna and made himself two sandwiches. He ate them slowly, to make them last.

He called Father Bob, who was surprised to hear the middle-aged man was back in the Valley and asked him to drop by. When he knocked on the sacristy's door, he was greeted by Bob and Buster, his big dog.

"You came just in time—happy hour started half an hour ago," said Father Bob as he walked in the kitchen. A bottle of vodka, glasses and olives waited on the counter.

"What are you doing back? It's like déjà vu," he said as he handed the middle-aged man a martini. "*The Golden Girls* was really funny today. You know I like to watch *Star Trek* at this time, but I'd rather talk to you," he said, smiling, as Buster came by to see if he could lick the frosty glasses. Father Bob had a big TV and enjoyed watching reruns in the afternoon while he sipped martinis.

"So, what the hell's going on?"

"I didn't get the job I was hoping for, didn't know what else I could do there." They sat on easy chairs by the piano. Buster had given up on his attempts to lick the glasses and was sleeping on the rug. The drink was cold and refreshing, and the vodka began to smooth the sharp edges of things.

Bob told him a little about his past. "I was an orphan, the couple that raised me, they were Catholic, and one Sunday morning, at church, as I watched the priest officiate mass, I thought to myself, 'That is what I want to do.' I must have been ten or eleven when I felt called, and from what you told me before, you felt a calling to become a philosophy professor a long time ago, but respiratory therapy, high school teaching—why?" Bob glanced at his watch and got up. "I need to go to the hall to change cassettes—there's a group of ladies who are watching a video on Saint Bernadette. I'll be right back," he said, as the middle-aged man chewed on the last ice chips left in the glass. A few minutes later, Bob returned and went in the kitchen to make two more martinis.

"So how's the church business? Have you written your homily for Sunday yet?" asked the middle-aged man.

"I don't want to talk shop," Bob said in an irritated voice from the kitchen. "Last week I had to deal with the secretary who stole money from the Sunday offerings, and I had to go to a conference and mingle with priests who wore expensive clothes, Italian designer socks, can you believe it? And they reeked of Aramis and Polo cologne." He handed the middle-aged man the drink and sat down again.

"Is that the reason you wear Old Spice? So you'll be considered one of the hoi polloi?"

"My dad used to wear it; I grew up with it. And maybe it keeps some of those lonely housewives from trying to seduce me. So many priests live cushy lives —hell, even me, in this town lost in the boondocks. I live for free in this nice house, I drive a comfy car, and you've seen the RV I have in the backyard. I take off for a month in the summer and go to the Rockies, near Bishop, camp out and fish. Not a bad life for a servant of God. But we were talking about vocations. What happened to yours?"

"When I call school districts, they tell me there are no philosophy teaching jobs, and if there is an opening, experience is required. Respiratory therapy was a way for me to make a living, but I don't like it."

"Nor teaching high school."

"I took a bunch of courses in education, for what? One of the professors was a school superintendent who told us to give C's to the students who deserve D's or F's, because they have to be moved through the system. When I worked at the high school, the principal told us we were not to give any student an F. They want them in class for money reasons, don't want to anger parents. The teachers are drowned in paperwork, made to fill charts and forms for accountability. They want to do away with tenure, because they blame it for 'bad' teachers. No, thank you."

"So you're back to square one."

"You'd think if God existed, he'd help me."

"How do you know he hasn't? Maybe he's been very patient with your sorry ass!"

"He probably doesn't exist."

"Maybe, who the hell knows. Like Kierkegaard says, at the end of the day you have to make a leap of faith."

"Yeah, yeah."

"Stay for dinner. I'm making my signature gourmet dish, Hamburger Helper. Buster loves it. And I'll make a salad, too," he said, as he finished his martini.

∽

THE MIDDLE-AGED MAN began working as a substitute teacher at the high school where he had been a full-time English teacher three years earlier. He walked to the office to use the copier, passed the library and entered classrooms stealthily, trying to make sure not to be seen by people he had worked with. He filled in three or four days a week, and on days off he looked through the job postings in the *San Diego Union-Tribune*. A home medical company in San Diego needed a respiratory therapist. He applied, went to the interview, and a few days later he received a call that he got the job.

DONNA, the respiratory therapy student who had taught him to run, who had been instrumental in getting him in shape, arranged for him to rent a room in a house she owned and where her daughter lived. By this time he had just enough money to pay for the first month's rent and for gas. He needed a little more for food until the first paycheck, so before he left El Centro he asked Ricardo for twenty dollars, which the old accountant gladly gave. Ricardo had a limp. "I need a new hip," he said as he sat on the creaky office chair, food stains on his shirt. "Pray to the Virgin; she'll help you. Every day when I go home I lay on the bed and say the rosary. It's a meditation. I'll pray for you, too."

When the middle-aged man returned from Italy, he had been determined to succeed, and people and events seemed to want to help him. He was surprised at how doors opened. It was strange, a new experience, like the day his car began to overheat because the radiator had a leak. He saw a man in front of a house, so he stopped and asked for help. The man helped him cool off the radiator with a water hose, said he had an old radiator that would fit the car and gave it to him.

ON THE LAST weekend of April, he drove from El Centro to the Clairemont area of San Diego with his belongings in the old white Impala, hoping it would not break down along the way. The old car survived Mountain Springs Grade, and as he drove past Live Oak Springs he thought of Penelope and her cabin. Larry had told him she had a boyfriend, her kids were doing well and she was happy. The sun hid behind the mountains, the sky became an intense, almost unreal blue and the majestic oaks and hillsides stood out sharply, as if wanting to move forward. *Transcendent* and *spiritual* were words that came to him, but he realized that what he saw was due to the cone cells in his eyes, stereoscopic vision and atmospheric conditions. It was breathtaking and uncanny but grounded in the physical. The experience of awe was special, to be treasured, but how ephemeral and ghostly. In the vast darkness of space, on a small rock circling a star, an organic being had a feeling of wonderment. What Wittgenstein had said came to mind: "It's not how the world is that is mystical, but that it is."

He arrived at the house in late evening. Donna's daughter, Karin, sat in the living room with her boyfriend as the middle-aged man carried his things in the room, and his new life in San Diego began.

The middle-aged man bought a pair of Asics and started jogging four or five times a week. He hadn't jogged in almost a year. He began by running around the neighborhood and on the Tecolote Canyon Trail, which was close by. He also liked to run in Torrey Pines State Park, downhill all the way to the beach. Sunny days, he flew down the narrow trail, the scent of yerba santa in his head. He would snap a fleshy leaf off, velvet smooth, break it with his fingers and sniff; it was like incense, and wasn't even this a cathedral, and his run a form of prayer? The sandstone cliffs buttresses, trees and shrubs holy statues, no need for stained-glass windows here, the cool breeze the holy spirit, the ocean in front of him the blessed mother, the sun the host of hosts. He ran on the beach for a couple of miles, listening to the restless waves, the briny smell of the ocean in the air, then jogged back up the steep hill to the road.

Abbey-Foster was a medical equipment company that employed three respiratory therapists. The job involved delivering medical devices and instructing patients, then assessing them. He began the workdays sitting at his desk going over files and arranging appointments over the phone, then he loaded equipment in the company van and headed for patients' homes. As he drove around San Diego in a white Suzuki van, he played "La Vita Mia" by Amedeo Minghi, the cassette his sister had given him for Christmas; the dreamy, nostalgic music became a soundtrack to his life in the land of plastic and concrete, of glaring billboards, gigantic American flags advertising gas stations and car dealerships. He yearned for umbrella pine trees, the Tyrrhenian Sea, the small towns with strange names. He wanted to stop at a bar and order a coffee, hear the huge espresso machine huff and puff. He had stopped at a coffee shop earlier and asked for a cappuccino. He was given a sixteen-ounce cup mostly full of milk. He wanted to *feel* a sense of history.

He began to wonder how he could get a certificate to teach English to foreign students so he could return to Italy and get a teaching job. He looked into university programs, but they would have required time and money, which he didn't have.

He was stuck, stranded again. Now that he was back in America he yearned to return to Italy. He wanted to smell the air as he walked in the Tuscan countryside, walk alongside the Arno in Florence in the rain.

But he suddenly realized that what he really wanted to do was to hold on to his brother as the Ducati banked on the curves, walk on the field in late afternoon as it started to snow, run after the chicken with his aunt Avia when they lived in the House of the Fig. He wanted to wade in the mountain stream looking at minnows dart away from his toes as the sun shone on the trees and warmed his skin, see Ornella again smiling from behind the desk as he recited by memory a poem by Leopardi. He wanted to climb the tree with his brother and laugh as they gorged themselves on cherries, feel cold drops of water from the fountain in Piazza de Ferrari baptize him as he walked on the rim, holding on to his father's hand. He wanted to see the fireworks again with his mother, sister and aunt, to walk with them at night in Genova, the shops' windows lit up, the trams like green caterpillars going down the shiny streets after it rained. He wanted to hear Christmas songs coming from the churches as golden light streamed from their open doors, admire the nativity scenes, smell the scent of the roasted chestnuts vendors sold in winter. He wanted to hear the church bells announce vespers, see the crepuscular light as he walked down the trail in Sella with his mother, sister and Giula after gathering mushrooms. He wanted to see his grandmother in her black dress, hair up in a bun, cut a thick slice of bread, rub one of the ripe tomatoes they had just picked from the vegetable garden, sprinkle salt, pour olive oil on it and hand it to him. He wanted to see her smile as her lips slightly trembled. He wanted to lie down on the sand and read science fiction stories after spending hours with his head underwater with mask and snorkel, on the summer days when his mother took him and his sister to the beach. He longed to go back, yearned to return to that time, but there was no going back; he was expelled from paradise, banished, irrevocably.

He spent most of his working days driving to homes, delivering oxygen concentrators, cylinders, masks and tubing, aerosol machines, oximeters and portable ventilators, and instructing and assessing patients. For lunch he'd bring a sandwich, for dinner another couple of sandwiches or some rice with half a can of garbanzo beans with some olive oil and vinegar. He couldn't eat out every day, after all, and he didn't want to cook in Karin's kitchen. He remembered that in the 1970s when he lived with Deborah on 27th Street, they went shopping downtown at Woo Chee Chong. The middle-aged man drove there, and as he walked around the aisles, he saw himself fifteen years earlier shopping, Deborah wearing her favorite leather sandals, him holding Michael. The smells were the same, but how much had changed. The middle-aged man let go of his reverie and picked up a small electric rice cooker so he could have warm rice with minimal use of Karin's kitchen.

On weekends, he drove to El Centro to see his son and take him to lunch and a movie, then he'd stop to visit Father Bob for a while before going back to San Diego. When the middle-aged man called the sacristy, the secretary answered. "Father Bob had a seizure while he was playing the piano for a group of parishioners. He's in Grossmont Hospital in La Mesa," she said. A couple of days later when he went to visit him, Bob was in the hospital bed propped up on pillows, half of his head shaved. He had a brain tumor, and the surgeons had operated on him right away. Was this another example of how God worked in strange and mysterious ways? *Playing the piano in his living room to a group of women and then waking up in a hospital bed, a doctor telling him he had a malignant brain tumor, Jesus,* thought the middle-aged man, as he took a deep breath on his way out of the hospital. It was only by ignoring the chaotic nature of life that humans managed to believe in a stable world regulated by natural and/or divine law. Bob had smiled, said he felt okay, was eager to get back home. He looked peevish, had glanced down as if ashamed. The middle-aged man wondered what Bob thought and felt about God as he lay in the hospital bed. Was Bob that very moment asking God, "Why, Lord? Is this a punishment for my sins, is this a test of my faith?"

I NEED TO STOP THIS, thought the old man. He turned on his left side and tried to fall asleep, but his mind would not leave him alone, so he got up and went into the study, turned on the light and sat down. He glanced at the framed print on the wall. The red angel was always above the gate, brandishing his sword, the dog asleep in the little bed by the Wittgenstein books. The old man turned his head toward the bookcase on the right side, glanced at the shelves of volumes on religion and recognized many he had bought so long ago, when he lived in Karin's house. Not far from there, he had found the Daughters of Saint Paul's bookstore. In a strip mall next to a Bank of America and a See's Candy store, the "media nuns" sold religious books and magazines, crucifixes, rosaries, statuettes of Jesus, Mary and the saints, cassettes and CDs of new age and religious music. He bought the complete *Summa Theologica* by Saint Thomas, books by Thomas Merton and Edith Stein. Why was he attracted to that place? Unlike the bank and the candy store, it sold hope, the possibility of transcendence. Browsing the shelves, relaxing meditative music playing, the nuns behind the counter, what was he looking for? He remembered when years earlier he'd go to the Revolutionary Bookstore, a space that offered hope of a better world, comradeship, purpose.

On a Saturday morning when everything looked drab and he felt stuck in the quicksand of his feelings, he drove to the bookstore. Maybe seeing the nuns behind the counter, so full of energy and commitment, would cheer him up. As he browsed around he saw an announcement on the bulletin board for a series of videos on the spiritual journey that was going to be shown at the Monastery of the Benedictine Sisters of Perpetual Adoration, near Pacific Beach. On the evening of the first video's showing, he drove the old white Impala and made sure to park far away from the parking lot, on a residential street.

He walked into the monastery's conference room. Chairs had been placed in front of a screen. A nun introduced the program, which consisted of videos narrated by Father Thomas Keating, a Trappist monk and priest. Sister Mary Gregory, a petite woman in her seventies, exuded kindness and caring. She had short, curly gray hair and big wire-rimmed glasses.

Among the people who sat there he noticed in the row in front of him, to his left, a woman with flowing red hair who wore a jacket embroidered in yellow. There was something mystical about her, and he felt an immediate attraction. He kept thinking about her, and a couple of weeks later, on a pretext, he succeeded in getting her phone number from Sister Mary. He called her one evening, and they talked for a long time about spirituality and meditation, but when he asked her if she wanted to have a cup of coffee with him, she declined.

Donna and her husband, Edwin, led a running group that met every week in different spots in San Diego for a one-hour jog. Hoping to take his mind off the woman with the red hair, he joined The Happy Wanderers one afternoon for a run. The eight or ten joggers were older than he; one man was in his early eighties, but even though he was slow, his stamina surprised the middle-aged man. The trail meandered through plants, boulders and oaks, and as he jogged, he couldn't stop thinking of the woman he felt so strongly attracted to. The rocks kept silent and aloof, the trees were busy with their vegetative lives and as they neared a house, a bougainvillea's outburst of intense red felt like an explosion, a rip in the veil of appearances through which blood flowed.

Then one evening, after the video and the meditation at the monastery, the red-haired woman agreed to have coffee and they met at the Java Express in Pacific Beach. Her name was Stephanie. She told him she had graduated from San Diego State University with a major in accounting, but spending all day at a desk dealing with numbers wasn't for her, so she began working in the landscaping department at Sea World. She sang in the Mission de Alcalá church choir, and was scheduled to sing two arias at a recital organized by her voice teacher. "I'm rather nervous about it," she said. "One of the arias is by the composer Stefano Donaudy; it's in Italian, and I'm not sure about the pronunciation."

"Let me borrow the sheet music book and I'll record the aria on tape. You can listen to the pronunciation and practice the words," he suggested, and she agreed.

The following day, after work, he went to Radio Shack to buy a tape recorder and a couple of blank cassettes, and back in his room, he recorded the words not only of the aria Stephanie was going to sing, "*Quando ti rivedrò,*" but the other eleven arias by

Donaudy in the sheet music book. He also translated the words into English and printed them on his dot matrix printer. He stapled the pages with a cover sheet illustrated with a bouquet of flowers, and on the evening of the video showing and meditation, he returned the music book with the cassette and the translations. Stephanie smiled and her eyes brightened. "Thank you," she said. "But now I won't have any excuses if I butcher the aria." She was anxious about the event, but a week later, when she sang it at the recital, she pronounced the words perfectly.

They made an appointment to meet at Balboa Park the following Saturday, by the Natural History Museum, near the huge Moreton Bay fig tree. Stephanie laid a blanket on the wet grass and from a picnic basket retrieved a thermos, two coffee mugs and some muffins. He had been there often, with his parents, his daughter Renée and his son Michael, who had climbed on the giant roots of the tree, but now everything was new, fresh, surprisingly radiant. It was early, the day just beginning; doves cooed from a tree, and even the traffic on Park Boulevard sounded like music. After the breakfast, they jogged across the park over the 163 bridge, then turned around. They made a date for the following Saturday to jog at Torrey Pines State Park.

They ran down the trail that led to the beach, the one flanked by yerba santa, brittle bush and California sage, the ancient sandstone cliffs and the tall, slender Torrey pines. They were in *his* cathedral, which was just as resplendent as the ones in Rome and Florence. On the beach, as they ran on the sand by the water, he spotted a coconut the waves had pushed ashore. He picked it up and walked near the cliffs, toward a boulder that looked like a small altar. He placed the coconut on top and hit it with a rock. It cracked in three pieces, and they ate the sweet, firm flesh and drank the milk that remained in the bigger piece. It was a communion, with an offering from the sea.

ONE WARM AUGUST EVENING, they met at Seaport Village. After a coffee at Upstart Crow, they browsed in the boutiques that sold candles, tee shirts, crystals, seashells and other tourist trinkets. In the hat shop they tried on different hats, then they sat on the low boardwalk wall and talked. He remembered how he had walked there years earlier when he had been alone, on his way to look for a book on acting. *Don't despair*, he would have told himself, *things will get better*. From the boardwalk they turned in the Embarcadero Marina Park, a small peninsula full of trees, picnic tables and benches barely illuminated by a few lampposts. The moon, a reddish, waning gibbous, peeked from the roofs of the village's buildings, and the air, finally cool after a hot day, was heavy with the sea. He drew her to him, embraced her and kissed her. Was it a dream? How many days had he suffered when she had refused to have coffee with him? Now she was in his arms, and the sound of the waves gently lapping serenaded them.

They went to restaurants and musical events, and one Saturday evening they drove to Symphony Hall to hear soprano Kathleen Battle sing. During the intermission they were greeted by Olive and Harry, an elderly couple who knew Stephanie and belonged to the Mission choir. Thus he began to become part of a larger social circle.

The Spiritual Journey video showings and the meditations were on Thursday evenings at the monastery, and there he befriended a fellow meditator, a man in his fifties who would later become his best man and the godfather of his son. Michael D. was a fervent Catholic who went to mass every day. A slim man full of energy, he told the middle-aged man and Stephanie about a novena that was going to be held at the Carmelite monastery in Normal Heights. In celebration of the feast day of Saint Teresa of Avila, every evening for nine days a mass would be celebrated, and so on Saturday, October 6, the middle-aged man found himself in the Carmelite church.

Built in the early 1930s, the Spanish-style church had a cream-colored facade with a red tile roof and double wooden doors decorated by reliefs of sacred hearts and other symbols. Inside, people sat on individual chairs with kneelers instead of pews. Above the altar, an image of José de Ribera's *The Holy Trinity* stood out on the white wall. The sisters sat behind iron gates on the right side of the altar so they couldn't be seen. The church had a simple elegance, a deeply spiritual feel. As he sat on a chair up front, he admired the small ornate crucifix above the tabernacle on the altar, the statues of Mary and Joseph, the Via Crucis on the walls. The soft white light created an ethereal atmosphere; it felt like a space beyond, untouched and unreachable by the mundane world outside.

The middle-aged man and Stephanie went almost every Saturday morning to the seven thirty mass held at the monastery. He made the acquaintance of some of her friends, including Anita, a woman in her forties who managed an apartment complex and was deeply religious. One morning just before the mass started, she stood next to him and began to pray. Then without turning, she said quietly, "I have lung cancer. And I don't even smoke." He didn't know what to say; then the mass started.

Meanwhile, Thomas Keating's video series continued. The Trappist priest promoted a process of overcoming the "false self" through silent prayer, or meditation. Sister Mary would begin the evening with a reading, then she would turn the VCR on and show a video, to be followed by a sitting and a walking meditation.

He was so inspired by his reading of the saints and by Keating's series that he wanted to become a spiritual counselor. He was back in the Church, but on his own terms. He interpreted scriptures symbolically; when the Nicene Creed was recited during mass he closed his eyes, remained silent and told himself the voices of the priest and the faithful were the sound of water flowing over rocks. The Creed was a series of dogmas he could not accept as literal truth. How could he believe that Jesus Christ was the only son of God born of the Virgin Mary, who was resurrected after dying on the cross and ascended to heaven? What appealed to him were not doctrines and beliefs, but the images, the art, the feeling of separation from the mundane; how the light changed as it passed through clouds of incense and burning candles, how it danced on the robes of the priest and shone on the faces of the people gathered there; the feeling of not being alone, but with others who, however briefly, yearned for love, meaning, hope, redemption.

He was directed to the Spiritual Ministry Center in Ocean Beach. The center was run by a few nuns who belonged to the Religious of the Sacred Heart. The sister he talked to was Betty Boyter, a woman in her sixties with light brown hair, who emitted serenity and acceptance. "Why do you want to become a spiritual counselor?" she asked him. She didn't seem convinced by his answers and told him that before thinking of becoming a spiritual counselor, he needed to have counseling himself.

Every week he went to a meeting with her, where she asked him to begin by praying aloud, not just the usual prayers, but to pray from his heart. He found it difficult but tried. One evening, he sat at his desk and began writing:

I thank You for the gift of this day. For clouds and rain, for loneliness and pain, for love and joy, for music and songs, for moon and stars, for bread and wine, for friends and enemies, for the confession and communion of a single day. You have given me so many days; so many journeys around the sun, so many springs, so many summers, so many falls, so many winters. What a splendor the trees' exuberance: leaves being born, growing under spring's caress, trembling under kiss of moon and breeze, rejoicing in summer's warmth, then heavy with gravity, with cold, just wanting to let go, surrendering, surrendering to You. Oh, what a sweet way down in the arms of the wind! Sweet free fall in brook, stream, on sidewalks, on fields, on roads. What a delight to become earth again, to become air, to become flowers, to become trees; it's just You, in different music, in different songs, in different faces, in different words; it's You, it's me, it's her, it's him. I kneel in the unfolding blossom of this day and open my arms to all it holds. This day, this hour, this minute, this moment, this suffering, this loneliness, this joy, this love: sanctify it, embrace it, because it is me and I came from You. This ground I've tilled, this seed I've planted, this water I've squeezed from my eyes await Your hand. This moment which is my time, this tiny space which is my body, this heart that wants to love, I offer to You. Live in me and through me, and when the last day is done, let me stand on the mountain top's edge, let me breathe pines' fragrance, let me turn around and send it all a kiss, let the rain wash me, before I too come to You.

Yes, the sister would have liked his prayer.

One day Sister Betty invited him to dinner in the afternoon, and he showed up with a bouquet of white roses. She put them in a vase and placed it in the middle of the round table. Another sister joined them for spaghetti, salad and bread. The sessions usually lasted an hour; what did they talk about? He couldn't remember. But once, before the session, Sister Betty said, "I've been diagnosed with non-alcoholic cirrhosis of the liver. I don't know how long I have left."

Driving on the way home, he kept hearing Sister Betty's words: "I don't know how long I have left." He saw himself as a child standing behind his grandmother as she, kneeling in front of the dead priest, recited the rosary. That priest had probably prayed to God to help him, as Bob must have prayed, as Sister

Betty probably prayed to God for healing. But it didn't seem to matter.

He and Stephanie filled their weekends with activities, had dinner together as often as they could, talked about everything for hours. He flew to Santa Rosa with her to spend Christmas at her parents' house and met her family. In the spring they decided to get married in July at the Carmelite Monastery Church.

They found a small house in the Normal Heights area and he moved out of the room he rented. His desk and computer fit in the bedroom, and he was even able to put a bookcase in the living room. The old Impala kept breaking down, so he bought a used Mazda hatchback, which proved to be more reliable.

The day of the wedding arrived. In the early afternoon, he drove to the church under an overcast sky. Many people attended, including his son Michael, Stephanie's parents and relatives from Santa Rosa, San Francisco and San Luis Obispo, and some of his friends, including Richard and Carol Hann, Bobbi and Pat, and sisters Mary Gregory and Betty Boyter. His friend Larry had refused the invitation, and Frank was somewhere in Utah, looking for fossils. The Mission de Alcalá church choir arrived, and the singing began to fill the nave.

Stephanie looked resplendent in her white wedding dress, and the choir's singing was angelic. They exchanged vows and rings, took communion and walked down the aisle out of the church. A simple reception was held under the monastery arcade and in the rose garden. He shook hands, thanked and hugged relatives and friends.

There was a lemon ricotta cake and bowls of fresh fruit and berries. People talked, laughed, ate and drank punch. He took deep breaths, felt light on his feet. He was warm in the black suit, though it wasn't a very hot day.

After the reception, he and Stephanie went to visit Anita at her house. She was in bed with a cannula connected to an oxygen tank. He felt odd sitting by her bed in his wedding suit, during one of the happiest days of his life, as Anita lay dying.

On their honeymoon they went to Europe for three weeks, visiting his relatives and traveling to Rome, Florence, Perugia, Assisi, Venice and Zürich. What did he remember of those days? Standing on the stairs of the Piazza di Spagna in Rome as the setting sun turned everything into gold. In the evening they happened by chance upon the Basilica of Santa Maria degli Angeli, another dream conjured by Michelangelo. They admired the marble floors with geometric designs, life-sized statues of angels holding bowls of holy water, massive Roman columns, arches, paintings and frescoes, the dome with its bright oculus. The ethereal lilting voices of nuns singing vespers reverberated in the church and made it come alive.

Not far from the main railway station they saw a church with a gray Baroque facade. An old woman sat by the door, begging. Inside, splendor lived: marble columns, golden Roman arches, white angels flying, blue skies and clouds, Mary, saints and putti on the ceiling and cupola. And then on the left side, in a chapel, an angel holds an arrow with a golden point and is about to pierce Saint Teresa, who is leaning back, her mouth open, her eyes closed. The angel smiles, his left hand delicately holding on to her robe; Teresa's naked foot hangs below the folds of her robe. Light from a window above the statue shone on the gilded bronze rays behind Bernini's sculpture. He remembered reading the saint's description of the vision when he bought Teresa's biography at the Book Nook, and now the vision was in front of him, given form in Bernini's masterpiece. The artist's rendering of the saint's vision enriched her words with material beauty and the sublime. *Every time I come back to Rome, I must come here*, thought the middle-aged man. After Rome, they stayed in a hotel in Albinia for two days so they could visit his parents and relatives, then continued on to Perugia.

Sandrina and Giuliano, her husband, drove them to a nearby mountain town where they had a long lunch on a veranda. Not many people were in the restaurant, and after dessert and coffee, at the insistence of Giuliano, Stephanie sang Donaudy's aria "Quando ti rivedrò," to the delight of the waiter. The middle-aged man was happy to see his sister; just a year earlier he had been alone, stranded at his parents' apartment, now he was back in Italy on his honeymoon. Sandrina and Stephanie got along well, and he and Giuliano had many conversations about cars and the culinary specialties of Perugia.

Venice in July was hot and humid. After a five hour ride, they stepped out of the Santa Lucia train station and instead of a square with buses and taxis, saw a wide canal with boats going back and forth in the musty breeze, palazzi and cupolas lining the sides. He had seen Venice often in movies, documentaries and photos, but being there was like stepping into a different world. They hauled their luggage onto a vaporetto, then a porter carried it on a cart across Piazza San Marco to their hotel, Antica Locanda al Gambero. Venice would have been wonderful if it hadn't been invaded by thousands of tourists. He felt like he was in Disneyland during the peak season or at the San Diego Comic-Con, but on a foggy night they went to the Church of Vivaldi for a concert and the tourists seemed to have mysteriously disappeared. Walking on the narrow streets by side canals and crossing the ubiquitous footbridges, surprised by small squares and ancient churches, water always flowing by, he thought of Carl Jung's idea that water in dreams represented the unconscious, the part of the psyche where hidden memories and impulses resided. Maybe that was the reason he had felt a loss of balance when he stepped in front of the Grand Canal. Palazzi and churches' domes seemed to have sprung up magically from a dreamy realm. What was more real? The ornate stone and marble buildings or the intangible world beneath them? And what about him? Hadn't he sprung from humankind's unconscious, from the memories and impulses of countless generations? How real was he? He needed to stop thinking and enjoy the interplay of water and stone, blue sky and seagulls flying low, the gentle lapping of water by the small canals, the scents of coffee and food that came from restaurants and bars.

From Venice they took the train to Zürich, from where they were to fly back home. What did he remember after thirty years? Vague images of the train station in Milan, where they had changed lines.

As the train labored uphill through the Alps, green meadows, firs and lofty snow-covered peaks reminded him of Thomas Mann's novel *The Magic Mountain*, when the protagonist, Hans Castorp, travels by train from Germany to Switzerland to visit his cousin. "Space, like time," says Mann, "engenders forgetfulness; but it does so by setting us bodily free from our surroundings and giving us back our primitive, unattached state." And indeed, as the middle-aged man sat by the window gazing at the massive white mountains crowned by clouds he entered in a trance, and forgot about time and space.

In the three days they spent in Zürich they explored the city, drank beer and wine outdoors, visited the Grossmünster church and ate lots of chocolate. He sat on a bench by Lake Zürich and wondered where the house of Carl Jung was. Richard Wagner, Lenin, Albert Einstein and James Joyce were just a few of the famous people who had lived in Zürich. Then the realization that he was married to the woman he had fallen in love with pushed those thoughts out of his mind. He watched Stephanie swim in the lake, she smiled at him and waved. Was this a bestowal of grace?

16

SAN DIEGO, 1991–1992

Back home, he was faced with the old problem of how to make a living. He had been laid off from the home medical company, so now he worked per diem at different hospitals. He had to wake up at four in the morning to be at work by six to do aerosol treatments and chest physical therapy, bring equipment into patients' rooms and be available for the occasional code blue. It was sporadic and certainly not what he wanted to do. He applied for part-time teaching jobs, and in the summer of 1991, Southwestern College in Chula Vista offered him an Introduction to Philosophy course for the fall semester.

He had never taught philosophy before, so he needed to brush up. The textbook he was going to use began with a chapter on Hesiod and Homer, the main ancient Greek representatives of a pre-philosophical worldview. To prepare, he reread *The Power of Myth* by Joseph Campbell, the book Pat had told him about long ago at the Book Nook. Campbell pointed out that religious narratives are not to be interpreted literally but metaphorically. If the stories are read as poetry, they can have healing effects on the individual and society. The middle-aged man reread *Theogony*, *The Iliad* and *The Odyssey*. In 1962, Ornella, his sixth-grade teacher, had assigned a selection from *The Iliad*, and at home, sitting on his bed, the heavy literature anthology on his lap, he had entered into Homer's world with fascination. Then at Imperial Valley College, he read the whole epic under the direction of professor Rosanne Hillhouse, and he learned to love that world where men and women, gods and goddesses, interacted, loved and hated, helped and hindered one another.

Hesiod was a Greek poet who lived in the second half of the eighth century BCE, and in the "Genealogy of the Gods" he narrates the creation of the world. Hesiod took ancient stories about gods and goddesses and wove them into a coherent history that gave order to the universe and humans' place in it.

The book begins with Hesiod tending his sheep on Mount Helicon, when the goddesses appear to him and inspire him to sing of the gods. In the beginning was Chaos, a primordial void, undifferentiated matter from which deep darkness and night were generated. They coupled and gave birth to sleep and death. Earth took form and separated from Sky, with whom she had many children including Mnemosyne, the goddess of memory and remembrance. But the Sky god behaved badly toward his children, so Earth asked Kronos, her son, to castrate him. When Sky, full of desire, came to spread himself on Earth, Kronos sliced off his father's genitals with a sharp sickle.

Kronos later became identified with the god of time, who having fathered children, devours them. *So it is Kronos who has been chasing me all my life, and the running away is how he has been devouring me*, thought the middle-aged man. But if he had stopped running, wouldn't he have died? Wasn't the running his life?

Emotions, thoughts, bodily drives, hopes and dreams; mountains, rivers, clouds, the ocean, love, death, sun, moon and stars—they were all gods and goddesses. How must it have been, to have lived in such a world? When the middle-aged man looked up at the moon, he knew it was a hunk of rock circling the earth; how mysterious and wonderful to have seen Selene, the goddess that shined her pale light on your path and looked over you! How could you feel lonely in such a world?

Kronos was defeated by Zeus and imprisoned, but he was still eating his children. Time, sucking the life out of humans, until only shriveled skin husks remain, slobbering demented things who had once been in the fullness of youth.

Zeus, the power principle, coupled with Mnemosyne, and the muses came into being. The muses went into the world and inspired humans. From this mythological poetic way of thinking, a shift took place in Greece, with thinkers who began to look for causes in the things themselves. After going over the early "nature philosophers," he introduced Socrates and Plato.

This is what he had dreamed of doing since he sat in Richard Hann's classroom at Imperial Valley College in 1969 and 1970, watched him walk back and forth in front of the class, writing on the chalkboard as he talked about free will, human nature and God. Finally, he was the one now who walked back and forth in front of the class and introduced Socrates, explained Plato's theory of the forms, laid out on the board the arguments and counterarguments for God's existence. Unfortunately, it was only one course, so he still had to work, usually on weekends, at hospitals as a respiratory therapist.

For the spring of 1992 he was assigned to teach two sections of humanities. According to the official course outline, he was expected to cover important works in literature, music, drama, painting, sculpture, architecture, philosophy and religion, from Mesopotamia and Egypt to the twentieth century.

To be better prepared, he read more books, including Gombrich's study of the great German art historian Aby Warburg, who lived for four years in Florence, studying Renaissance paintings. The middle-aged man was fascinated by Warburg's analysis of certain images, including Ghirlandaio's frescoes in the Basilica of Santa Maria Novella in Florence. Warburg devoted much time to the study of Botticelli's *The Birth of Venus*, from its mythological origins to the flowing drapery, which he traced back to influences by Poliziano, Duccio and ancient sarcophagi. The middle-aged man remembered the first time he stood in front of the painting, in July of 1987, when he and Penelope had taken the bus to Florence for the day. There had been no Plexiglas over the canvas, and he stood there as if time had stopped. He had gone to the Uffizi on other occasions, but it hadn't been the same; the plate protecting the work reflected light and the direct, sensual connection with Botticelli's masterpiece was gone.

Every time he visited Florence, he went to the Basilica of Santa Maria Novella to admire Masaccio's fresco of the Trinity. Masaccio was a Florentine artist who worked on the fresco in 1427. Twenty-two feet tall and ten feet wide, on the basilica's left wall, God the Father holds the cross on which a dead Christ is crucified. In single-point perspective within a classical architectural space, it had a trompe l'oeil effect: it looked three dimensional on the flat wall. Below the Trinity, a skeleton lies on a sarcophagus; an inscription below it reads, *I was once like you and what I am you will be*. Why did he find the fresco so enthralling? "Only by faith in the Trinity can death be overcome" was probably what the devout read in it, but he was captivated by the composition and the colors, by the memento mori of the skeleton and the wish for life everlasting symbolized by the Father, the Son and the Holy Spirit.

He couldn't see the other frescoes in the chapels clearly, due to the lack of light, but in the book he bought at the church's gift shop, they were displayed in all their beauty. Aby Warburg analyzed how the figures were dressed, signs that could reveal the psychological motivations of the artist, the cultural, economic forces dominant at the time, the stresses and strains in them. If you looked deeply at works of art, you could discern how different historical epochs and cultures, through the lives of the artist, made them possible. They were time machines that transported you into different times and places.

He went to the Adams Avenue Bookstore weekly

and spent an hour there, browsing the shelves. Upstairs was the philosophy section, and Jeff, the owner, always kept it well stocked. He had first met Jeff the year before, when he sold him a few boxes of books he no longer wanted. An ordained minister, Jeff expanded the store when the upstairs became available, and unlike some of the other used bookstores around, he kept the shelves well organized with serious literature and nonfiction. The store mascot, a fat cat, usually slept on a shelf.

Jeff had bought a batch of used books heavily underlined in blue and red pencil, with occasional notes in the margins. "I usually hate used books with underlining in them," he told Jeff, "but these I don't mind." Indeed, the neat markings and notes showed that someone had seriously studied the books. The previous owner had written his name, "Stanley R. Hopper," on the front flyleaf of the volumes. The more books he bought from Mr. Hopper's former library, the more curious the middle-aged man became about him. Hopper had extensively marked works of philosophy, literature, history and religion. One day, at the bookstore, he found a book that had been written by Stanley Romaine Hopper. *The Way of Transfiguration* was a collection of essays Hopper had written on "theopoetics," a way of thinking about religion that incorporated poetry, philosophy and psychology. In chapter four he concluded that "although we may be but the minutest minuscule of dust on a grain of sand tossed in a galactic sea, the whole is given in the part and we are permitted—from the deep centrum of our being—to be both the eyes of becoming and a tongue for utterance: the manifest of glory, the resonance of praise."

Hopper had been a professor at Syracuse University in New York. Born in 1907, he had been ordained an elder of the Methodist Episcopalian Church, studied theology in Zürich and the Greek classics at Oxford, and according to a biographical sketch by Tony Stoneburner, upon the recommendation of Heidegger and Jung, Hopper traveled to Japan, where he stayed for a year. Reading the books the professor had meticulously underlined, deciphering the remarks written in the margins in pencil, then reading the essays where Hopper referenced many of those books made him feel like he knew Stanley R. Hopper a little, could see the links between the professor's reading and how it had informed his thinking.

Hopper's essays sparkled with philosophical and poetic flair, he had been such a presence and had taught for decades, but now he was dead, and his books were sold to a used bookstore, traces of his intellectual life that continued living in others' libraries. Sad to think that those books once were in the library of a scholar who had treasured them, reading and studying them, and after his death, their link to the man was gone; they became dusty things to be disposed of. But some of Hopper's books were now in the middle-aged man's library, and they had inspired and increased his knowledge. *As long as I live, I'll safeguard your books, and I'll think of you. Thank you, Dr. Hopper,* he thought.

Whenever he walked into the bookstore, he greeted Jeff or Craig, who stood behind the counter sorting and pricing books. Craig, a young man who had gone to San Diego State University and had taken some philosophy courses, eventually opened his own bookstore in La Mesa.

One Friday, when after doing the grocery shopping, he stopped at the bookstore to see what he could find on the shelves, he noticed several hardbound copies of Carl Jung's *Collected Works*. They were used but in good condition, so he bought some. As his library grew and his reading increased, he realized he was not going to be able to read all the books he wanted to, and so there were times when he'd sit on the sofa, look at the books on the shelves and not know what to read.

The middle-aged man struggled with religion. He read a work by the scholar-priest Ernesto Balducci, in which he elaborated the idea that "Western man doesn't listen to anyone, his philosophy is an inexhaustible monologue." He wrote that cultures give rise to religious expressions that become ideologies—systems of beliefs that support and sacralize social and political power. God as defined by the system is an edited God, a representation that validates what the groups in power want us to believe and value. But if we are sincere in our spiritual quest, we must strive to search for the unedited God. Wasn't that what the mystics attempted? Saint Francis, butting heads with the Pope, or Saint John of the Cross, or *The Cloud of Unknowing*. Whoever wrote it in fourteenth-century England must have been a mystic. God is hidden in a cloud of unknowing, and reason cannot see through it, but we can penetrate the cloud with our love. In this contemplative prayer we must let go of images and thoughts, forge a cloud of forgetting, letting go even of ourselves, and to help us in our contemplation, come up with a one-syllable word that we can recite if we are distracted by thoughts or images.

This reminded him of Meister Eckhart, the German mystic he had read the year before. In Eckhart's view, there comes a time in the spiritual journey when God becomes the ultimate obstacle. If we are to continue the journey, then what we believe about God, our representations of God, must be overcome. In one of his sermons, he says that if something is perceived in God and if some names are attached to him, then that is not God, because God is beyond names and words.

But, the middle-aged man thought, *if God is beyond names and words, beyond representations, aren't we left with nothingness? If I don't know what is in the cloud, what sense does it make to "send" my love to it? Wouldn't I assume that "God" was there? And if I cannot know God, how can I love God? What would I be loving?* He heard it often: "God is love." Such a vague statement. *If God is love, why is the world in such a sorry state? Full of pain, fear, suffering? Yes, the apologists will answer with theodicean arguments at this point, but they are not convincing. Perhaps the problem would disappear if God was not thought of in representational ways, or as a being. But then, reduced to a fuzzy concept, it dissolved into irrelevance.*

During his shifts at University Hospital, one of the patients on the floor he was assigned to was a 23-year-old man with cystic fibrosis. Robert was a gifted painter, but as is the case for many cystic fibrosis patients, he was in and out of the hospital frequently.

He was discharged after a few weeks of treatments, but his disease had worsened, and he was readmitted. This time the doctors told him there was nothing more that could be done. During one of Robert's respiratory therapy sessions, the middle-aged man told him, "When you get better, I would appreciate it if you could come have dinner with my wife and me." Robert had looked at him and replied, "I would really like that." A few days later, when he was called to cover a shift, he found out that Robert had died. Having been informed that the end was near, he had requested morphine and died peacefully with his parents at his bedside.

The old man got up from the chair and went downstairs to let the dog out. Twenty-eight years had passed, but he still remembered Robert. Thin and frail, Robert had told him that when he went to the gym, after a workout he stood on a scale and some people stared at him because he was so thin, so he looked at them and said, "Damn, I need to lose more weight." Robert was a likable, smart and talented young man. How must he have felt, lying in the hospital bed, his whole life up to that point a struggle to keep his lungs clear enough so he could breathe? To be young, so eager to paint, travel, love, and to know that it was all denied.

The old man sat on one of the patio chairs while Berry sniffed the plants, and felt a twinge of sorrow, even after so long. Then he thought of the young man he had seen at the Yuma hospital, the one who had committed suicide. He had felt anger then also. He remembered a psychiatrist he talked to once. "You look depressed," the doctor had declared, taking a pipe out of his mouth. "How can I be happy when millions of people are suffering?" he had replied. "The problem with you is that you have weak ego boundaries," the psychiatrist replied. Weak ego boundaries? Did he have to strengthen them, in order not to let others' suffering affect him? Yes, it was important to have ego boundaries; how else to maintain one's sense of self and not fall into madness? But was it weakness to feel sadness for the suffering of others, anger at the injustice, capriciousness and absurdity of life?

As the old man enjoyed the silence, the night and the cool air in the backyard, he traveled back to the time in 1992 when he began to teach philosophy at Southwestern College. He was forty-four years old.

THE MORE THE middle-aged man read about evolutionary biology and cognitive science, the harder it became to make sense of the conventional concept of God. And yet, he couldn't simply dismiss religion. It had been part of his life in many ways. There had been his mother dragging him and his sister to church; the priests, yes, even the dead one his grandmother had prayed for, and the one who called him Chou En-lai, or the one who told him to write in a black book his bad thoughts; the woman who came to the house to teach him the catechism; the hour of religious instruction in elementary school; finding some peace in reciting the rosary; Ricardo Jimenez inviting him and Mike Maxwell to the yearly retreat in Redlands; the religious images, the candles, the incense, the magic and mystery of the Latin liturgy. *Dominus vobiscum—et cum spiritu tuo.*

The books the middle-aged man read, and the films he watched as preparation for his teaching and for their own sake, expanded his intellectual horizons, made him want to be in Italy again, but now he knew he had to built a life where he was. He was married to a woman he loved and who loved him, had been given the opportunity to teach at the community college level. He still went to Italy during the summer for three weeks to visit his parents, and he found a way to be close to the land of his birth through Italian writers and poets and by watching Italian films.

When the spring semester ended in late May, he was told by the dean that in the fall he could have two courses in philosophy.

The middle-aged man drove to El Centro to visit his son, and before returning to San Diego, he stopped to see Ricardo. The receptionist wasn't there, and as the bell above the door rang, announcing his presence, Ricardo came out of the office.

"Shiggy! Come in, come in," he said as he limped down the hall back to his lair. He sat down with a grimace in the faded leather chair.

"I was listening to a talk by Fulton Sheen," he said, as he moved a small cassette player to the side.

"I came down to see my son and wanted to say hi before driving back," said the middle-aged man as he sat down on one of the chairs.

"Had a good visit?" he asked as he leaned forward.

His brown eyes, magnified by his glasses, seemed to float on limpid pools.

"We go to Burger King and the movies, that's about it. He doesn't say much."

"They don't like to talk to their parents at that age. At least you get together, do things with him—that's the important thing," Ricardo replied as he shifted his weight and rubbed his side.

"How's your hip?" asked the middle-age man.

"Dr. Haworth says I need a new one, but I'm a chicken. We'll see...What are you up to?"

"I'm going to teach two more courses at the college next semester, and I still have my hospital work. Stephanie got a promotion as the manager of horticulture at Sea World, and she sings in the Mission choir on Sundays."

"You've had your ups and downs, but the good lord has been smiling at you."

"Maybe."

"The Knights of Columbus Retreat will be on the first weekend of June; I'd love to see you in Redlands. Two days away from home, contemplation in a beautiful place, good food. Think about it."

"I will," said the middle-aged man as the phone rang and Ricardo picked it up. The middle-aged man looked at the bulletin board on the left side of the wall, right next to the desk. There were faded color photos of Ricardo's children, a large black-and-white one with a younger Ricardo and Bishop Sheen, holy cards of the Virgin Mary and Saint Joseph, an old church bulletin, a newspaper clipping of one of Ricardo's letters to the editor. The old accountant was a prolific writer of letters to the *Imperial Valley Press*.

They were often long articles about the history of the Valley.

"That was Mae, my wife," he said when he got off the phone. "She was wondering what I wanted for dinner. We've been married for almost fifty years, and she still makes me feel like a king. I'll send you a letter with the details for the retreat." They talked for a while longer, then the middle-aged man drove back to San Diego. When he and Mike had taken advantage of Ricardo's offer, it had been just a pretext for getting out of the Valley for a couple of days. Twenty-four years later, he wanted to take it seriously. Perhaps he could come to terms with his doubts and anxieties. He was married now, but employment was still problematic. Working weekends in hospitals, teaching a class or two per semester, he wanted a full-time teaching job.

El Carmelo Retreat was a Carmelite Catholic "spiritual sanctuary" on twenty-nine acres in Redlands, overlooking the San Bernardino Mountains. Once there, the middle-aged man walked under trees and listened to fountains as birds chirped. Flowers were everywhere—geraniums, daisies, poppies. The theme for the retreat was evangelization. The pope and the bishops were concerned about the increasing number of Catholics who left the church to join other religious sects, so the questions were why, and what can be done? The middle-aged man forced himself to attend the talks. He had wanted to spend more time in solitude, but almost every hour was planned with discussions and group activities. He was happy to be there with Ricardo, who, with graying hair neatly trimmed, still looked like Anthony Quinn, albeit a much older version.

On Sunday afternoon, as everyone left, he remembered the twenty dollars Ricardo had loaned him almost two years earlier. Ricardo was already in the backseat of a car. "Ricardo!" the middle-aged man called out, knocking on the car's window. As it rolled down, the middle-aged man gave Ricardo the twenty dollars. "Thank you!" he said to the old accountant, who had never lost faith in him.

As he drove back to San Diego, he wondered if the retreat had been worth it. He felt pulled to the Church, with its two thousand years of tradition, the iconography, the art and architecture, the belief in a center of love and pure consciousness beyond space and time, the claim of eternal life, but at the same time felt repulsed by the dogmatic rigidity, by the authoritarian mechanics of the institution. And he could not believe in a literal interpretation of the Christian narrative. It had been good to be there with Ricardo, who had started organizing the yearly retreat when he was young and was now an old man limping around with his worn-out hip. The middle-aged man had enjoyed walking under the trees, and the quiet times spent sitting in a pew in the chapel, looking at the San Bernardino Mountains, still with snow on their peaks, from the window behind the altar.

His father had written to him that his mother was not doing well and would be spending a few days in the hospital. He wanted to see her, so he made plans to go to Italy for three weeks.

17

ITALY, 1992

Tuscany in late spring; haystack wheels on harvested wheat fields, sunflowers like platoons of soldiers at attention, saluting the sky, the cocktail of scents as the breeze brought the sea inland.

They were waiting for him at the airport. His mother frailer, unsteady on her feet. He hugged her; she seemed shorter, her back humped. As a child when he ran to her crying because he had skinned a knee, she was tall and strong as she lifted him up to her and consoled him. Now he was a middle-aged man and his mother was in her final years. *That's the way it is; why even think about it?* And yet the passing of time embodied in his mother's physical decay wounded him.

The day after his arrival, he woke up at 4 a.m. on the sofa bed in his parents' apartment. It was so familiar: the clock's dry ticking, the kitchenette faucet dripping, the sound of his father snoring through the wall. The trains passed through town with the *ka-ching, ka-*

ching, ka-ching of wheels on rails. Through the slits of the shutter, lightning flashed.

Later in the morning, he and his father drove to Orbetello; his mother didn't feel like going. They drove south on the Via Aurelia, then after a few kilometers, turned right into the strip of land that on a map looked like a fat finger pointing at the promontory that was home to Monte Argentario and the fishing villages of Porto Ercole and Porto Santo Stefano. They passed by the cemetery, the park and the entrance to the old hydroplane airport, from which in 1930, the famous aviator Italo Balbo made his transatlantic flight in a hydroplane. Then they drove through the fifth-century gates, huge stone blocks with three archways. It was not easy to find parking there in summer, but they succeeded. While his father took care of some business, the middle-aged man walked up and down the main street, went in the Duomo and noticed a large, thick volume on a stand in the entrance. It was a record of members of the parish who had died. He found the names of his grandparents, and their images flashed in his mind: his grandmother, usually in dark clothes, her hair up in a bun, working in the vegetable garden, sitting on a chair reciting the rosary, making fresh pasta. His mother told him that when he was a boy, during dinner at the *cantoniera*, he had moved his grandmother's chair, so when she returned from the kitchen and sat down, she fell on the floor. His grandfather, a stern-looking, imposing man with a handlebar mustache, liked to smoke short Toscano cigars and drink red wine. As a six-year-old he had watched his grandfather split wood by the side of the house when under a heavy blow of the mallet, the chisel flew off, grazed the boy's left eyebrow ridge and embedded itself in a steel drum. The boy began to cry uncontrollably as blood covered his face, and his uncles Gaetano and Libero put him in the bed of their three-wheeled Piaggio pickup truck and rushed him to the hospital, where the doctor closed the wound with three stitches. The middle-aged man ran his fingers on the scar as he remembered the panic of his uncles, the warm, salty taste of blood, the rush of air as Libero held him in the open truck's bed. If the chisel had hit him just half an inch lower, it would have penetrated his eye and embedded itself in his brain.

Still lost in his memories, he left the church and waited on a bench for his father. It was 10 a.m., and everybody seemed to be out, drinking coffees in bars, shopping, walking or just standing around the piazza, gesticulating and talking. A priest in fervent conversation with two older men, women carrying shopping bags, groups of twos or threes stood on the cobblestones, lost in their discussions, as if time didn't exist. How different this was from life in San Diego!

That night, he woke up at 3 a.m. and couldn't go back to sleep, so he lay in bed reading yesterday's newspapers. Then at six he got up and went jogging. Swallows screeched overhead, feasting on mosquitoes. He ran by the bird preserve in the cool air as colors asserted themselves in purple, red, white and yellow wildflowers lining the road. The pools of water sparkled green with algae, frogs chattered and black locusts and pines slowly shook the night from their branches in the breeze.

On the way back, he saw Franco the vet in the side yard playing with a big German shepherd. "This is Attila," he said. "They were going to euthanize him for being aggressive, but I brought him home. Many people keep them in cages and beat them, but dogs need love, too." The middle-aged man talked to Franco for a while, then crossed the street and went back to his parents' apartment.

It was a long trek up the coast, past Livorno, Massa-Carrara and La Spezia, the sparkling Tyrrhenian Sea on the left. When they arrived in Genova, they drove up the narrow mountain road to Davagna, where his brother Noé had built his house. They were greeted by Bruna, the middle-aged man's sister-in-law, Fabrizio, his nephew, and Fabrizio's wife, Elena.

Sella, the little village he had lived in with his mother and sister from 1953 to 1955, was adjacent to Davagna, and just past Sella was Moranego, with the church. Bruna had prepared lunch with linguine al pesto. She made it with basil from her garden, pine nuts from local trees and olive oil produced not far from Genova, and she added chunks of potato and green beans to the dish.

On the fourth of July he woke up at the sound of the church bell ringing six times. A rooster in the distance was answered by other roosters. The rushing sound of a mountain stream came through the shutters. He got up and looked out the window: steep green mountains left and right, white and ochre houses perched on the sides, the sky silver and charcoal gray, a sea over which clouds seemed to float by, a tinge of pink filtering through them. He opened the window and the air, fragrant with jasmine, cooled his face. *Tweet, tweet, tweet,* sang birds in cherry trees and poplars.

After breakfast he went for a long hike with his father and Fabrizio. By the trail's sides were extended rows of pines and chestnut trees, grassy meadows and the ruins of old stone houses. He remembered their neighbor Maria, returning in late afternoon with a load of grass on her bent back, a handkerchief over her head. That was in 1953. Almost forty years had passed, and that way of life had disappeared. They returned by eleven thirty, as it began to rain. *It's probably a hot day in San Diego,* the middle-aged man thought. What a wonderful way to spend the Fourth of July, away from the Southern California heat and people celebrating with burgers, hot dogs and beer.

The next day it rained and thundered. He woke up and saw lightning flash through the wooden shutters. The rumbles reverberated, distant explosions. Later in the morning the downpour stopped, and he went with his nephew to buy the paper. As they walked to the bar, his nephew said, "Look, there's someone you knew a long time ago, according to what my father told me. It's Gianni." Fabrizio stopped the white-haired man and talked to him for a few seconds, then the man walked up to the middle-aged man and, embarrassed, shook his hand and left. He and Gianni used to play together as children, climb up the tree by the house on the hill, sit on the branches, look at the mountains and eat the fat green figs. He and Gianni had been childhood friends, but after thirty years, they were different people, some fading memories all that remained of those years when they talked, laughed and played together.

The middle-aged man and his father took the bus to Genova. His mother didn't want to go, she tired easily and only walked short distances. The International Exposition celebrating five hundred years since Columbus discovered America had opened in May, so they bought tickets. They walked in Columbus's house, climbed Genova's famous lighthouse, toured ships and went through the new aquarium. Then, tired, they sat outside a bar in Piazza de Ferrari, where the middle-aged man wrote a postcard to Stephanie. The legendary fountain still sent its jets of water in the air and Giuseppe Garibaldi still stood on his bronze horse in front of the classic facade of the Carlo Fenice Theater, as he had since the late 1800s. The only indignity Garibaldi's statue suffered was the occasional seagull that perched on his head.

THE OLD MAN smiled at the thought of Garibaldi with the seagull on his head. Unfortunately, the fountain had been "renovated" by a German architect in the early 1990s, had been enlarged, so the low wall was no longer reachable. Why couldn't they have left it alone? It was a disease, the need to change something, to somehow "bring it up" to the new aesthetic tastes of those in power. As he wrote the postcard to Stephanie he had missed her and little Joseph, but in retrospect, it had been good to spend time with his father.

The full moon traveled swiftly behind clouds, and

trees and shrubs on the slope made the old man feel like he was in a forest. Berry had done his business and had grown tired of wandering around the yard, so he picked him up, brought him upstairs and laid him in the little bed by the bookcase. He petted the dog as it made itself comfortable. It hurt him to think Berry, who had been a rambunctious, playful dog and now was deaf and blind, could barely walk. Time had passed, and it had sucked the life out of the little creature, as it sucked being out of all things. The old man sat in the chair for a while, his eyes fixed on Masaccio's *Expulsion*, then went to bed, thinking about that time, so long ago, when he began to teach philosophy.

18

SAN DIEGO, 1992–1993

Classes at Southwestern College began on the nineteenth of August. He was only scheduled to teach two sections of Introduction to Philosophy and one in humanities, so he still worked two or three days a week as a respiratory therapist at various hospitals around the city.

There was the middle-aged woman who sat up in bed screaming. "What's wrong, honey, are you in pain?" asked the nurse as she walked in and injected morphine in the patient's IV. Her suitcase was in front of the closet—she was never going to take it home; he knew that. Breast cancer had metastasized throughout her body; she had come to die.

There was the crying toddler the EMTs brought to the ER with a kitchen knife stuck to the hilt in his eye; the police were there, one taking photographs as the child was brought to the OR. Or the young pregnant woman who had fallen unconscious in her garden. The middle-aged man had been called to the ER to do chest compressions. The woman was attractive, her breasts getting ready for her baby, but nothing worked, not even the injection of epinephrine in her heart, and after an hour, the head doctor said, "Okay, I think we have to call it; thank you very much." The middle-aged man left and went to the cafeteria to have a cup of coffee. *You wake up in the morning, have your breakfast, go in the garden to plant some flowers, feel dizzy and an hour later you're declared dead. Nothing can be counted on; you could drop dead at any minute.* He remembered the cousin he hadn't met when he arrived in America in 1963. Marylin had been a young woman, married with a child, a teacher, who collapsed in front of the class and died of a brain aneurism. *Life is so unpredictable and fragile; I don't want to be reminded of it in such painful ways in my work*, he thought as he finished his coffee. He yearned to be in the classroom, teaching philosophy.

IN THE SPRING of 1993 he applied for full-time community college positions, but openings were rare and competition high. He heard of a "jobs in education fair" that was going to be held at the San Diego Convention Center, so on the appointed day he drove downtown. He took the escalator upstairs and saw rows of tables covered with flyers and brochures. Representatives from various colleges and schools talked to prospective applicants. At the table for Santa Ana College, he noticed a stack of flyers advertising a full-time philosophy position. One of the men behind the table was a philosophy professor by the name of John Velasquez, who encouraged him to apply. It was a long shot. How many times had he applied for jobs that never materialized? But this time he could list under "experience" the courses in philosophy and humanities he'd taught and was teaching at Southwestern College.

To distract himself from his job problems he went to see a film by Fellini, *Intervista*. Framed by the device of an interview, the film seemed at times a documentary, but it was a well-woven tapestry of "the present-day reality" of Fellini making the film and the past unfolding in the Fascist era. In one segment, Fellini reenacts his arrival at Cinecittà when as a young man he is sent to interview an actress. We see the director and his crew in 1986, when the film was made, searching for the old trams that ran in the 1940s. Two trams are found in an old warehouse and repaired for the shoot. Actors in costumes take their seats, we see tractors pull the tram cars, soon we're in the countryside, and when the actor playing the young Fellini begins to talk to a girl sitting next to him, we assume we're still in 1986, but on the way to Cinecittà, from the top of a green hill a group of joyful farm workers come down and the tram stops. The viewers have been seamlessly transported to 1942. Smiling girls singing *"Reginella Campagnola"* offer bunches of sweet grapes to the passengers, and the middle-aged man felt a dull, distant ache at this time shift, the ache of time and life that have passed, and the pain became sharper when in a later sequence he saw Marcello Mastroianni and Anita Ekberg meet after many years and watch themselves in the famous scene from *La Dolce Vita*, where they dance in the Trevi Fountain. Mastroianni, his face full of wrinkles, slightly bent, and the divine Swedish actress, now old and stocky, watch the shadowy black-and-white images from twenty-six years earlier, glance at each other, then with a smile dance.

The middle-aged man didn't recall the first time he had seen *La Dolce Vita*. He became aware of the film in 1960 when he saw a billboard advertising it, as he walked with his friend Giulio by the Bisagno River. Perhaps he first watched it in Professor Scott's film appreciation class at Imperial Valley College, or at the Ken theater in San Diego, but it had become one of his favorites. It's the story of Marcello, a young tabloid journalist in Rome who aspires to be a literary writer but loses himself in the shallow, pleasure-seeking lives of the rich and famous. Whenever the middle-aged man watched *La Dolce Vita* he was impressed by the aesthetics of the film, the cinematography, the music by Nino Rota, the script, the editing, the director's vision; all those elements came together to create an artistic whole that he appreciated on its own terms. One was overwhelmed by it, yet much of it worked at a subconscious level. It was a social commentary, it raised spiritual and philosophical issues, ultimately it posed a fundamental question: what is happiness? Perhaps he could talk about the film to his class when he covered Socrates, Plato and Aristotle.

He collected films released by the Criterion Collection because in addition to their impeccable technical quality, the discs often included supplemental interviews with the director, actors and others associated with the productions. Many of the films he had seen as a boy or a young man, when the actors were young. In the interviews the actors were old, sometimes almost unrecognizably wrinkled and shriveled, and the contrast between watching them in the films and then in interviews given thirty or forty years later filled the middle-aged man with nostalgia and sadness. The abrupt shift in time often brought tears to his eyes. Even a film from the 1970s seemed so distant now. Yes, it was amusing to see people dressed in bell-bottom pants and with bushy hair and long sideburns, but he felt a pang of melancholia even for that era, when he was young.

HOPING to be called for an interview by Santa Ana College, he continued working per diem in hospitals, but at least he was an adjunct philosophy instructor now, and even though he taught only two or three courses per semester, they anchored him to a profession and a vocation, grounded him and made even his hospital work seem valuable. What he saw there, his interaction with patients, nurses and doctors, had existential, ethical, metaphysical import.

The alarm went off at 4 a.m., and he forced himself out of bed. It was a Saturday morning. This weekend he was scheduled to work at Grossmont Hospital. Last week he had worked at Children's, the week before at University. From the freeway, as he neared the exit, still in darkness, the hospital looked like a sleeping alien giant, its several eyes beginning to wake up. He parked and walked toward the entrance. It was five forty-five. The shift started at six, and he had to be there for twelve hours. Even though as a per diem worker he was given the simpler, more routine procedures, he still had to respond to code blues, run to the emergency room to do CPR or draw arterial blood for blood gas analysis. By the end of the shift, he was tired, and his feet and lower back hurt. He would drive home knowing that at six the following morning he had to be there again.

At Children's Hospital he had seen a premature newborn in the neonatal ICU, sleeping on his stomach in a small plastic box set on a table near the nurse's station. A note scotch-taped on the box said the little boy was dying, nothing could be done; it was just a matter of hours. They had put a tiny blue woolen cap on his head. Some nurses had written short notes on the piece of paper: "Bye, Jake, we love you!" and "You're leaving so soon, Jake, but you touched our hearts." The middle-aged man looked at the little boy who had entered the world condemned to leave it right away. But there he was, sleeping on his tummy on a warm blanket. Did he dream?

In other beds, machines, monitors with blinking lights and all kinds of tubes were attached to the small bodies of boys and girls. They looked like hungry, monstrous parasites sucking life out of the children, but they were keeping those frail, emaciated little bodies alive. Cancer does not wait until adulthood. He remembered the preadolescent girl he had talked to one day at University Hospital. She had a terminal disease, and it was beginning to dawn on her that she might not live to become a woman. The middle-aged man could not forget her eyes, full of foreboding, incomprehension, disbelief.

There was the man who woke up to find out he could no longer walk, because he had been involved in a car accident and was paralyzed from the waist down. He lay in bed in a daze, in denial.

They called the patients on the eighth floor the "Cabbage Patch Kids," because that's where the young men who had been in motorcycle accidents and had sustained massive brain damage were kept. In vegetative states, they needed to have their aerosol masks changed, their airways suctioned, their bodies moved every four hours to prevent bed sores. They would eventually be sent to convalescent homes, to live out the rest of their lives.

Life was precarious, fragile; you could not count on tomorrow, only hope that it would come and that you would be okay. So much suffering, so much pain, so much death. And there was no place to hide, no fortress to keep you safe. Your own body could betray you, and there was nothing you could do; you would grow old and feeble, get sick and die. But he was driving home now. His wife waited for him, and they would eat a good dinner and relax on the sofa for a while, watching something on TV. She was going to give birth in a few months; he was going to be a father again. He thought of his students, mostly young people, bursting with energy and eagerness, hungry for fun, adventure and success. Maybe he could help them to think for themselves, help them become more authentic. *Be careful*, he wanted to tell them. *You may feel immortal, but let me tell you what I see in hospitals. Be vigilant; a moment's distraction and poof! You're gone. Don't ride a motorcycle, but if you must, wear a helmet and be extra cautious. Savor every day; be present to the wonder and beauty around you. Everyone else out there is also on the road to old age, sickness and death. Be compassionate. Be loving. And as Joseph Campbell said, "Follow your bliss."* Of course, he would not say it so directly, but through stories, philosophical discussions and readings. But would they listen?

FATHER BOB'S tumor was in remission, and he continued to devote himself to ministry. He convinced the parishioners' representatives to fund improvements to the church, commissioned an artist to restore a statue of Mary and began to hold weekly classes on the gospels. The middle-aged man hadn't seen him since the hospital visit; on the phone Bob sounded like his old self, upbeat and welcoming. When Bob opened the sacristy's door, Buster thrust his head forward, as if wanting to protect his master. "You look good," said the middle-aged man as he scratched the dog's ears.

"My hair hasn't grown back yet. Don't I look weird, with half of my head bald?" asked Bob.

"Looks like a new style—you might start a trend." After a few minutes of talk, the middle-aged man finished the glass of water Bob had offered him.

"I'll drive, so I can show off my new ride," said Bob. "Let's go to the Country Club restaurant—they have good tuna sandwiches there."

"I love that smell of new car," said the middle-aged man as he got in the passenger seat. "But why is a servant of God driving a plush Buick LeSabre?"

"I wanted to get myself something nice, maybe to distract myself."

As they drove down the highway, the middle-aged

man remembered the dead priest he had seen as a child.

"You're a priest, you work hard to take care of your parish; you must have wondered why God didn't help you. You've dedicated your life to him, and there's a shortage of you guys."

"It's something that happened to me, and I have to deal with it. Maybe God isn't some big guy sitting up there on a throne looking at everyone's body, thinking, 'Oh, there's a cancer beginning in that guy's head; I better get rid of it.' Maybe it doesn't work like that. I still have my faith." The middle-aged man didn't say anything. They talked, ate the tuna sandwiches with iced tea, then back at the sacristy talked some more, after which the middle-aged man returned to San Diego.

The semester was ending. He had gone over the art of courtly love, showed slides of Gothic cathedrals, said something about Dante. What an impossible task —to cover the cultural history of the world in a semester. It became a question of emphases and distillation to essences.

For the summer he had been offered a humanities class again. It was only one course, so he still worked per diem as a respiratory therapist, but he found time to read, watch movies and to apply to college districts.

He received a letter from Santa Ana College informing him he had an interview the following week. Finally, an interview! He drove to Santa Ana early in the morning, dressed in the new slacks and sport coat he had bought at Macy's a few days earlier. It was still dark outside, wind and road noise roaring in the Mazda hatchback as he drove on Interstate 5.

An interview. It doesn't mean much, he thought, *but it's a chance*. He was sure dozens of applicants with much more experience applied for the job, it was probably an exercise in futility, but he had to try. He parked in the visitor's lot and walked up to the fifth floor of the humanities building. At the division office he waited to be called, then stepped into the conference room. Five or six people sat around an oblong table, including the philosophy professor he had met at the job fair. They asked questions, and then at the end they asked him to give a teaching demonstration. He stood up and began to explain Plato's theory of the forms.

Back home, he tried not to think about the interview by going to the movies. He and Stephanie went to the Ken one evening to watch a restored 35-millimeter print of Fellini's *8 1/2*, a surreal comedy about the creative struggles of a film director starring Marcello Mastroianni. The middle-aged man was not only entranced by the acting, the black-and-white cinematography, the editing, the script, but its depiction of the early 1960s. The film spoke to him of youth, of a simpler, poorer Italy, of a time to which he could never return. There were certain films he never tired of seeing, and *8 1/2* was one of them.

A week after the interview, the dean of the Social Studies Division at Santa Ana College called to tell him he was one of the semifinalists for the position, so they had to schedule a second interview. He was ecstatic, but he needed to remind himself that he couldn't count on getting the job.

The second interview was at the district office with the chancellor, the president and the dean. He thought he'd done okay, and the following morning he went on a retreat to the Prince of Peace Abbey in Oceanside. Perched on a hill a few miles from the ocean, the Benedictine monastery had several rooms for retreatants. He sat at a table in the garden of the monastery. It was a clear, warm day with a light wind, which made the flag slap around and the tree's branches restless. He liked the sound of the wind through the trees and shrubs—it reminded him of the surf. A palm tree with a short, thick trunk shaded him, and a white bird landed on a branch at the top of a eucalyptus. Past the garden he could see queen palms, a Hollywood juniper, pines and bottlebrush trees. He had come there to think about his life and ultimate things: God, the spiritual, death.

He had found a good person who loved him, and they were about to have a child. However, he still didn't have full-time employment. *When I get back tomorrow, I must intensify my search*, he thought. And as far as the spiritual journey was concerned, he was stuck, and had been for a while. He closed his eyes, quieted his mind and tried to just listen, but it was always there, right under the veil of silence and peace: the fear, the anxiety, slowly gnawing.

He got up and walked to the library. It was quiet, just thirty thousand books, comfortable chairs and tables. In the evening, after dinner, he went to the church. A modern structure designed by the Mexican architect and artist Gabriel Chávez de la Mora and built in the early 1980s, it was a mix of simplicity and beauty, with gray bricks, a blue-tiled roof and a bell tower. He walked in. The windows behind him, made of red, yellow and white swirling rectangles of stained glass, threw faint splashes of color on the stone floor.

He sat on the pew closest to the door, by the left side of the aisle, and gazed at the large wooden icon of Jesus, also designed by Chávez de la Mora, that had center stage, behind the altar. A stylized brown Jesus in a white robe sat with his right hand in a sign of benediction and held a book with his left hand on which was written the word *Pax*. The altar was flanked by choir stalls where monks sat during prayers and mass. Wide windows on the side walls let in light and views of plants, trees and the ocean during the day, but the sun had set, and only tinges of red came through the windows on the right side. Looking up at the wooden slanted roof crisscrossed by rafters, he had the impression of being in a ship. He took deep breaths; no one else was there. Spotlights brought Chávez de la Mora's icon to life, and the colors reflected on the dark floor. With eyes closed, he emptied his mind and let go of feelings.

Then he got up and wandered in the chapel of the Black Madonna, knelt in front of her and prayed for a long time, both for forgiveness and for the philosophy teaching job. The Black Madonna, holding her child, looked at him. A while later, when he was in his room, a brother knocked on the door to tell him someone wanted him on the phone. It was his wife, who told him the dean had called: he had gotten the full-time teaching position. His prayers had been answered. He was grateful and awed, found it hard to believe.

19

SAN DIEGO, 1993

In the following days, he kept thinking about what happened. He had prayed fervently for the job and he had gotten it. But to believe that Mary had granted his petition would have been an example of the fallacy of false cause. That he received the news of having been selected for the teaching position right after he prayed for it didn't mean the praying caused the event. It could have been a coincidence. Besides, there was the standard of plausibility to consider. For him to accept the claim that Mary had answered his prayers, he would have had to accept the whole Christian theology: that God existed, that Jesus literally was the son of God, that Mary was somehow in heaven and had heard his prayer and caused events to turn out as he had wished. All this was too much to accept. And yet, he was left with a sense of wonder.

∾

THE THIRD WEEK in August he was to report to the college for meetings, but on weekends he had shifts at the hospital, a world of pain and suffering, another reality. When he got a couple of days off, he returned to the Prince of Peace Abbey. He drove up the hill behind Oceanside, crossed the narrow, primitive bridge and went around the curves until he reached the parking lot. He was only going to spend two days there; he wanted to reflect, think and meditate in a place where silence was a value and a virtue, where men who had renounced worldly things spent their days in work and prayer.

He attended mass, had lunch, spent time in his room reading, went to the library and to the church for the divine office, and in the evening, after dinner, talked for a while with two retreatants. When the middle-aged man mentioned that he had been raised in Italy and spoke Italian, one of the men told him that the community had an Italian monk who was visiting from Rome. "You could talk to him tomorrow," he said.

The following day at lunch, the middle-aged man was standing in line with a tray, waiting to get a bowl of soup with some vegetables and bread, when the monks began to enter. "Hey, there's Salvatore," said the retreatant from the evening before, as he pointed to a tall monk with bushy black hair and thick eyeglasses. "Salvatore, this guy is Italian!" the retreatant said pointing at the middle-aged man, who said, "I'm only half Italian." The tall monk smiled. "Which half?"

In the afternoon he went to talk to Salvatore, who was working in the vegetable garden. He was snipping off white flowers from the tops of tall basil plants. In the long conversation that followed, Salvatore told him his monastery was in Rome, at the Basilica of Saint Paul Outside the Walls. There had been some problems at the monastery; he had experienced a crisis and was sent to Oceanside for a year. "I like it here," he said. "The monks are friendly and I enjoy working in this vegetable patch and feeding the pigs. I planted this basil; I made pesto for the community here, and they raved about it. But my stay is coming to an end. I'm scheduled to return to Rome next month." It was time to go to vespers. "I wish you luck on your new teaching position," Salvatore said. "We'll talk again."

What attracted the middle-aged man to monasteries was the idea of dedicating one's life to something transcendent. He remembered the long talks he and his college friend Mike had back in 1971, when they fantasized about living in a community dedicated to the pursuit of truth.

Before Salvatore left for Rome, the middle-aged man went to the monastery again. The monk offered him a cup of coffee, which he made in a moka pot on a hotplate in his room. Afterward they walked to the vegetable garden, where the tall basil plants were going to seed. Salvatore told him he was born in Naples, and at the age of seven or eight, his mother sent him to work as an apprentice in a shoe repairer's shop. The owner of the shop sexually abused him countless times until the age of eleven, when his mother brought him back home so he could work. At twenty-one, he went to do his military service and then worked in Florence for a hotel. When he was twenty-nine or thirty, he suffered a great crisis and decided to enter the Benedictine Monastery Order. After two months, he discovered piles of gay pornographic magazines in the room of the spiritual director and was very disturbed by it. After his ordination, he was sent to the Monastery of Saint Paul Outside the Walls in Rome, where he discovered that the civilian supplier of foodstuffs cheated the monastery with the full knowledge of the prior, who received kickbacks. He reported it to the abbot, who rectified the situation.

Salvatore was frustrated and disillusioned by monastic life. A few old monks in their late eighties controlled the administration of the monastery and kept all the younger monks from having any input in the life of the community. Many felt oppressed and sought escape in food, TV, or illicit affairs. One night Salvatore was awakened by screams. He opened the door of his room and saw on the hall's marble floor a monk in a pool of blood. He had been killed by another monk with a hatchet. Traumatized, no longer able to attend to his daily duties, Salvatore was sent for a year to the Prince of Peace Abbey in Oceanside. What the monk had told him popped the inflated idea the middle-aged man had of monasticism, but in Salvatore he saw a gentle and searching soul who read books on science, theology and literature, someone with whom he could communicate in Italian about ideas, theories, worldviews. Too bad Salvatore had to return to his monastery in Rome.

∼

On August 23, the middle-aged man began teaching classes at Santa Ana College as a full-time assistant professor. After so many years and so many detours, he had finally achieved his goal. It was hard at first: there was the commute, learning how things worked, campus politics and suddenly having to teach five courses per semester, but he adjusted. The college was eighty-five miles from his home, so he rented a room in Santa Ana where he could stay two nights a week, and since he had Fridays off, he was home by Thursday afternoon.

In the middle of October, autumn weather finally arrived. The middle-aged man was tired of the hot, humid days, fans and air conditioners, the noise of children playing on the street and the crazy guy that mowed his lawn every single day.

They moved into a charming bungalow in the Normal Heights area, and they were happy with their first home. It had wooden floors, a fireplace, a spacious master bedroom with an alcove window overlooking a juniper tree and a star pine, an airy kitchen and two smaller bedrooms. But the house, built in 1928, was in front of Saint Didacus, and the church, especially on weekends, was a major source of noise. Even so, in twilight, the white church's façade turned golden, and when the bells rang, he felt transported to other times. As the weather changed, pumpkins began to appear in front of stores, the leaves of liquid ambers and sycamores had begun to turn red, purple and brown, and soon it would be time for sweaters and jackets. Halloween would arrive, and then Thanksgiving.

Joseph was born on October 22. The middle-aged man was in the hospital room when his wife gave birth. What a wonderful event seeing the little boy appear in the world. In awe he cut the newborn's umbilical cord, it seemed a sacred moment. And he had a full-time job now, and not just any job but the teaching position he had dreamed of since his first year at Imperial Valley College.

Besides teaching Introduction to Philosophy and Critical Thinking, he had to teach the course on the world's religions. He needed to prepare. The more he read, the more he lost the desire to reconnect to the Church. He liked the rituals, the scent of incense and candles, holy cards, art and architecture, but could not accept the dogmas. He could not believe in a personal God or that a man who lived two thousand years ago had been the son of God. The belief system was not plausible.

Teaching religions was not what he wanted to do, but he had to, so he chose Huston Smith's *Religions of the World* as the main text. He liked the book's approach, which was to stress the spiritual message and not the historical/cultural aspects of religions. To supplement Smith's text, he picked *On Reading the Bible* by Thomas Merton and *The Heart of Understanding* by Thich Nhat Hanh. He drove to a Muslim bookstore in Garden Grove and bought a copy of the Koran. Translated into English, it lost much of the literary beauty he was told it had in Arabic.

He studied the Dhammapada, the writings of D.T. Suzuki and the Buddhist philosophers of the Kyoto

School. He reread different translations of the Bible and supplementary material, the Gita and the Upanishads. He continued to read more works by Carl Jung. Opening the black hardbound books, he plunged into an ocean of psychological concepts that revealed the contents and workings of the psyche richly explained through mythology, religions, fables, literature, art and philosophy. After teaching the night class, back in his Santa Ana rented room, he went to bed and read Jung for an hour. The clothbound volume felt solid, the paper thick and soft to the touch, the ideas exciting. He incorporated Jungian ideas in his teaching of religion, especially the archetypes of the collective unconscious, which explained the apparent similarity of mythological/religious motifs worldwide.

He resented having to teach the course in the beginning, but he came to like it as time went on. Religions had a spiritual kernel that needed to be considered. That was what Joseph Campbell tried to impress in his books. The middle-aged man stood in front of the class and explained that religion was basically the human response to the mystery at the heart of things, at the wonder of being alive. Art, music and writings have given form to this mystery in many ways. The question was, what form will our response to the mystery take in our lives? This is what he told them at the end of the course, but how many took seriously what he said? He often had the impression he was just talking to himself.

∼

IN A LETTER, Salvatore said the first few days back in Rome had been nightmarish. In addition to the jet lag, it was hot and humid and he had plunged back into depression. He found the situation at the monastery very difficult and had asked the abbot at Prince of Peace if he could be accepted in their community, but received a negative reply, so Salvatore was stuck in Rome.

During the fall semester, the middle-aged man was busy with teaching, office hours, meetings, grading papers and tests, and when at home he was occupied with family life. One day while reading the newspaper he found out that the new film by the Italian director Nanni Moretti was playing in downtown San Diego. On a Saturday afternoon, he went to see *Caro Diario*, an anthology of three events in the life of the director. He found the film, with Moretti driving around Rome in a Vespa, fascinating. Mordant social commentary, funny and moving scenes and pulsating Latin American music fed the nostalgia the middle-aged man felt for Rome. Since he had been only one year old when his parents moved to Genova, the first time he had seen it was in the summer vacation of 1987. All his stays in the eternal city amounted to just a few weeks. He wondered how it would have been to have lived in Rome for years. It wasn't just a thought; it was something that burrowed deep inside and stirred, painfully. But when he saw postcards of Genova, he felt the same pain. In June of 1963, as a fifteen-year-old boy, he had excitedly gotten in his brother's Fiat 600 and had looked behind at the two old ladies sitting on chairs outside of the apartment building, as the car sped off to the harbor. His life's dream had been to go to America, but now when he thought of Genova, he ached deep inside. Still, he realized it was a longing he could not satisfy by returning there, because what he longed for no longer existed.

HE RECEIVED in the mail an elegant facsimile of Robert Hooke's *Micrographia,* originally published in 1665, the first work with detailed illustrations of insects based on using a microscope. In the preface, Hooke wrote that humans are prone to mistakes and errors in thinking because our senses, memory and understanding are not always to be trusted. Even natural science has been relegated to thinking and conjecturing, which can lead us into error. "It is now high time," he says, "that it should return to the plainness and soundness of observations in material and obvious things." There were obviously questions of philosophy and values not amenable to being resolved by this method, but philosophy had to consider what had been ascertained to be the case based on accurate observation and experimentation. In the hundreds of following pages and in the breathtaking details of what Hooke observed with his microscope, he demonstrated this method. A thirst for reading more about science was kindled in the middle-aged man. He remembered his eagerness to read the weekly issues of the encyclopedia as a boy and his love of science in high school; the excitement he felt when he peered into the microscope during lab and observed the paramecia swimming around in a drop of water. The more he read about science, the more he studied critical thinking, the harder it became for him to take mysticism seriously.

Mystical experiences were subjective. The intense, deeply interior feeling of unity with a supreme being or some other form of transcendent power was beyond words, ineffable, so there was no way to ascertain the veracity of mystical claims. Much of the "evidence" for mystical experiences was anecdotal. He had hoped, after reading William James and the saints, that mysticism could have been a path beyond reason, a way to another kind of knowledge, but while mystical experiences could feel like knowledge in the sense of a strong belief, they lacked verifiable evidence. They could be more simply explained by psychology and cognitive science.

20

SAN DIEGO AND ITALY, 1994

When the first year of the middle-aged man's teaching at Santa Ana College ended, he flew to Rome. His mother had been in the hospital for a few days with pneumonia, and he looked forward to seeing her again.

As the plane approached Fiumicino Airport, the symmetrical patchwork of fields, green hills, farmhouses with red roofs and the sea came into view. It was the land where historical events converged to bring together a Japanese American soldier and an Italian woman. Their lives met like two lines on a piece of paper, and he came into being. It was the land that gave him birth, his first language, the ground for his tentative steps as a toddler.

After passing through customs, he saw his father, who looked trim and youthful in spite of his seventy-two years. His mother sat on a chair with a distant expression on her face. She broke into a smile when she saw him, and got up. He hugged her and kissed her on the cheek. "See how old your little mother has gotten," she said. The day was hot and the ride home, without air-conditioning, turned out to be too much for his father, who as soon as he parked the car in front of their apartment building began to feel dizzy. He barely made it up the flights of stairs, went straight to the bedroom and plopped on the bed. He got up after twenty minutes, saying he was fine, but the event made the middle-aged man realize his father was getting more physically fragile.

He went to see his uncle Libero, who lived in a five-story apartment building on the northernmost part of town, just a few blocks away. It was a cloudy, breezy day, and from a distance he saw Libero in his vegetable garden, breaking up soil with a rototiller. His uncle looked thinner and toothless. Four years had passed since the days when the middle-aged man kept him company in the truck. Libero said he had suffered a stroke, and now his arm and shoulder felt tingly.

The middle-aged man visited Libero and his sons again during his stay, went to see his uncle Gaetano and Aunt Lilia, bought some books, walked with his parents to the bar by the beach, strolled down Albinia's tree-lined main street and had coffee in the afternoon, ice cream in the evening. He recognized most of the shop owners: the butchers, the grocers, the bakers, the jeweler, the barber, the pharmacist, the owners of the newspaper kiosks, the photographer. They all knew his father and were used to seeing the middle-aged man every year, greeted him warmly and asked him how he was doing. The middle-aged man enjoyed sitting at a table outside the bars, drink coffees or Campari and sodas, reading the papers and watch people pass by on the sidewalk. This is what he liked so much about Albinia; the sense of community and how everything was within walking distance, including the sea.

But he also ached to go to Florence, and after a week in Albinia, he took the train for a four-day stay there. He found a room in a hotel near the Basilica of Santa Maria Novella, his favorite church. In the following days he went to the Duomo square to study the doors of the Baptistery, went up the four hundred steps of Giotto's campanile, walked to the Museo dell'-Opera del Duomo and admired Michelangelo's *Pietà*, Donatello's *Saint Mary Magdalen*, the *Zuccone* and other works. It wasn't just aesthetics he was after, but the experience of traveling back in time, moving in spaces created centuries earlier, standing on floors and touching walls built by human beings now gone forever.

He had lunch at a snack bar in Piazza San Marco, then went to visit Michelangelo's *David* at the Galleria dell'Accademia; he never tired of looking up at the giant, half expecting the statue to start moving. He walked to the Basilica of Santa Croce to see the Giottos. When had he become aware of the Italian painter? Probably in one of the encyclopedia entries he used to read as a child. The colors were not as exuberant as in the Assisi frescoes, but there was the naturalness, the ethereal humanness that he could discern in all of Giotto's works. He bought his wife a pair of gold earrings in a shop on Ponte Vecchio, stopped for pizza and beer at a restaurant called Pinocchio, then headed back to his room, where he fell into a deep sleep.

He began the next day early, with a cappuccino and a brioche at a bar, then crossed the square to Santa Maria Novella, where he meditated in front of the Holy Trinity. He had been impressed by the church the first time he saw the graceful and imposing facade that had been worked, in part, by the Renaissance artist and philosopher Leon Battista Alberti. The middle-aged man had read Alberti's *On Painting*, a short but dense book where the author explained the techniques painters ought to master if they wanted to create beauty. He talked about perspective and composition, how to portray living creatures and by what means to show movement in inanimate things like hair, branches, leaves and clouds. For Alberti, painting was the mistress of all the arts. "Whatever beauty is in things," he said, "has been derived from painting," since architects, stonemasons and sculptors are guided by the painter's art.

Alberti was also a priest and an architect, and when he began work on the basilica's facade, the lower part had already been built in a Gothic style. Alberti harmoniously extended it with a classically inspired design. Inside, the basilica, with its Gothic vaults and pointed arches, high and narrow stained-glass windows, was a treasure trove, including a nineteen-foot-tall crucifix by Giotto in front of the nave, an ornate recessed sink by Della Robbia, frescoes by Ghirlandaio and works by Brunelleschi, Paolo Uccello and Masaccio.

In that sacred space full of time frozen into pieces of art, the middle-aged man forgot mundane concerns, forgot himself. His breathing deepened and slowed, his shoulders relaxed, he felt connected as he walked on the stone floor to what had been able to overcome, at least for a while, impermanence and death.

On the last day in Florence he wanted to visit the church of Santo Spirito, but it was closed, so he went to see the Brancacci Chapel in Santa Maria del Carmine, where he stood in front of Masaccio's *Expulsion from Eden* for as long as he could. Then on the way out, in the gift shop he bought a print of the *Expulsion*. When he left, it began to rain. He put the plastic bag with the print under his shirt and walked on the cobblestone streets as purifying drops of cool water baptized him.

The middle-aged man stayed another three days in Albinia, then left for San Diego.

AS THE MONTHS PASSED, he called his parents every few weeks, and talking to his mother made him want to go visit her. "I just got out of the hospital yesterday; I almost forgot how to walk. Your father does most of the cooking now," she said over the phone, in a weak, tentative voice.

"Take good care of yourself. I'll come see you in the summer and you have to be strong, so we can go for some nice walks," he told her.

THE OLD MAN couldn't fall asleep. He'd turn on one side and after a few minutes, turn on the other. One hundred thousand cases of Covid-19 were reported in one day in the United States, many hospitals had tents outside to accommodate the overflow of patients, thousands died every day. Due to shortages, triage protocols were in effect, so the very old and sick in some cases were not given treatment. Parks and beaches were still closed. The old man sought refuge in his memories. He remembered that in the 1990s he went to Italy almost every year to visit his parents, especially his mother, who was in poor health. His wife couldn't take time off from work and didn't want to go anyway, since he spent most of the time visiting his relatives. While on every trip he went to mostly the same places and saw the same people, time seemed to change everything, sometimes drastically, often imperceptibly. He found truth in the Buddhist saying that you cannot kiss the same person twice because the second time, everything will have slightly altered.

When the 1994 spring semester ended, he made preparations to visit his parents. His mother had been a fast typist and usually wrote long letters, but the last one he received was a single sheet of paper with handwritten scribbling he could barely decipher: "Dear son, as you can see I can't write anymore, but I wanted to send you these few words. Your father was so worried because when he came home from the store he found me on the floor. I fell and couldn't get up. I wish you, Stephanie and dear little Joseph are well, I love you, mamma."

21

ITALY AND SAN DIEGO, 1995

In June, when he hugged his mother at the airport she seemed smaller, as if she had shrunk since the previous year. The curvature of her spine had increased, and there were more wrinkles around her eyes. It always felt good to hug her and kiss her on the cheeks. His mother didn't feel well, so one afternoon she stayed home while he and his father walked to the bar by the beach. They sat at a table on the terrace while on the sand, bathers lay on towels shaded by umbrellas and children played by the water under the watchful eyes of their parents. The air smelled of sunscreen and sea. He remembered how he and Stephanie had played in the waves when they came here on their honeymoon. As they waded near the shore she hugged him and said, "you're my calamari!" It surprised him to think that four years had already passed since that day.

"Hey look, there's Franco," said his father. The veterinarian walked up from the beach, muscular and tanned; he was drying his hair and face with a towel.

"Franco, would you like a coffee?" asked the middle-aged man's father.

"Sure," he replied with a smile as he sat at the table. The bar's owner, the older man who had left the running of the bar to his son and who liked to clean tables and talk to customers, was nearby, so they asked him for the coffees. "My daughter is in Florida visiting her mother, and here I am trying to wind surf," said Franco. He couldn't go on vacation because he was the only veterinarian in Albinia, but in the afternoons, if he had no appointments, he spent some time at the beach. The older man arrived with a tray and gave them the steaming shots of espresso. They talked for a while, then Franco said he had to go home; someone was going to bring him a sick dog to examine. "*Grazie* for the coffee," he said as he left. The middle-aged man felt slightly envious of Franco; he was young and athletic, had a house within walking distance of the beach.

Some kids played foosball nearby, and Mango's recent song, "*Dove Vai?*" began to play on the jukebox. They sat there for a while longer, gazing at the sea. They didn't talk much, but for the middle-aged man, being near his father enjoying the air, looking at the waves' constant arrival and departure, felt like a conversation.

Walking back to the apartment they kept by the side of the road. It was odd how that walk to the beach had become part of the mythology of his life. The scents of hay and sea, the red poppies in green fields, the warm shoosh of a car or Vespa as it passed by, Albinia's apartment buildings and the campanile in the distance, framed by a bright blue sky and white clouds. It was as if every time he had walked that way, something had remained in the air and the scenery, an imprint of himself at particular times, and now all those moments, all those traces, entered into him. On the left side, as they crossed the culvert bridge, was the small house an elderly man had worked on years before. In early spring of 1990, on his daily walks he used to see him slowly pour water and cement in a small mixer in front of the partially built structure. Every day the man made a little progress on the walls, and now the tiny house was finished. Was he still alive?

IN FLORENCE FOR TWO DAYS. On Monday morning he went to an exhibit of Fellini's artwork and the original outfits that were used in some of his films. This was the closest to Fellini he had been. On display were many of the director's drawings of women with gigantic breasts and buttocks and the costumes used in the famous scene of the film *Roma*, where new ecclesiastical garments were displayed to a group of aristocrats and church officials. The surreal fashion show, with nuns in crazy headgear and priests on roller skates, was one of the most unforgettable scenes of the film, and it surprised the middle-aged man to see that the costumes were made of paper, cheap fabric, plastic gemstones and glitter.

On Tuesday he woke up early; the morning would be dedicated to Fra Angelico. He walked to the Baptistery and turned left on Via de Martelli. What a strange mix; massive stone facades and iron grates on the windows of Medici era palazzi, kitschy shop windows displaying shoes and clothes, smells of fumes and coffee, the sounds of church bells and traffic. He finally reached Piazza San Marco. The oldest part of the Dominican monastery had been converted into a museum, famous for Fra Angelico's frescoes. Fra Angelico was a friar and a painter, and in the fifteenth century, besides decorating other areas of the convent, in each friar's cell he painted a fresco depicting a scene from the gospels. When the middle-aged man climbed the stairs leading to the monks' dormitories, he was met at the top by a large fresco of the Annunciation. In an open loggia, Mary sits on a stool and is greeted by the angel Gabriel. The colors, the shapes, the light that seemed to emanate from within, made of the fresco a vision. And in cell number three was another, simpler and smaller Annunciation, which also impressed him. Why was he drawn to these images? He liked the idea of a messenger from another realm appearing and announcing the arrival in the world of a momentous event; the triumph of love, the defeat of death. The transcendent breaking into the monotony of everydayness, a crack in reality revealing an eternal, shining truth.

When the time to return home arrived, there was the sadness of leaving his mother and not knowing if he was going to see her again. She was ill and frail, taking several medications a day, managed by his father, who had made a chart of all the pills she had to take at different times.

The middle-aged man left Albinia for Rome on June 6. His parents had gone to see him off at the

Orbetello train station. "I'll see you next year," he told his mother as he hugged her.

THE OLD MAN had returned from grocery shopping. People wore masks, some even gloves. Taped arrows on the floor indicated you should only go through store aisles in one direction, in order to maintain six feet of distance. Many shelves were bare. After he put the groceries away he went up the stairs to the study, but on the landing, through the window that overlooked the side of the house, he noticed on a shrub's branch a nest with a green hummingbird in it. After a few weeks, he could see two tiny beaks protrude from the side of the nest when the mama hummingbird wasn't there. The old man often stood in front of the window looking at the nest, then one day he saw two little heads. The mama hummingbird would take off and come back every half hour or so to feed the two babies, and with the passing of the days they grew bigger. They looked up and all around impatiently for their mother until she came to feed them; then they would calm down. As the days passed, they began to preen and test their wings, until one afternoon the bigger one after much effort flew onto a higher branch. The smaller bird continued beating its wings but couldn't fly, so the bigger bird came back and stayed with its sibling until they both flew to another branch. The mama bird would still come back, find them and feed them. Late one afternoon they all left, and now seeing the empty nest made him sad. He was happy both baby hummingbirds survived, but at the same time he felt a sense of loss. Another example of the Buddha's first noble truth: due to impermanence, even joyful events have an aspect of suffering.

So the hummingbirds were gone. He went in the study and sat in the easy chair, looking at the photo of his mother he kept propped up on a shelf. It was a black-and-white photograph from the 1940s, and his mother looked beautiful, with a full head of hair, a Roman nose and gold loop earrings. When was the last time he had seen her? It was in 1996, when after the spring semester ended, he flew to Italy.

22

ITALY AND SAN DIEGO, 1996–1997

As he walked out of the airport's sliding glass doors, he saw his parents before they noticed him. His mother took slow, hesitant steps helped by his father, who walked slightly bent. His mother looked better than the middle-aged man expected, but at eighty-two, with all her health problems, he doubted she was going to be able to walk for much longer. When he hugged her he wished he could hold her for a long time. He could feel her bony shoulders, the beating of her tired heart.

They stopped on the way home for a cappuccino, then he drove the rest of the way to Albinia, through the countryside: emerald hills, fields dotted with rolled haystacks, the deep blue Tyrrhenian Sea accompanied him on the left side, houses with red-shingled roofs and walls the colors of the earth on the right. The air sparkled, perfumed by sea, sun and pines. He sighed, inhaled deeply.

He sat on the balcony at dusk watching the swallows streak and screech in the air, weaving arcs above rooftops and the church campanile. He gazed at the street below, the other apartment buildings, trees and mountains in the distance. The setting sun turned the houses' walls into bronze. In 1987, from the balcony looking west he could have seen the sea, but a new building had gone up, and the strip of deep blue was gone.

HIS MOTHER COULD NO LONGER WALK the mile from the apartment to the beach, so in late afternoon his father dropped him and his mother off at the path that led to the beach and went looking for a parking place. The middle-aged man walked with his mother down the narrow road lined by trees. She walked slowly as she held on to his arm. When they arrived, they sat down at a table on the bar's terrace and soon after, his father joined them. The old guy, the bar's owner, came over with a smile. "You came to visit again this year—welcome back," he said. They had coffee and tonic water, talked and enjoyed the air and the view. It was a cool day, and not many people were on the beach. A few umbrellas, some children playing in the waves. Then his father went to get the car and the middle-aged man and his mother walked slowly back. Behind wire fences lining the road stood tall pines whose crowns embraced to form a green ceiling. Growing along the west-side fence, creamy white petals of sweet mock orange bushes perfumed the air. His mother held his arm and walked with a determined look. "I'm so happy you've come. Here I am, walking with my son. I wasn't sure I'd see you again." She squeezed his arm with her trembling hand and smiled.

When he went to visit his uncle Libero his aunt answered the door, greeted him and made coffee. As they sat in the living room talking, his uncle came in from the bedroom and crossed the living room to the bathroom. "Libero, how are you?" he asked his uncle, who glanced at him and said, "Bad, bad." That's all he said. A few minutes later, his uncle crossed the living room again looking straight ahead, went in the bedroom and closed the door. "What's wrong with Libero?" he asked his aunt, who just looked at him and said nothing. The middle-aged man walked back to his parents' apartment. What had happened to Libero? The shy youth who played guns with him behind the House of the Fig in Sella? The confident young man who showed up in Genova in a big car? The jovial uncle who drove him and Penelope to Porto Santo Stefano in his new Alfa Romeo and bought them ice cream? Who gave him a ride on his Lambretta to Talamone? The spirited, charming driver that "showed him Italy" from the cabin of the truck?

IT WAS a long and tiring drive in his father's Fiat Panda, especially for the middle-aged man's mother. When they arrived in Perugia, he was happy to see his sister and her children.

His mother was too old and sick to walk without help. His father dragged her along, but it was painful to see. The following morning they went to the center of Perugia. They walked down Corso Vannucci and had coffee at an outdoor table, something he doubted would happen again.

In the early evening, Sandrina took them to a Chinese restaurant. His mother's shaking hands caused food to fall on the table; his father had to help her. The young, tall, strong woman who had bought him his notebook and pencils and taught him how to write the letters of the alphabet a year before he had to go to school, the woman who raised him and his sister, was now ravaged by congestive heart failure and Parkinson's.

The middle-aged man took a last walk with his parents to the bar by the beach. They sat at a table on the terrace, and besides the usual tonic water and coffee they had Maxibon ice cream bars. He hated the feeling he had the day before leaving. He didn't know if he was going to see his mother again.

On the day of departure, he got up at 6 a.m. Through the blind's slats the sun awakened, and cool air flowed in as the swallows screeched over trees and buildings faintly visible. They left Albinia at seven o'clock and arrived at Fiumicino Airport by nine. He kissed his mother goodbye. "I'll see you next year," he said, but she looked at him and cried.

BACK HOME, the middle-aged man kept seeing his mother coming into the living room of the apartment in Albinia to wish him a good night, then shuffle down the hall to the bedroom. She wore a light green nightgown, his father helping her. Hunched over, leaning heavily toward her right side, she took small, tentative steps in her slippers; then they turned right and disappeared in the bedroom. After a while he got up from the sofa and went to wish her good night again. She lay in bed, the covers up to her chin. The big suitcases his parents brought when they left San Diego were still at the top of the closet, a layer of dust on them. His mother often missed her house in El Centro. Yes, it was a desert town, but she had her plants and trees, the vegetable garden; she could step out the door early in the morning and go for a walk around the neighborhood. Trapped in the little apartment in Albinia, she dreamed of returning to California, and maybe to an earlier time, when she was younger.

"Good night," he said. She looked at him, a death's skull asserting itself more and more as her face's skin retreated.

"You know, I pray to Jesus that I may live a little bit more," she replied. He kissed her good night.

THE FAMILIAR ANXIETY at the beginning of a new semester, then teaching classes, office hours, curriculum meetings, grading tests and papers. At home he went to grocery stores, the Adams Avenue Bookstore, played with his three-year-old son. Often, on weekends, with Stephanie and the baby, they'd go for hikes, little Joseph in a backpack carrier.

On October 4 the middle-aged man received a phone call from his father. "Your mother is gone," he said, almost in a whisper. "For a few days she stayed in bed and refused food and water. I gave her ice chips. She didn't speak."

Your mother is gone. He heard his father's words again but felt nothing. Many years earlier, the death of his mother would have been incomprehensible. It had seemed like something he could not possibly have survived, but now he felt nothing. She was going to be buried the following day; there was no time for him to get a flight. He was relieved.

In the summer of 1997, he and his wife planned to buy a house in a different area of San Diego, and his father was going to come to California for a family reunion. He had hoped to spend the summer vacation reading and writing, but those hopes were dashed. His father was going to stay with them for several months, and since he had been told by his Italian doctor that he had heart problems, he needed to see a cardiologist.

Was peace to be found only in death? The middle-aged man lay on his bed and thought about his first day of school, how he had cried holding on to his mother's hand. He remembered the single-room school, the young teacher, other children, the black smocks with white plastic collars and blue ribbons. Who knows what he did that day after school? It was 1955; he was seven years old. Why couldn't he return to that time? "Why would you want to?" a voice said. "Hadn't you suffered, lived in fear, anxiety, and shame?" "But I was at the beginning of the story, my whole life ahead of me. I could dream of so many different lives," another voice answered.

Italy in 1955. Still poor but imbued with an austere beauty, purer. He thought of his childhood, of that time long gone, often with melancholy. As he walked all alone in late afternoon on that field as it began to snow—thick, heavy flakes blanketing everything in white—he had felt joy and wonder, acceptance and love. It had been a gift, a grace he had treasured all his life. An event that embedded itself in his being. No matter how miserable and full of woe he would find himself, that event was there, inside of him, and it told him, "Yes, there is pain, fear, loneliness, anger, suffering—but don't forget that day, don't forget the sky opening and the baptism of snow."

HE CALLED Bob to find out if he was still alive. The secretary said he had died six months earlier. When was the last time he had talked to Bob? Probably eight months ago, over the phone. Bob could no longer attend to his priestly duties, so he had moved up north to live with some people who could take care of him. "They worry so much about me, but I'm okay. Doctors, what do they know?" he had said in a dismissive tone. The middle-aged man wondered what happened to Buster. He remembered the morning he had gone to Saint Joseph's to talk to Bob, to tell him he wanted to get back in the Church. He had looked healthy, full of energy and vigor. *I'll miss you, Bob*, thought the middle-aged man. *I'll miss drinking a martini while watching a* Star Trek *rerun in*

the afternoon as Buster tries to lick the frosty glass. I'll miss talking about scriptures, the Church and philosophy. Father Bob never lost his faith, but to the middle-aged man, Bob's death was another reason for concluding that God didn't exist. *Once we die, we're gone*, thought the middle-aged man. *And as essential selves, as independently existing entities, we never existed. We are temporary manifestations of being in a form that has self-consciousness, that's all.* It was certainly comforting to believe in eternal life, whatever that meant, but the middle-aged man couldn't stand the thought of living a lie. Much better to be sober, in the truth. But what was truth? It was the way he saw things to the best of his critical thinking, supported by scientific and cogent arguments when possible. A rather subjective and limited answer; perhaps ultimately, he would have to say, "I don't know." But he found it repulsive to think that so many people went from "I don't know" to "I believe." If he didn't know, he had to live in the bosom of that unknowing. The problem was that truth was a vague word. There were different kinds of truth. There was empirical truth, semantic truth, logical truth, and there were different kinds of statements people made. When it came to value judgments, to the understanding of historical events, there might be different interpretations, but it irritated the old man to think that so many people talked of "my truth," or said, "That's his truth, who are you to judge?" *Well, sorry*, he thought, *you shouldn't use the word* truth, *but* belief. *Maybe you believe* x *to be true, but that doesn't mean it's true. Whether Napoleon was a great military strategist might be open to different views, but not the statement that immunizations historically have been a boon for humankind. That is true, as verified by data.*

HE RUMINATED over his father's arrival. He, his wife and child lived in a small house that needed to be sold; they were looking at different areas to move. Where was his father going to sleep? He needed to buy a cot and set it up in the study. To get his mind off these things, he kept thinking about Dante. "In the middle of our life's journey..." The first time he had read Dante was as a freshman at Imperial Valley College, in Mrs. Hillhouse's class. They had read selections from the *Inferno*. Twenty years later, during one of his trips to Italy he bought a copy of the *Commedia* in the original Italian, and even though it still required looking up the meaning of many archaic words, he fell in love with the poetry and the vision. It was an aesthetic whole, a long poem in which language comes alive as music even as it explores different levels of being, the historical as seen through the poet's experience/subjectivity, the theological as an adventure into the Catholic worldview, and the existential as the struggle of the inner self, as Jung saw it, to transcend the ego and the id and find unity. The *Commedia* was a spiritual epic, an investigation of the varying layers of the psyche. The middle-aged man joined the Dante Society and subscribed to the journal *Dante Studies*, but he seldom read the long, technical articles.

The Italian language. *L'Italiano*. His mother tongue. That day on the deck of the ship that brought him to America, when he talked about literature with the boy from first class, words had flown out of his mouth effortlessly for the last time in his life. Upon arriving in the new world, he'd had to learn another language, and the strange words struggled to escape from his throat, tentatively, awkwardly, deformed. And even after he learned English, the words never flew easily out of him as they had once in Italian. And when he spoke Italian now, the words came out clumsily, since he seldom spoke it and his vocabulary was poor.

The church bells rang nine; they were the bells of his memories, slivers of reality lost in the flesh of forgetfulness, of myth, of imagination. Their search for a house had narrowed to a few areas he didn't like. He wished they could have lived in Florence, the city where Dante was born in 1265. The city where Lorenzo Ghiberti worked on the Baptistery Doors, where Machiavelli was born, where Savonarola was burned at the stake, where Michelangelo and Leonardo worked. Brunelleschi and Fra Angelico at San Marco. Art, history, so much of the past coexisting with the present.

To wake up early, drink a cappuccino at the bar, cross the piazza and in the Basilica of Santa Maria Novella, meditate in front of Masaccio's *Holy Trinity*. God. *Theos. Deus.* What a strange word. What did it mean? October in Italy. The scents after a brief rain as he walked in the garden of the Pazzi Chapel in Florence, walking along the Arno in twilight, the facades of palazzi coloring the murky green water. The grape harvest, the children who return to school, the aroma of roasted chestnuts as he roamed the sidewalks in the center of Genova. He could believe in all that. In the beauty of sunset and dawn, the distant ringing of vesper bells, climbing a tree with his brother and eating cherries. The scents of the forest after the rain, reading Dante aloud, wandering in the Roman Forum.

Mozart, Beethoven, Haydn. Michelangelo, Leonardo, Van Gogh. Plato, Hegel and Heidegger. Renee', Michael, Stephanie and Joseph. Yes, he could believe in all that. Maybe that was God. A creative force. Creation? A violence done to the status quo, a breaking of routine. To cause a change to take place. Was there a plan? Just plain spontaneity? The sound of steps on the street, sense organs, beliefs, opinions. So, his father was going to stay with them for several weeks, then return to Albinia. He thought, *Once we're dead, it's as if we were never born as far as our consciousness/memory are concerned. We're just passing through the experience of consciousness, awareness of being, just passing through, so why spend so much of our lives chasing after status, prestige, material things? Why be slaves of a materialistic, market/consumer society that molds its members to fit nicely in its machinery?*

Capitalism had molded society with the values of acquisition, greed and immediate gratification. He didn't want to be of that society; he didn't want to be a cog in the machine. He didn't want his mind to be hijacked by ideologies, by beliefs. He wanted to live authentically, soberly, experiencing life joyfully in the face of death, but he found himself caught in the machine, distracted by material objects. How much time did he spend shopping, buying things? A lot of time. A lot of time that was his life. *My life*, he thought. But who was that "he"? Did he exist? As an organism, a conscious animal being, he existed. It was a temporary, ever-changing, ephemeral existence to be sure, but existence, nevertheless. All this swirled in his head as he sat in the drab waiting room of the optometry shop waiting for the frames of his glasses to be fixed. The sun on his back, a shadow on his hand and the open pages of the magazine he was looking at. People talking, engines idling, the reflection of the words "Eyeglass Frame Repair" on the greenish carpet. It was June of 1997. His brother was dead, his aunt was dead, his uncle was dead, his mother was dead, Lloyd and Bob were dead. Time flowed.

HIS FATHER HAD ARRIVED the evening before and was now watching television. It was Sunday. The religious machine hummed outside. The middle-aged man sat on the living room sofa drinking a cup of coffee, his father read the paper and Joseph watched *The Big Comfy Couch* on TV. When his son saw his grandfather for the first time that morning he had been timid, looked down and sucked his thumb, but it didn't take long for Joseph to get used to him, and as he sat on the sofa next to the middle-aged man, sometimes he'd take his eyes off the TV and glance at his grandfather, who smiled broadly at him. Joseph broke into a smile and went on watching the show.

They went to a Japanese restaurant so his father could finally eat some sashimi after so many years, took a walk in Balboa Park and watched a movie on TV; then it was time to go to bed.

∼

His brother sat on the floor, scraping paint off with a spatula. The middle-aged man hesitated, then sat down in front of him, took a spatula and began to scrape. His brother looked on and smiled. "You're using the wrong one —here you go," he said and handed him the right one. His brother looked happy that the middle-aged man was there, even though he had a melancholy look. "Did you die?" his brother asked. "Not yet," the middle-aged man replied. "How is it like to be dead?" he asked his brother. "It's not bad, but we don't go anywhere," his brother replied. He seemed pleased to see him and was amused at the middle-aged man's tears. Then his brother began to do something else.

The middle-aged man awakened. It was time to get out of bed. The last time he had seen his brother was in the ship's cabin that day in June of 1963. Now his brother was dead, he was forty-nine years old, Italy was choking with automobiles, trucks and smog, and America was no longer a dream, but an ambivalent reality.

∼

On July 11, the middle-aged man, his father, Stephanie and Joseph drove to San Luis Obispo, the first stop on the trip up north for the family reunion. Family reunion. An attempt to reunite for a day or two what time had torn asunder. Children now men and women had scattered around the country or the world, parents and relatives with white hair and bent backs. They stopped for the day in San Luis Obispo, at the house of his wife's sister and family. Craig, engineer and long-distance runner, was in the backyard grilling salmon, and Janice was making a salad and serving drinks as their children, Kevin and Caroline, played with Joseph. The cat, disturbed by the sudden invasion, made a quick exit into the backyard.

The following morning they drove to El Cerrito, where the family reunion was being held. At the family picnic, uncle Caesar, who he first saw in 1963 in the front yard barbecuing, tall, muscular and smiling, now sat hunched over in a wheelchair with a cannula in his nostrils connected to a small green oxygen tank. His eyes looked watery and tired, and Gary's father, Joe, walked slowly with a cane. Uncles and aunts, cousins and nephews, people he hadn't seen in decades had been transformed as if by a magical spell; in his mind he still saw them as they had been long ago.

The old man tried to reconstruct more of that day, but he only remembered lying on a blanket with his wife and son while his father talked to his brother. It seemed like the families kept mostly to themselves. If he could go back to that day, he would get up from the blanket and go talk to Caesar, to his cousins and the others, but it was too late. He could not step into the same river twice.

FINALLY BACK HOME, he was busy working, commuting, engaging in family activities, going to grocery stores, playing with his son and taking his father to doctor's appointments. Going to Kensington Video to browse through their extensive foreign film collection and talk to Winnie, whose son Guy ran the place, relaxed him. A woman in her eighties, full of energy and information about movies, Winnie always had time to talk to customers. And perhaps on the way back he'd stop at the bookstore and chat with Jeff or Craig.

He had installed an update on his Apple Performa computer, had a modem installed and now had the internet. It all seemed exciting at first, but he wasn't sure if at the end of the day it represented an advance. And then the internet took over and life became unthinkable without it. Shopping and paying bills online, social media—everything seemed to lose materiality and became ghostly; photos and music were in the cloud, letter writing became rarer, anonymity allowed many people to be truly themselves, hateful trolls, intolerant, spiteful, malicious. He wished he could go back in time before the internet, back when electric typewriters were state-of-the-art technology. If you needed information, you went to the library or consulted your encyclopedia, twenty heavy volumes on a bookshelf. If you had to make a phone call and you were not at home, you found a pay phone, and if you wanted to watch the news, you had to wait until Walter Cronkite was on. As the years passed, as he read fewer books and spent more time on the internet, he had the impression he had become shallower, that his *feel* of the world and himself had faded. But he knew there was no going back.

JULY WAS GONE, and with it his vacation was practically over. He'd have to wake up at four in the morning on Mondays and Tuesdays, drive to Santa Ana and teach classes until Thursday night. He steeled himself for the long meetings, the stacks of papers to grade. But when he stood in front of the class and lectured, wrote on the blackboard with white chalk, asked questions and made comments, he was *doing philosophy* and he felt centered. *I can't believe they are paying me for doing what I enjoy*, he thought.

Through the bedroom window he could see the left side of the star pine that grew in front of the house, green branches on a foggy background. The white and red "For Sale" sign was partially visible, along with the telephone pole reaching upward; everything else was lost in mist. And so today was the first of August. August with its angst. He began to think about ways he could improve his teaching of critical thinking. The fog was rapidly dissipating; things outside became more three-dimensional. The roar of traffic on the 805 freeway sounded like a gargantuan machine humming.

HE DROVE his father to Sharp Memorial Hospital for an angiogram. After the procedure, the cardiologist came into the room and said it was necessary to perform a coronary bypass as soon as possible.

The middle-aged man sat in the lobby during the surgery. He had talked to his sister on the phone earlier to inform her about their father's operation. He had worked in that hospital from 1983 to 1984 in the equipment room, then in 1985 as a respiratory therapist, taking arterial blood samples, turning comatose patients over for chest physical therapy, suctioning secretions from their lungs, managing ventilators, responding to code blues and doing CPR in the emergency room.

As he shifted his weight in the uncomfortable chair he felt anxious about his father's surgery, about moving, about having to go back to work, about his own health. At eleven forty-five, Dr. Adamson came to tell him the surgery was over. Everything had gone well, no complications. That night they would take out his father's endotracheal tube, and in four to five days he would be able to go home.

Seeing his father in the ICU connected to a ventilator after open heart surgery shook the middle-aged man. His father had always been strong, and when he became a postal worker, he walked ten miles a day. He didn't drink or smoke, and yet there he was in intensive care, helpless, hooked up to machines.

His father came home from the hospital, seventy-five years old, widowed, convalescing from open heart surgery. He sat in the easy chair in the living room reading the *San Diego Union-Tribune* and spy novels, went for short walks around the block and watched TV. It was hot and the house had no air-conditioning, the cot was uncomfortable and at times prospective buyers came to look at the house. Mary, his older sister, came to pick him up and drove him to her house in El Centro, where he stayed for a couple of months.

The middle-aged man and his wife bought a new house and moved before the beginning of the fall semester. They were happy with the larger house, even though it was going to take some time to get used to the new neighborhood. They welcomed a new addition to the family, a Brittany Spaniel puppy with a shining white and dark red coat. They called him Billy, and Joseph was ecstatic. The middle-aged man's father returned to Albinia in early December. He looked relaxed and healthy, and seemed eager to be back in his own apartment and see his friends. "I'll come see you next year," the middle-aged man told his father as he hugged him goodbye at the airport.

23

SAN DIEGO AND ITALY, 1998

At the end of the spring semester in late May of 1998, the middle-aged man found himself sitting in the commuter terminal waiting for a flight to Los Angeles. He had seen his father just six months earlier, but he wanted to visit his mother's grave, see his relatives, be in Italy again. He arrived in Rome late at night, where his father was waiting for him, and it was past midnight when they arrived in Albinia.

The following morning, he went to the cemetery with his father. It was a sunny day, and the middle-aged man sat in the narrow passenger seat of the Fiat Panda and looked out the window at two stilt birds flying low over the preserve. White bodies and black wings, slim pointed beaks and long red legs, the "Italian Knights" glided gracefully over reeds and shrubs. The cemetery was not far, just on the outskirts of Orbetello. He bought flowers from the vendor at the entrance of the cemetery and walked with his father to his mother's grave. It consisted of a slab of marble on a platform about a foot above ground, a headstone with her name in gold lettering under her photo.

His father had gone to the cemetery every day. "I asked one of the women who visits her husband's tomb if the dead can see us, and she believed they did," his father told him. How strange to believe that your loved one is up there beyond the sky looking down on you. *Where are they, and how can they see if they have no eyes? And if they can see you, do they watch you even when you wouldn't want to be seen?* Maybe it gave his father some solace, the thought that the woman he met after the war, had married and lived with for half a century, was up there, looking down at him, still loving him and keeping him company. The last time the middle-aged man had seen his mother was in front of the airport's entrance, when he hugged her and told her he would see her the following year, and now her remains were underneath that marble slab.

A field of graves, photographs of the dead on headstones, flowers on marble rectangles. A cult of remembrance and grieving, signs of people's feelings of love, caring, attachment to dear ones now forever gone. Two green lizards darted on the ground between the graves, a butterfly landed on a tombstone's flower and a tractor cut the grass in the olive grove next to the cemetery. The north part of the lagoon was a deep blue, and the fragrance of the plants growing by the wall separating the cemetery from the olive grove reached him, together with the musty scent of the lagoon. By the western wall, a water faucet dripped in a bucket and a broom seemed to stand guard. His father swept the marble slab, filled the permanent golden vase at the bottom of the grave with water and arranged the red and yellow lilies, white daisies and greenery. "See, your son has come to visit you," said his father as he stood in front of the grave, "and brought you flowers."

Then he and his father drove to Perugia. When Sandrina was a year old, in 1954, the middle-aged man was six, and while visiting their grandparents in Orbetello, he remembered how in front of the *cantoniera* he'd call his sister, wave and then hide behind a wall. She'd start sobbing, he'd come out and smile, and she'd stop crying. He would do this repeatedly, finding it amusing. Then as older kids, he talked her into playing cowboys and Indians, until their exasperated mother yelled at them to stop.

He hadn't seen her in two years, but she looked the same. The passing of time showed more in Sofia, her daughter, who had grown taller. In the next couple of days, Sandrina took them to Assisi for lunch, to Deruta to see how ceramics were made and to an ancient, abandoned church that had been converted into a textile shop that wove cloth on ancient looms.

After they drove back to Albinia, the middle-aged man took the train to Florence. Spending a few days there was the gift he gave himself.

As he walked in front of the Museum of the Hospital of Innocents, he noticed posters advertising a Chagall art exhibit. Built in the early part of the fifteenth century and designed by Filippo Brunelleschi, the hospital was the first in Europe to provide a sanctuary for orphans and abandoned infants, and the Museum of Art was housed on its grounds. A Belarusian-French artist who lived almost a hundred years, Chagall worked in many artistic styles and formats, but the middle-aged man had only seen a few of his works in art books. It was early, and the tourist hordes hadn't arrived yet. He was in one of his favorite cities, in a building designed by Brunelleschi, who had also designed and built the great cupola of the Duomo, and on that morning, the middle-aged man was surrounded by dazzling paintings of lovers flying over towns, of angels and animals, bright colors, geometric designs, prophets and naked women. After more than two hours, tired and hungry, he left and had lunch at a nearby snack bar, then walked back to his room to rest.

He bought books at the Feltrinelli store, made his usual pilgrimage to the Basilica Santa Maria Novella and the Opera del Duomo, then in the late afternoon he went to Santa Maria Maggiore, one of the oldest churches in Florence, built in the eleventh century. Past the Valentino and Gucci shops, the loud noise of traffic, buses and scooters, the stink of exhaust fumes, he stepped into the shadowy space where silence reigned. Rustic stone columns held up pointed arches that split the nave from the aisles. He looked up at the bare groined vaults and as his eyes adjusted to the low light, he saw that frescoes decorated some of the side vault ceilings. He sat in a pew in the back as the priest, so old he had to be helped as he walked in little rapid steps, approached the altar. The priest preached interesting homilies to the few old men and women there, and the middle-aged man, enclosed in that space, forgot himself and his concerns.

In the evening he decided to see Nanni Moretti's new film, *Aprile,* a comedy dealing with the Italian national elections, the creative difficulties of the director and the birth of his son. What a day! Browsing and buying books in Italian, going to his favorite sights, seeing a film by a director he admired and walking on the ancient cobblestones on the way to his hotel room, the Arno shimmering with moonlight, a light breeze cooling his face, the earthy scent of the river wafting by. In bed in the hotel room, he read some poems from one of the books he'd bought that afternoon, until he fell asleep.

He took rolls of photos with the Olympus camera he had recently bought, and one day it rained all morning. *I'm not far from paradise*, he thought as he walked alongside the Arno under the rain, sought respite in a bar with a shot of coffee, then greeted the stone faces of statues. In the Duomo, he tried to see Domenico de Michelino's fifteenth-century painting of Dante offering his *Commedia* to the city of Florence, with images of hell, purgatory and paradise in the background, but no matter how much he squinted at the work high on the left wall, in penumbra, he could never see it clearly.

BACK IN ALBINIA, the middle-aged man and his father went for a walk. At the end of the town's main street, they turned left on a parallel road to the Aurelia highway. The sky darkened and the air felt heavy with humidity. On the left side, two-story houses with white walls and orange-red tiled roofs were partially hidden by pines, oleanders and olive trees. On the right side, beyond the guardrail, trucks and cars whizzed by on the highway. The middle aged man thought of his mother; they often walked this way and being here only with his father made her absence more noticeable. "We should go back, it'll rain soon," his father said as he looked at the sky with a worried look. "Let's go a bit further, we need to stretch our legs," replied the middle-aged man. When they turned back it began to rain hard. They sought refuge in a phone booth. Drenched, raindrops violently slamming on the stall, they waited for a few minutes until the rain subsided. "I told you it was going to rain!" complained his father as the water running down the booth's plastic walls seemed to melt trees and buildings. On the way home, they stopped at a bar and had coffee with grappa. Decades later, when as an old man he remembered that day, he would smile. It had been exciting—the sudden rainstorm, then seeking shelter in a phone booth with his father.

HIS INTEREST in Buddhism led him to frequent the Buddha's Light Bookstore on Park Boulevard; there through the years he bought several books, including the *Shobogenzo*, by Dogen Zenji, a thirteenth-century Buddhist monk who founded the Zen school, became an abbot and wrote ninety-five essays that became *The Eye and Treasury of the True Law*. Some of the essays were cryptic, but much of what Dogen said made sense: "Our life is nothing more than a handful of dirt from a graveyard; we should not overvalue or be attached to it. If we have no resolve, who will have pity on us? If you see an abandoned corpse in a field, look at it closely and develop correct vision." He agreed with those words, and when he read the essay "Being-Time" he saw a similarity between Dogen's view and Heidegger's. "We, ourselves, are time," Dogen said.

According to Masao Abe's essay "Time and Buddhism," the conventional understanding of time as linear is only part of the story, it is to view it from the outside, but time must also be viewed from the inside, subjectively. "Accordingly, we must say that time has two aspects: the aspect of continuity or forward movement and the aspect of discontinuity or transcending movement. And these two aspects are dynamically linked together at each and every moment."

For Abe, "time is not a unidirectional movement but a sheer series of independent moments that can move reciprocally. A sort of reversibility of time is realized here." Was it possible to travel in time backwards and forward? Perhaps past and future could be glimpsed by "movement" in subjective time. If the mind was stilled, cleared of all concepts and images, could someone go beyond the present moment?

The middle-aged man may have experienced an intimation of this years earlier in Siena, in the Basilica of San Domenico. In one of the chapels, as he had stood in front of the wooden Christ crucified on the white wall with dim light filtering through the narrow double-lancet window, he had lost the anchor to the present, it could have been any time. He wondered, if he went into a thirteenth-century church, sat in isolation and lost himself in meditation, could he possibly experience or see images or presences from other times? Not just the past, but also the future?

His childhood had been difficult. His father mostly absent, his mother, left to raise him and his sister by herself with sporadic financial support, was often irritable and moody. At school or in public places, he was the child with the slanted eyes and the funny name. He was often sick in bed with chronic asthmatic bronchitis. But retroactively, he could reconsider those years, see them in a different light, still honor the painful memories but bestow on those years beauty and grace. He could remember his brother as a young man with his red Ducati; his aunt Avia with her exuberance and zest for life; his grandmother working in the vegetable garden, showing up at the door with bags full of smoked eels, sausages and cheeses. But now they were all dead. Time passed and they disappeared. "Our life is nothing more than a handful of dirt from a graveyard…" That was the truth. All those moments were gone, but their faint traces still smoldered in his aging brain, dimming rapidly as the second law of thermodynamics took effect. *Oh, Father in heaven! Most Holy Mother! Pray for us!*

24

SAN DIEGO AND ITALY, 2000–2004

The old man got up from his chair, a memory diver running out of air. It was almost midnight. He went downstairs, poured water in a mug and walked out into the backyard. It was cold and clear, stars visible between trees' branches. He took a sip and searched for the moon; a sliver peeked above the silhouette of a nearby house. What an ambivalent thing the past, a Janus face. Most of his life had been stained with the corroding acid of anxiety, and as he was getting older and closer to sickness and death, it increased.

He had taught philosophy for twenty-five years—had stood in front of the class, walked back and forth lecturing, asking and answering questions, giving tests, grading papers, talking to students. That was what he'd wanted to do ever since a freshman in college, but now those twenty-five years were gone, and the thousands of students that took his classes—did they even remember anything he tried to impart to them? He had hoped to help them think more critically, to open their minds a little, to spark in them wonder for being alive, to introduce them to the ideas of some of the great philosophers, but had he been successful? Semester followed semester; year followed year; vacation followed vacation.

As he stood in the backyard, he glanced at the tree to his left. The summer he walked for the last time with his mother to the beach under the pines, he had picked up a few seeds from a cone he found on the ground. Back home, he had put the seeds in a pot, and one grew. When they moved into their new home, he had planted the tiny pine tree in the backyard, and now it was taller than the house. He drank the last sip of water from the mug, which was handmade in Deruta. His sister gave it to him in 1999, when she came to San Diego with her husband and children for a year.

Sandrina and Giuliano rented an apartment in San Diego, bought a car and began to investigate the possibility of selling ceramics from Umbria. She registered Sofia and Daniel in local public schools, then she began an intense search for ways to market the stoneware. The middle-aged man liked to have his sister and her family nearby—they could visit often, have dinner together, go places—but her plans didn't work out, so they returned to Italy. Before leaving, she gave him the mug.

~

THE YEAR 2000 ARRIVED. The year that had been emblematic of the future. When as a child he watched the film *On the Beach*, in one scene a calendar had

Struggles Against Time

shown the year 1964. To him, as a child in 1959, 1964 was so far away. And as he read science fiction stories, the year 2000 heralded sentient robots and flying cars. That year had arrived, but there were no bases on the moon or Mars, no robots walking around and interacting with humans. Personal computers, the internet and smartphones were real, but not as exciting as interplanetary travel or robots. As a young man, when he thought of the year 2000, unthinkably distant, he assumed human beings would have become more rational, more understanding and accepting, less prone to fear and aggression, but he had been badly mistaken.

In late November of 2000, the middle-aged man received a letter from Salvatore. He'd had a heart attack and needed to have a bypass operation. He was already suffering from angina, and the stress of working on the Jubilee probably contributed to the cardiac crisis. "They say it's in suffering that we are closer to God; it's all bullshit. During the heart attack, which lasted almost ten hours, I asked God to make himself present in some way, to help me believe in something. Absolute silence. Maybe God has more important things to think about."

THE MIDDLE-AGED MAN took a sabbatical year. He missed taking courses in philosophy; he wanted to be in a classroom as a student, listen to lectures, write papers, so he registered at San Diego State University. Almost all the professors he had known in the 1970s had retired, but his thesis chairman, Dr. Feenberg, and Dr. Leon Rosenstein were still there. Walking around campus with a backpack, the middle-aged man felt out of place, awkward. He had been in his early twenties when he was a student there; now he was a 52-year-old man. Sitting at a desk, he looked at the other students—young men and women who could have been his children, with fresh, smooth skin, emanating energy and eagerness.

Dr. Feenberg, the fiery young professor who in 1973 paced back and forth in the classroom chain-smoking Marlboros, was now frail; he stood in front of the podium and lectured in a soft voice. Professor Rosenstein, who in the 1970s looked like a youthful Apollo, had gained weight but still had an elegant, classic way of moving and speaking. Even after so many years at San Diego State University, he had not forgotten Mount Olympus.

SEPTEMBER 11, 2001. As he walked Joseph to his classroom, the middle-aged man noticed in the library some teachers intently watching CNN on a TV. Back home, he turned on the news and saw black smoke rise from one of the World Trade Center's towers. He noticed something falling from a window and realized a person had jumped out. A fireman sat on a bench being interviewed, when suddenly, behind him, a plane plowed into the other tower. At the loud explosion, the firefighter jumped up and looked up. "What the hell?" he cried out.

The middle-aged man drove to the university, where he had Dr. Rosenstein's course at eleven o'clock. When the professor walked in, he said that due to the events in New York, the university was closing for the day and everyone was dismissed. Getting out of the parking structure took more than an hour.

In subsequent days, many vehicles the middle-aged man saw on the roads had American flags waving from radio antennas. Then tall fences went up around the perimeter of Miramar Lake, where he liked to go for walks. Surveillance cameras sprang up everywhere and privacy became a thing of the past. President Bush invaded Iraq and Afghanistan in retaliation for the terrorist attack. The invasion of two countries, the intense fear exhibited by so many, the beatings and killings of Sikhs, Muslims and others who looked Middle Eastern—these were symptoms of a fearful, troubled and vindictive nation. How could this happen in the land of the brave and the just?

THE MIDDLE-AGED MAN began to teach two classes in the summer session, so his yearly trip to Italy had to wait until the winter break. It took him more than an hour to get through security at the San Diego airport, where soldiers with M16s stood guard, and when he landed at Fiumicino in Rome, on December 30, Italian policemen armed with submachine guns patrolled the terminal. After the attacks on 9/11, the world had drastically changed. The internet and "the war on terror" had eroded privacy. He couldn't help think of Orwell's *1984*, where people were under constant surveillance.

His father informed him that Franco had shot himself the previous day and the funeral was held that very morning. Franco: dedicated and caring veterinarian, a handsome middle-aged man. What despair led him to kill himself? "He called his mother on the phone after he pulled the trigger, and she ran to his house and he died in her arms," his father said. The middle-aged man imagined Franco's mother seeing him on the bed in a pool of blood, so dark and red on the white sheets. Maybe she held her son's head up as she cried, "My son! My son! What have you done?" The middle-aged man stood on the balcony looking across the street at Franco's house. The plastic "*Veterinario*" sign in the front yard, the closed green shutters upstairs, the deserted side yard. The dog nowhere in sight. It was chilly and the trees were bare, but in a few months, spring would come and then summer. But Franco would never again go to the beach and wind surf, never again see his daughter or play with the dog in the yard.

On New Year's Eve the middle-aged man stayed up with his father to wait for 2002. It was cold in the apartment, as his father was reluctant to turn the heater on, worried about the expense. They had made little sandwiches like they used to do every year, and at midnight they toasted with a glass of spumante, his father bundled up in a heavy sweater and a red wool cap, looked like an elf.

That was the winter he also went to Genova with his father in the old Fiat to visit his nephew Fabrizio, the middle-aged man's sister-in-law, her mother

Giula, his nephew's wife Elena and her mother. There were long dinners, with local wine and shots of his nephew's grappa that he made with cherries from his trees.

One evening Fabrizio took him to a nearby bar. It was warm inside and crowded. Everyone knew his nephew, and a white-haired man who stood at the counter drinking white wine greeted the middle-aged man profusely and offered him a drink. He introduced himself as Gianfranco. The middle-aged man noticed at a table a group of men bundled up in coats looking at him. His nephew introduced them to him. They had been the children he used to play with when he had lived there. He smiled and shook their hands but didn't know what to say. He didn't remember them, and when he left the bar, he thought of the childhood years he spent in that mountain village. They had been heavy with anxiety and fear, but the passing of time had effaced the pain, so only the promise of childhood remained, only the beauty of nature. *Children play after school, laugh as they run after a ball, then they turn around and are middle-aged, the scars of the years on their faces. So what? Time passes, doesn't it? Yes, impermanence is imbedded in existence and what makes it possible, but it may still be experienced as a violent process of negation. We must go with the flow; that's the nature of things; it's childish to resist the passing of time.* He rebelled at such attempts, his whole being a middle finger in the face of time, impermanence and death.

Before returning to San Diego, he went to Saint Paul Outside the Walls. Salvatore had undergone the heart bypass operation several months earlier but didn't feel much better. His room was spacious, with a high ceiling and a window overlooking the garden. Metal cases six feet high crammed with books gave one the impression of having wandered into a library, and beyond the book stacks, on the right side, was a large mahogany desk with a computer, magazines and newspapers, and on the left side, a bed flanked by a small table and a couple of chairs. On the table, besides several containers of medicines was a stack of CDs and a small boom box. "I mostly listen to operas and read," Salvatore said as he lit a cigarette. "I've been listening to *Lucia di Lammermoor*, my favorite opera by Donizetti. When I lie on the bed, close my eyes and listen to Montserrat Caballé, I feel transported to some other place."

"I'll get it when I get back," replied the middle-aged man. "I like opera, but I'm not familiar with Donizetti."

"You like opera and don't know Donizetti? You've never heard *L'elisir d'amore*? You must have heard the aria 'Una furtiva lagrima.'"

"The aria, yes, but not the whole opera."

"If you listen to *Lucia di Lammermoor*, get the version with Caballé—it's the best."

Salvatore took two tablets from a medication bottle and swallowed them. "I'm following a hard diet; I already lost seven pounds in less than a month. They tell me that this will help my heart to recover; let's hope. But I pass most of the time in my room. I leave an hour during the day to walk, but I find it hard; my chest hurts and I don't feel like doing anything. The only thing I'd like to do is to go to the countryside and await death."

"I'm afraid of death," said the middle-aged man.

"Now more than ever, I'm ready to die. The boredom is terrible; I don't find anything that gives me joy in life," said Salvatore, as he took a drag from his cigarette.

"What about operas, reading?

"They help pass the time, but joy, no."

"You're a monk and a priest. Is there no meaning in prayer, in saying mass, chanting the office? You live surrounded by art and beauty, and there must be some comradeship in the community here."

"I live in a museum. The abbot is aloof and authoritarian; it's every man for himself. God is absent and beauty is not enough. I killed myself working on the Jubilee, for what? So all those cardinals who came from every part of the world could have the vestments ready for their show. You're a philosopher; you need to let go of the romantic ideas you have of the monastic life, see clearly through the appearances."

He made coffee in a small moka pot and as they sat and sipped the dense brew, the middle-aged man began to complain about his father. Salvatore listened attentively, then said, "I don't think my parents were even aware of having caused me so much suffering. The fact is we can no longer blame them; what's the use of remaining angry with them? Nothing will change. At this point your father is old. Try to be a father for him; act so that the few years left will be serene for him. At least later you'll have no regrets of things you would have wanted to do but didn't."

They talked until nine; then the middle-aged man had to leave to take the subway to the hotel. Early the following morning he had to go to the airport. "*Ciao*, Salvatore. Get better, so next time I come to Italy, we'll go to Naples to visit your family, and you can show me around. I'd like to see Pompeii."

"Let's hope," replied the monk. A hug, then the middle-aged man left.

A COYOTE's cry shook the old man from his memories. Often, at night, they would venture from the preserve onto the streets, looking for food. As the humans expanded, they razed more and more hills to build houses and condos, destroying the natural habitats. He was still in the backyard, lost in the past. He walked back in the kitchen and locked the door. He glanced at the clock; it was past midnight. On his way to bed, he thought again of the evening his nephew brought him to the bar in Davagna and he had a glass of wine at the counter with the friendly man. "I'm Gianfranco," the man had said, the same man he had met a couple of years earlier, when he and his father had taken the bus from Genova and gotten off at the wrong stop. Once under the covers, the old man adjusted his pillow and turned on his right side. He was digging into his memories, trying to glue together the pieces of Gianfranco. He recalled that when his father had visited them for a few weeks in Sella, back in 1956, a young man would drop by and talk with his father, arguing that the earth could be flat. That young man was Gianfranco. He was the son of Luigi, the owner of the restaurant in Moranego, the man who was almost shot by the retreating German soldiers in 1945, spared only because his wife had pleaded for his life and offered the German officer all her gold. He wondered what Gianfranco had done with his life in the past forty years. The middle-aged man had been a child and Gianfranco, eighteen or nineteen. He couldn't remember any more; all that remained of those years were a few ephemeral, vague images—wasn't that death? When the old man had asked his sister if she remembered their father visiting them in Sella, she said it never happened. Why did he have that memory, then? He wished he could have asked his father about it, but he was dead, and besides, he might not have recalled. Again he experienced his inability to clearly remember as a kind of dementia. His memories were fragmented, vague images seen through veils, as in dreams; they were all that remained of vivid, lived life. He couldn't sleep, so he went into the study, turned on the lamp and sat in his chair. It was late at night, when he felt his whole life had dissipated like smoke or vapor, that a dark mood fell on him and the world bled colors, lost substance and threatened to collapse like an untethered lace curtain. Then he picked up a book. As he read, he found structure and order in the words as they followed one another until they conjured the world back into being.

THE OLD MAN often thought of his mother and wondered why he hadn't felt much sadness at the news of her death. Perhaps making himself feel nothing was a shield against pain. He remembered that he cried some time later, and wrote her a letter. His mother lived in him and in his memories. At times she visited him in his dreams.

IN JANUARY OF 2003, the middle-aged man received a letter from Salvatore. He said his health had worsened, and in the last few months he had also been diagnosed with diabetes. He took seventeen medications every day to decrease the risk of another heart attack. His cardiologist told him that such a situation could not go on for long. "I left your address in the list of people to be notified in case of my death," he wrote. "The abbot and I get along better; we ignore each other and find ways to not exist the one for the other, which works well for both of us. I salute you with friendship, Salvatore." Then, in March of 2004, the middle-aged man received a small envelope from the monastery, enclosing a funerary card with a photo of Salvatore. On the back it read, "In the silence and solitude of the night, God has recalled to Himself suddenly, but not unexpectedly, our brother, Father Salvatore Romano O.S.B."

The old man was in the study again, late at night. He had opened the window and the breeze made the venetian blind rattle. He thought of Salvatore. They had met in 1993, had mostly an epistolary relationship, even though he went to see him a few times in Rome. Salvatore had been a priest and a monk, had been for the middle-aged man a living connection to the Church, in some ways, to God, even if only mediated by the faith, at times faltering, of another. Had the middle-aged man being a good friend to Salvatore? He didn't think so. They had planned to go to Naples in 1996 to visit his family, but he hadn't even called Salvatore to let him know he wasn't coming. And as the years passed, the correspondence dwindled. Salvatore hoped to find love in God and the Church but found mostly indifference and regimentation. But was that the whole story? He had been a monk and a priest for decades, performed masses, listened to confessions, served as the sacristan, said the office every day. Perhaps he found some meaning and purpose in the Church, in his vocation, even if often he felt alone and abandoned.

It was past one in the morning, but the old man fought going to bed. He picked up his smartphone to check his calendar, and just before turning it on he saw his reflection on the glass screen. The face that looked at him so grudgingly was his own. Those brown spots on the puffy cheeks, those wrinkles, were an old man's, but inside, his consciousness, his sense of being alive, didn't seem to have any connection to that image. What did the reflection on the smartphone's screen have to do with him? What connection did it have to his awareness, his being? And yet he could not escape the face looking back at him. He was a prisoner; he was looking through that ancient man's eyes and couldn't get out. He forced himself to go to sleep.

THE YEAR ENDED with Trump losing the election, and 2021 began with an angry mob attacking the Capitol building while Congress was in session. Something was definitively rotten in the United States of America. But while at the level of ideology liberals and conservatives, progressives and right-wingers struggled and bickered, the rich, to use a worn-out cliché, laughed all the way to the bank. The military budget increased as usual, arms manufacturers prospered, billionaires proliferated. At least Covid vaccines became available in the spring, and in the summer California lifted restrictions. The old man felt freer, but he still wore a mask in crowded areas and was reluctant to go to movie theaters and concerts. Travel to Italy was possible now without a quarantine period, but it was still too early for him to go. As he sat in his chair in the study, he glanced at a postcard of Florence he had nailed on the wall and felt pulled by the past. He wanted to go back to Italy; he would do it by traveling in time.

25

ITALY AND SAN DIEGO, 2004–2014

June 2004. He was in Rome again, but this time with his wife and ten-year-old son. They gazed at the sea of gilded buildings, basilicas and domes from the roof of Castel Sant'Angelo at sunset. Built in the second century AD by the emperor Hadrian as a mausoleum, it later became a papal residence, a castle and a prison. His son looked with interest in the cells where many had been held through the centuries. Joseph also liked the Colosseum and the catacombs, but tired easily in museums and art galleries. "After this we'll go get some gelato," he would tell the boy when he complained. When they climbed the stairs to the top of Saint Peter's Basilica, his son led the way, and when they found a coffee shop on the roof, he and Stephanie had a cappuccino while Joseph had an orange Fanta, his favorite drink. In the evening, as they walked around the Trastevere neighborhood, loud chanting broke the silence, then dim lights began to flicker on the walls of nearby buildings as men carrying a cart with a statue of a saint appeared. They shouted, "Long live Saint Anthony!" The cart with the statue was followed by a procession of people carrying candles. Joseph stood still, his mouth open. He would never have seen anything like it in San Diego.

They visited his sister in Perugia, with short trips to Assisi, Deruta and Etruscan tombs, then drove to Florence, where his son looked at Michelangelo's *David* in awe. In the Uffizi Gallery, the middle-aged man became entranced by the paintings of Uccello and Titian and began to pay particular attention to the backgrounds. Beyond the figures in the foreground, often through windows or doors, villages or houses beckoned. What kind of people lived there? What hopes, dreams and sufferings were they experiencing? He would put himself there, in one of the houses, and fantasize a life. He saw himself sitting at a table, reading Dante's *Commedia*, cool air entering through the open window, a church bell intoning the hours. He could have lived whole lives in those paintings' backgrounds.

While in Albinia to see his father they drove to Talamone on a Sunday morning. The sun was bright and hot, the town teeming with tourists and the narrow beach crowded with bathers. His wife and son went swimming while he stayed with his father, who fatigued easily and had a hard time climbing the steep, narrow alleys. It was late in the morning and bars and restaurants were full, all the inside and outside tables taken. They sat on the steps near a wall and waited. It had been a mistake to drag his father to Talamone; he walked slowly and seemed in distress. But the visit had been worthwhile; at least his father was able to spend some time with his grandson. Joseph was ten, and liked to sit on the balcony with his grandfather and eat peanuts as they watched the swallows flying around. And in the evenings they walked to the ice cream parlor, where they sat at a table outside and enjoyed gelato.

A FEW DAYS later they were home. Now that he taught two courses during summer session he couldn't go to Italy for the usual three weeks, but in 2006 he wanted to see his father, who had been diagnosed with congestive heart failure and had spent a few days in the hospital. This time the middle-aged man could stay in Italy just a week.

His father had lost weight, walked unsteadily and tired easily. They went to Perugia for a short visit, but the day after arriving his father had to be taken to the hospital, where he waited on a gurney in a hallway for hours before a bed could be found for him. The next day the middle-aged man went to see him and said goodbye; he had to return to Albinia to pick up his bag and drive to the airport the following morning. "Get better. I'll come see you next year," he told his father. "I love you."

WHEN THE MIDDLE-AGED man called his sister from San Diego, she said that after a two-week stay at the hospital their father returned to his apartment in Albinia. In the following weeks he seemed to be doing well but was getting weaker. He needed a caregiver now, who cooked his meals and cleaned, and toward the end of 2007 he became ill again and an ambulance took him to the Orbetello hospital. He sounded short of breath on the phone, had complained of being cold and of wanting to buy himself some wool pants. When the middle-aged man called again, the nurse gave the phone to the caregiver, who said his father was extremely sick and couldn't talk. She said the doctors expected him to live one or two weeks at most. He called again the following day, and the nurse handed the phone to his father, who kept repeating in a whisper that he couldn't hear anything. The middle-aged man kept speaking loudly into the phone, but his father could not hear. Rustling of sheets and moans were the only sounds that came through. "I love you," he told his father, "I love you," then he hung up. The next day his sister informed him their father had died. He didn't feel anything—perhaps some sadness, but not much else. Planning to go to the funeral was out of the question; his sister took care of the arrangements.

THE OLD MAN looked at his father's Army insignias framed on the wall of the study. Perhaps he should have taken time off from work and flown to Italy to be with him as he lay in the hospital dying. He retrieved a photo album from the top of a bookcase, sat down again and began to flip the pages. There was his father as a little boy standing next to his brother and sisters in a family portrait with his parents; in another photo the little boy had a sailor's cap on, wore a sleeveless white tee shirt, and at the family farm, looked at boxes of tomatoes. In his senior picture in the 1940 high school yearbook, he had a strange expression, a faint smile mingled with sadness. Then as a soldier in the 442nd Regiment, he was washing clothes next to a pup tent, playing baseball, driving a jeep. There were photos from his trips on the USS *Exchester*, when he worked in the merchant marine, then pictures of the period when he settled down, when he left the merchant marine and found a job with the US Postal Service. Faded images of family picnics, vacations, holidays, of his retirement party, of the two years he spent in San Diego before moving to Italy.

The old man closed the album and put it back on the top shelf of the bookcase. When he was a child, he had looked up to his father, had been proud of him; then as a teenager he found him a crude, inarticulate, shallow person, and began to increasingly dislike him. But now he missed his father. He wished they could go for a walk down the bird preserve in Albinia, cross the street and stroll under the pine groves to the bar overlooking the beach. Sit outside on the terrace, have a coffee and talk. He wished he could invite his father to San Diego, take him to a Japanese restaurant and have a nice lunch with sashimi and rice.

In 2007 his parents were dead and he taught summer sessions, so he no longer went to Italy every year. Ten years passed before he would see the country of his birth again. He didn't remember much of those ten years. He commuted, taught classes and attended department meetings, graded papers and tests, went shopping on Fridays, spent time at home. During the summers he went on vacations with his family, to the Grand Caymans and Alaska, on camping trips in the Sierras, visited Stephanie's family in San Luis Obispo, San Francisco, Santa Rosa and Healdsburg.

He discovered the films of the great Hungarian director Béla Tarr. In *Sátántangó*, a seven-and-a-half-hour black-and-white film, Tarr did justice to time. No Hollywood fast editing, but very long takes. Cows roam on a muddy field for eight minutes, two men walk on a windswept street for almost two minutes, saying nothing, as the wind blows newspapers and empty paper cups around. The film, based on a novel by László Krasznahorkai, was truly the work of an artistic genius; the cinematography, the acting, the soundtrack and themes left the middle-aged man drained. After watching it, he felt as if a giant spoon had stirred wildly his thoughts and feelings. He had cried, been amused, been questioned, made afraid, horrified, touched by beauty, left to wonder.

He reread Hegel's *Logic*, despairing at the high level of abstractness. Did he truly understand it? Probably not. He began to see the films of Andrei Tarkovsky, including *Stalker* and *The Sacrifice*. The Russian director was truly a poet and a visionary, a deeply spiritual man who liked to shoot long scenes of detritus in water and levitating women. The old man began reading Proust's *In Search of Lost Time* and enjoyed the richness of the writing, dialogue and descriptions, but the last part, which dealt mostly with the relationship between Marcel and Albertine, was the reef on which he crashed. He hated Albertine and couldn't stand Marcel's obsession with her.

In June of 2011 Bruna, his sister-in-law, died. He remembered her as the young girl his brother had fallen in love with; the nervous, excited woman at the wedding; years later, when she returned home from the hospital with the newborn Fabrizio; in 1987, when he saw her after twenty-four years; and the last time in 2004, when he and his father had gone to Genova. The young couple who went on Sunday drives on the Ducati to make love was no more. They had lived out their lives, and now their remains rested in the little cemetery a short distance from the home they built in the mountains.

Semester followed semester; his son Joseph graduated from high school and went to Northern Arizona University. The middle-aged man and Stephanie drove him to the dorm, and on the way home, the car felt like a submarine gliding in an ocean of sadness. Their son was no longer a boy; time had passed, and he was a university student now, living far from home. The middle-aged man smiled as he remembered Joseph as a five year old boy running after the ball in soccer peewee league, playing tennis and basketball as he got older. The piano lessons which he wasn't very excited about, the trumpet, which he enjoyed and the concert band he had belonged to in middle school. His excitement when he caught a trout on a camping trip, the video games they played together, the Harry Potter books. Joseph's four years in high school had gone in a flash it seemed, and now he longed to be away from home, to be a college student.

In the fall of 2014 the middle-aged man received a

call from his daughter Renée, who said her mother's heart was failing, she didn't have long to live. "I'll call her," he had replied, and one evening, when he was in his office at work, he called Roberta. She sounded happy he had phoned, and they reminisced, talking about old times, the day he took her to the prom, the year she was elected "Queen of Seeley." Roberta sounded short of breath, but they talked for a long time, then said their goodbyes. They both knew she didn't have long. And indeed, on the eighteenth of December, she died. He called Renee', sent flowers, then logged on Facebook to see if there were any photos of Roberta. There were a few, and one moved him in particular. It showed Roberta sitting in a restaurant booth, an old woman with a cable protruding from her shirt connected to a battery pack by her side. Her white hair was cut short, crew-cut style, her face ashen, a cannula in her nostrils. She attempted a smile, but her hazy blue eyes were gray, and gone was the expression of mirth that usually graced her face. He remembered the high school junior he fell for, in 1967. *She's too beautiful for you*, his mother had blurted out when she saw her in the Seeley parade. They had been high school sweethearts, had a daughter, then went their separate ways. Roberta had a tumultuous life; she had married five times but never found the right person. At least she died in the care of Renée, her daughter.

When her mother died, Renée had been battling MS for sixteen years. She did her best to take care of her daughter Lexi, but there were times when her daughter wound up taking care of her.

26

ITALY AND SAN DIEGO, 2016–2017

In May of 2016 his son Joseph graduated from Northern Arizona University with a degree in geology. It was a joyous event attended by his parents, grandmother, aunts and cousins. Soon after, Joseph found a position in San Diego, so when in the summer the old man and Stephanie traveled to Italy, his son could take care of little Berry.

The last time he had seen his sister was ten years earlier, those two days he spent at her house in 2006 when his father had to be taken to the hospital. Sandrina had gained some weight and had cut her hair short, but she still had the same sparkling smile. Her children had grown into successful adults.

They took a walk down Corso Vannucci, had a cappuccino and an almond pastry at Santino's bakery, visited Piazza Italia in the rain and saw red, white and orange koi in the fountain, circling the rocky pedestal on which sat the greenish sculpture of a youth. Lily pads, one with a purple lotus, floated on the surface. It was the twentieth of June, but it was cool. He had walked up and down Corso Vannucci so often with Penelope, Michael, his parents and sister, with Stephanie, in so many frames of mind.

He, his wife and sister drove to nearby picturesque towns, like Bevagna and Corciano, medieval villages transformed by time into tourist destinations. It was hot; the old man needed to remember to come to Italy in late fall or winter. As they walked on the cobblestone streets he glanced at his sister and wished they could have seen each other more often, have dinners together, talk. It saddened him that he only saw her for a few days as the years passed.

The old man and Stephanie drove to Orbetello to visit his parents' grave and see his nephews and cousin. They rented an apartment for three days on the fifth floor of a building not far from the center of town. They could see the sea on the right side of the balcony, roofs of stores and houses below, Monte Argentario on the left, in the distance. When as a child he visited his grandparents, the promontory of Monte Argentario was part of the scenery that imbedded itself in his psyche. His grandmother and mother were born in the fishing village of Porto Santo Stefano, on the promontory's north side. He had, in a way, a genetic connection to that mountain, and as he gazed at it from the balcony, it sparked inside him a feeling of primordial familiarity.

The following morning they drove to the cemetery. This was the first time he had been there since his father's remains were interred in his mother's grave. He stood in front of his mother's tomb as he had stood with his father in the summer of 1998. Now his father's ashes were inside it. So this was it, this was all it came down to, at the end of the day. Behind the veil of appearances, there was nothing.

They also visited the graves of his uncle Gaetano, aunt Lilia and Libero. On the white marble headstone above his name, Libero's photo was on the left side; on the right, a mosaic of his Mercedes truck, the truck in which he had kept Libero company on many drives up and down Italy, chain-smoking cigarettes and talking for hours. *Dear Libero, you don't believe in the witches!* The old man often wondered what his uncle had meant by that statement.

After the cemetery they went to Albinia. They walked down Via Fattori, where his parents had lived. On the right side, Franco's veterinary office had been converted into a window coverings shop, and as the old man looked at the apartment building on the left side, he saw on the third floor the balcony from which his mother had stood and greeted him when he came to visit. How often had he sat on a chair up there and read the paper or watched people go by as he talked to his mother or father? Other people lived there now; his mother's flowerpots were gone. Farther up the street on the left side, the house of Franco's mother was partially hidden by trees and shrubs; on the right was the furniture store, the photographer's shop and the hardware store. He had known the owners of all those businesses, used to talk to them during his stays in town, but as he looked in the windows, he didn't recognize anyone. As they walked down the main street, he experienced a moment of disorientation. The tall pines lining both sides were gone, wider sidewalks in their place. They went in a bar, ordered two coffees, and he asked the server what happened to the trees. "We had a flood in November of 2012, a nightmare—all the trees had to be cut down," he said. The old man and Stephanie sat at an outside table and sipped their cappuccinos. The main street with its majestic trees was what he had liked best in Albinia, and now they were gone. As he finished his coffee, he felt the passing of time as something sinister, as a force that had pushed him into a different world, one that still held some semblance to the one he remembered, but different, somehow alien. He knew what a Buddhist would say: "You're experiencing impermanence. Things change; there was a natural upheaval; the trees are gone. Understand this fully; don't be attached to how things were. Let go; embrace the now."

In the evening they went to visit his cousin Anna Maria and her husband, Rolando. They lived in a spacious house near Grosseto. It was a balmy late June day. They were greeted warmly, talked for a long time in the garden, then Rolando went in the kitchen and cooked spaghetti alla carbonara and made a salad. They ate, drank wine and talked until late, then he and Stephanie said their goodbyes and promised to come back to visit soon.

He remembered when as a child his mother had taken him and his sister on summer vacation to Orbetello. Everyone had gone to the Feniglia beach—his mother and sister, uncle and aunts and his cousin. He had dived under the warm, crystalline water and had looked up at Anna Maria's legs. How old had he been? Twelve? Anna Maria must have been sixteen. Now they were almost seventy. As he sat in his cousin's living room talking to a stocky old woman with white hair, he saw the svelte sixteen-year-old girl who laughed as they splashed water on each other at the beach. The sun shining in a clear blue sky, the cool air full of that fresh scent of the sea, he wanted so desperately to be there again, but time had passed, and now they were two old people and there was no going back.

The following morning the old man and his wife left for Genova, but on the way, they stopped in Pisa for a few hours. It was a hot day with the usual crowd of tourists. The famous leaning tower was closed to the public, but he had climbed it with his father in 1990, when he lived at his parents' apartment in Albinia, waiting for the return ticket to California. Sixteen years had passed, his father had been dead for a decade. When the old man was young, so was the world, and the places he went to were new, fresh. But as he aged, the world lost its purity; places became encrusted with layers upon layers of past experiences, so that as he gazed at the tower, he saw himself and his father looking down from the top. Then he remembered the Zen teaching of being present. He was there with Stephanie for the first time; she smiled, radiant, and he took a photo of her as she moved her hand toward the tower's side, as if to keep it from falling.

In Genova they stayed in an apartment not far from Piazza de Ferrari. That square was close to the old man's heart. He had been there often as a child, and the fountain had become emblematic of his youth. They had only three days there. Before they left, his nephew and his wife, Elena, came to see them after work, drove them all over Genova. They passed the Corso Italia promenade, where he had gone for a walk with his parents and relatives on the day of his sister's first communion; the promenade from where he and his brother tried to send a message to his father, whose ship was visible in the distance. They had stenciled his father's name on a piece of cardboard and rode at night to the promenade. Noé ran the cut-out message over the Ducati's headlight, "Maybe someone on deck will see it and let him know," he had said, and he, thirteen or fourteen, had wanted to believe it. They went by Portofino, where according to Nietzsche, "the bay of Genova ends its melody." He had gone to Portofino on a picnic with his parents, sister and his brother, Bruna and Fabrizio, who was not yet a year old. Now Fabrizio was a middle-aged man with two adult sons, and he was driving him around Genova.

From Genova, he and Stephanie drove to Milan because they wanted to see Leonardo's *The Last Supper*. They stopped at an Autogrill on the way. The building on the highway bridge looked familiar; it was the same one where Libero had stopped on one of the truck runs. He remembered that he and Libero had dinner there, and now Libero was gone.

His first experience of Milan was the torture of finding a parking place. Tired after the long drive from Genova, they finally found a parking structure and dragged their carry-ons a few blocks to the apartment they rented. They woke up early and walked to the Church of Santa Maria delle Grazie. He was still sleepy, but enjoyed the cool air and the scents of coffee and pastries that came from the bars. They already had reserved tickets on a tour. When they entered what had been the monastery's dining hall, Leonardo's famous work silenced everyone. The fresco, unearthly in the white room, warmed by the spotlights, hovered above them. Behind Jesus, through the windows, green hills beckoned. He imagined himself behind one of the hills, on a narrow road leading to the house where Jesus presided over the last supper. He saw himself walking on the road on a warm spring day, and a young woman passing by, pulling a squeaky cart full of baskets almost overflowing with plump reddish dates. He turned to look at her as she disappeared behind a bend when he heard a voice. "Will you take a photo of me?" his wife asked, and he was back in the oratorio, gazing at the mural. He took many photos; then, after a rest sitting outside a café, they walked down streets lined with imposing trees, palazzi's pale yellow, rusty facades, tall windows with brown shutters, ornate pediments, terraces overflowing with potted greenery and flowers, the traffic heavy, the tram's rails in the middle of the street, then the towers of the Sforzesco Castle in the distance.

It was only ten thirty in the morning, but he was already tired. Once inside, he contemplated a Madonna and Child with angels by Benedetto Bembo that he found ugly, Filippo Lippi's and Andrea Mantegna's Madonnas more naturalistic; then paintings of murders and tortures, martyrdoms of saints, roasted alive, heads split open with cleavers. *Leave it to human beings to turn tortures and killings into martyrdoms and art. Human beings, what a sad, murderous species*, thought the old man, but then he came across Michelangelo's last work, the *Rondanini Pietà*. In the unfinished marble sculpture, Jesus, slim and frail, his chest crisscrossed by chisel marks and his face just beginning to appear, Mary behind him, emerges out of stone. *Humankind is redeemed by works such as this*, he thought. Afterward, they had lunch at a La Scala restaurant, where the food was mediocre and the atmosphere pretentious.

As they approached the Milan Cathedral, begun in 1386, he thought of Vittorio de Sica's 1951 film *Miracle in Milan*, where in the last scene, the good people fly above the Duomo on broomsticks, and of the faded color photos of his parents and his daughter who had gone to Italy in 1976. They had landed at the airport in Milan, and Noé had picked them up and taken them to see the Duomo before driving to Genova. The old man remembered a faded photo of his daughter, seven years old, holding out her hand as a pigeon lands on it, and of his brother beaming, happy to see his mother after thirteen years. Now, forty years later, he could see them in his mind, could feel their presence in the air.

BACK HOME, it was time to get ready for the fall semester.

In December of 2016, his father-in-law died at eighty-four after a long battle with dementia. Loy had played the bugle in the Boy Scouts, had joined the Marines and fought in the Korean War. Soon after the conflict ended, he married Norma, a petite brunette with hazel eyes. They had four children and lived the American dream in Santa Rosa, California. Loy had a distinguished career in management and ran marathons in his fifties. He was fifty-eight when the middle-aged man met him, a tall, athletic gentleman who had been kind and generous. One day Loy took the middle-aged man to a fisherman's shop in Santa Rosa and bought him an Orvis Madison fly-fishing reel. He made him a fishing rod and in the backyard taught the middle-aged man how to cast it. Loy jogged, played golf, fished, and rode a bike that was custom made in Italy. The old man still had the Orvis Madison reel but had never gone fly fishing. He went in the garage and found it in the bottom drawer of his filing cabinet. It still looked new. *I want to try it,* he thought. *I want to hear this reel sing as it releases the fishing line. Loy would have liked that.*

THE OLD MAN was approaching the seventh decade of his life. It was time to retire, especially since major structural changes were being made to the campus. Bulldozers leveled the grassy mounds he liked so much, cut down all the trees, and as the months passed, the college became a huge construction site teeming with workers, excavators, trucks, jackhammers, noise, dirt and dust. For twenty-four years he had walked from one end of the campus to the other, past the music building, the humanities hall, the fountain, the library and the administration building, the bookstore, the cafeteria, the astronomy observatory, the science hall, and now everything was changing, cut down, torn apart, in the name of renovation. *Trees' roots in the long run damage sewage and water*

lines, they break the concrete in parking lots, the grassy mounds have to be mowed—let's do away with all the trees, let's just have a flat sea of cement. It's cheaper.

He was glad to leave. As he walked down the corridor to his office, he didn't recognize anyone; the professors he had known for years had all retired, and now bright, young new faces smiled at him from inside their offices. They had been hired the previous year; he was now the oldest faculty member in the humanities division. He had to clear out his office, had to somehow get rid of various editions of texts, books, magazines, journals and mementos, the detritus of twenty-four years of teaching.

And so this was the last week at the college. In late afternoon, as was his routine, he had driven to the Main Place Mall, parked at the South end, by the Gym that had recently replaced a furniture store. As he walked in the covered gallery a wave of familiarity and peace washed over him. In that enclosed space full of bright colors, music, voices and children's laughter, disease and death were inconceivable. He passed display windows, a parade of jewelry and watches, shoes, fashionable clothes, video games, Playstations and Xboxes. Scents of cookies and cinnamon rolls just out of the ovens wafted from the second tier of shops above his head. In the center of the gallery small trees struggled to grow in huge pots, tired shoppers rested on benches. If he looked up he could see clouds in the cerulean sky. Often, the store clerks were his former students. "Hello, professor, remember me?" they would ask, smiling.

He had seen many stores open, then after a few years close, to be replaced by other businesses. Even

Nordstrom closed, along with the restaurant and the coffee shop. He'd go to the restaurant with his friend Karim; they'd order salads with salmon and tomato soup. They talked about campus politics, about the fava beans that were ready to pick. Karim described in detail how to make *fattoush* salad or the best way to prepare halibut. He'd meet Gus and over coffee talk about writing projects, their mutual interests in mythology and current world events. But he was retiring; he would probably never go back to that mall he had frequented for almost a quarter century.

On June 6, he went to the last graduation he would have to attend, and as he sat on a chair among other faculty members on the city's football field, students' family and friends crowding the bleachers, listening to the names of the graduates being called in the cool air of the evening, he was filled with emotions. Twenty-four years had passed; it seemed like he had just been hired and now he was retiring. "It feels like it was just yesterday…" What a cliché, and yet there he was, sitting on a folding chair on the field where every year he sat for the students' graduation, the air cooling down, the breeze on his cheeks, the scent of freshly cut grass in his head, his back hurting, the graduates' excitement palpable, one of hundreds of faculty members, the end of the school year, but this was the last time he would be on that field, and while it didn't literally seem like yesterday that he had started teaching at the college, the past twenty-four years were gone, poof! He looked forward to retirement: no more long commutes, no more meetings to attend and tedious paperwork, no more difficult students to deal with. But he liked being in the classroom; walking back and forth, lecturing, asking questions, writing on the board, talking to students. He would miss that part, and he would miss seeing Beatrice sitting at her desk in the admissions office, or Victor standing behind the counter helping students register, or the librarians and the custodians, with whom he would talk, or seeing students he knew as he walked around, or Debbie at the coffee stand. But the college he knew was gone. It was time to leave.

27

EUROPE, 2017

To celebrate his retirement, he and his wife flew to London in late September. His sister met them there and after a week followed them to Amsterdam; then she flew back to Perugia, and they took the train to Germany.

Norwegian Air landed at Gatwick in early afternoon, and after a painless ride on the express train and a quick taxi trip they were at the Lime Tree Hotel in Belgravia.

After resting, they walked to Buckingham Palace, not far from the hotel. Gray against a luminous sky in late afternoon, the palace's facade, with its marble columns and Corinthian capitals, subtly changed its hues, from charcoal to rust and violet. The golden statues of *Victory*, *Courage* and *Constancy* stood at the top of the Victoria Memorial, and *Truth*, winged and bare-breasted, held a mirror.

The people who created the monument would no doubt have believed it true that England had the right to subjugate and exploit other continents and peoples. They would have claimed it to be true that the English were racially superior to Indians, Africans or Asians. What they saw in the mirror of truth was themselves, their values, their way of life. He looked around. How strange to be in San Diego one day and the next at the Memorial Gardens with their flower beds and wonder if at that very time, the Queen was relaxing in her residence. It was almost six in the evening. The sun hid behind the upper right corner of the palace, a white disc dissolving in yellow and orange swaths flanked by dark elongated clouds crowned by gold, and above, a pale expanse given texture by dark streaks. He looked up at *Justice*; her right hand held the arm of a man on his knees, her left hand was on the hilt of a sword. Queen Victoria, holding a globe and scepter, eighteen feet high in Carrara marble, looked severe. Who could stand against her, with Victory, Courage, Constancy, Truth and Justice at her side?

It proved more difficult to go to Karl Marx's memorial. Two subway runs, a bus ride and a long walk to Waterlow Park in Highgate village, past Saint Joseph's Church, with its green copper dome, then Highgate Cemetery. On one of the cracked concrete paths flanked by tombstones, on the right side, stood the imposing monument of the great philosopher, economist and political activist. His massive head in bronze rested on top of a granite pedestal. "Workers of all lands unite" was emblazoned in gold at the top of the pedestal, "The philosophers have only interpreted the world in various ways, the point however is to change it" at the bottom.

In high school he thought of Marx with ambivalence, but his view had changed when in college he read the *Manifesto* and *Capital*. And the more he read by Marx, the more value he found in the philosopher's ideas. True to his convictions, Marx didn't just spend his days sitting at a desk at the British Museum, but actively participated in progressive organizations, a bridge between theory and practice.

In philosophy classes, when he assigned the *Communist Manifesto*, some students balked at reading it because at the name "Karl Marx" their heads filled with images of Stalinist gulags or the killing fields of the Khmer Rouge under Pol Pot. But would you blame Jesus for the Inquisition, for all the atrocities committed in his name? Human beings have an uncanny ability to rationalize their murderous acts by invoking the words of the Buddha, Yahweh or anyone else they can hide behind. Would you flush the Bible down the toilet because of all the bigotry and pain caused throughout history by true believers who used it to legitimize their nefarious ends? "Have your read the three volumes of *Capital*? *The German Ideology*, *The Civil War in France*, *The Philosophic and Political Manuscripts of 1844*, *Grundrisse*?" They would stare at him with blank eyes. "Don't you think it unfair to condemn a philosopher without having read his books? How lazy to reach for the easy answer, just dismiss Marx by blaming his work for how others have chosen to interpret it, distort it or use it. Let's do justice to Marx; let's read his works with an open mind, approach the texts with charity and a suspension of judgment. After having read the texts and making sure we understand them, then we can critically evaluate them," he would tell them. Did they heed his words?

THE OLD MAN looked up from the recliner at the row of books by Marx on the shelves. He had read recently that the philosopher's memorial had been repeatedly vandalized at Highgate to the extent that cameras had been placed on nearby trees to discourage further attacks. He tried to imagine the mindset of people who defaced or vandalized graves and tombstones but couldn't. Marx was a philosopher who elaborated a method for social analysis, he tried to predict certain courses of events based on the conditions at the time, but his method was historical. And Marxism is not a monolithic doctrine; there are different schools of thought and divergent interpretations. "I am not a Marxist," Marx wrote once, when confronted with the views of some Marxists.

In the 1960s and 1970s he had believed that things were improving: there was the war on poverty, the Civil Rights Act, the free speech movement. But now in the name of justice, free speech was curtailed, books, monuments and people attacked or erased. Truth, facts, objectivity, rationality and open-mindedness retreated under the onslaught of fake news, conspiracy thinking, political correctness, identity politics and tribalism.

The old man picked up his phone and opened the photo album of the London trip. They had gone to the Tate, and he had taken several photos of paintings. He stopped scrolling when he saw *Ophelia,* the painting by John Everett Millais. In Shakespeare's *Hamlet*, Ophelia, before drowning in a river, sings. In Millais's painting, her golden flowing skirt floats among flowers on the surface of a river; only her outstretched hands and her upper torso are above the water. Elizabeth Siddal, the nineteen-year-old model for Ophelia, later became an artist and poet, married the artist Dante Gabriel Rossetti and died at thirty-two. She was buried at Highgate Cemetery. He couldn't remember seeing her tomb and felt a desire to go back and spend more time walking down the lanes of the old cemetery, under the trees and the sky of London, and find her grave. He also found out that Mary Ann Evans, who wrote under the pen name of George Eliot, was buried there. In English class at Central Union High School they had been assigned *Silas Marner,* one of the first novels in English he had ever read. He had roamed in the place where she was buried but hadn't noticed her grave. He felt a pang of regret.

THEY FLEW from London to Amsterdam, where they spent a week. What did the old man remember? Not much: the rain; getting almost run over by an onslaught of bicycle traffic when he made the mistake of standing like a fool in the bike lane; tall glasses of golden Brand Weizen beer; the Rijksmuseum under a brooding October sky; Vermeer's maiden pouring milk; noisy birds hiding in restless crowns of trees in Vondelpark; boats moored alongside canals; rippling water reflecting pearl light; the wind; two bicycles rattling by over a bridge; the smallest car he had ever laid eyes on, red, like one of the toy cars his aunt Avia used to surprise him with; cheeses on shops' shelves like precious tomes in a medieval library. The reason they were there was to go to the Van Gogh Museum, where they spent a morning walking through galleries of the great artist's paintings. As a student at Imperial Valley College he had checked out of the library a huge art book of the artist's works, and he had spent hours looking at the illustrations, dreaming of seeing the paintings one day, and now he was surrounded by them. He felt like a pilgrim who finally made it to the holy site. As they walked around in the afternoon, the old man came across a stylized statue of René Descartes holding a huge book close to his chest. The French philosopher lived there for many years in the early part of the seventeenth century, since in Amsterdam there was freedom of thought. The house they rented, with the steepest staircases he had ever seen, was spacious and comfortable, and the old man liked to rest on the bed looking at the imperious elms behind the bedroom window and listen to the sighing of the wind through the branches. Yes, he did fondly remember that: resting on the bed in the afternoon looking at the leaves shake as if alive, the branches struggling, and beyond them, other houses, where people lived, had probably lived for years, unlike him, who was just passing through. He didn't speak Dutch; he was just a tourist, an ephemeral apparition.

∽

Struggles Against Time

THEY DEPARTED Amsterdam for Braunschweig on a cold, overcast morning to visit Stephanie's friend Edith and her husband, then went on to Berlin. What was in Berlin? The Pergamon Museum and Hegel's grave.

Edith had studied art history before embarking on an adventure in South America in the 1970s. She eventually found her way to San Diego, where she befriended Stephanie. Edith worked for a while at the Unicorn, a small theater in the back of the Mithras bookstore in La Jolla, and the old man wondered if perhaps she had stood behind the counter when he and his friend Larry went there to buy books and watch art films at the Unicorn. Edith moved back to Germany and married, and in the early nineties came to visit with Carl.

The morning after they arrived in Braunschweig, Edith took them to the Altstadtmarkt, a short walk from the hotel. Rows of tables protected by red canopies were flanked by the radiating chapels of the Church of Saint Martin and the old town hall, featuring pumpkins, apples, pomegranates, grapes, cauliflowers, eggs, meats and cheeses, amid the scent of baked bread and pastries. The market had been in existence for 700 years, and the old man, walking on cobblestones, felt deep inside a shift in time. As he looked at the church's Gothic spires, with clouds passing behind them, it could have been the twelfth century.

While Carl, an architect, worked in a spacious studio downtown, Edith took them to the picturesque town of Goslar, to the Jakob-Kemenate Art Gallery, to museums, the Bibliotheca Augusta and Lessinghaus in Wolfenbüttel.

As the old man walked inside the main building of the library, built in the late 1800s in the style of a Florentine palazzo, he held his breath at the sight of red stone columns with gilded Corinthian capitals and a million books on three levels, from floor to ceiling. What would he have thought as the child who sat on the living room floor and gazed at the few books and magazines on the shelves of his bookcase?

Near the Bibliotheca Augusta stood the yellow house of Gotthold Lessing, the eighteenth-century philosopher and art critic who wrote *Laocoön, An Essay on the Limits of Painting and Poetry,* one of the texts Professor Rosenstein had assigned for his course in aesthetics at San Diego State University. The title of Lessing's essay refers to a statue group representing the Trojan priest Laocoön, who is struggling with his two sons against a giant snake. The old man had seen the *Laocoön* at the Vatican Museums almost thirty years earlier, had marveled at the 2,000-year-old statue, and now he was standing in front of Lessing's house, the author of the text he had read as a student. Space and time seemed to contract, disparate events to coalesce. A long dead philosopher's book, a 2,000-year-old Greek statue brought to Rome, and in a different part of the globe at a different time, a young student had read the book and would decades later see the statue, and now as an old man, stand in front of Lessing's house.

Then on to Berlin. Edith and Carl were going to visit a friend there, so they gave the old man and Stephanie a ride. On the way they stopped at Potsdam to take a walk in the Park Sanssouci, and they crossed a street named after Schopenhauer. Professor Polich, in his course on the diplomatic history of Europe, had lectured on the Potsdam Conference. Stalin, Truman, Churchill and Chiang Kai-shek had met there to discuss the terms for the surrender of Japan. And now, more than half a century later, the old man was there. Under an opalescent sky the gilded arches of King Frederick the Great's palace shone in contrast to the green dome and the dark roof. A vast park with more than a thousand sculptures, trees and plants, stately buildings in Neoclassic and German Romantic styles, it made history palpable, something he could feel in the cold air.

He remembered *Wings of Desire*, the film by Wim Wenders where angels stand on the tallest buildings and look over the German capital. *Berlin Alexanderplatz*, the fifteen-hour miniseries by Rainer Werner Fassbinder; *Before the Deluge*, a history of Berlin in the 1920s, and how many more films and books had he seen and read about the city? So much history, art and architecture in Berlin. The State Museum, the Brandenburg Gate, Republic Square, the Art Library. But they had only three days in the city—not enough.

They could spend barely two hours in the afternoon at the Gemäldegalerie, with works by Caravaggio, Giotto, Botticelli, Veronese, Ghirlandaio and so many others. He recognized paintings he had admired in art books, savored late at night sitting in his chair, the study in penumbra, the lamp illuminating the plates. He had felt an intimate, personal bond with them, and now he stood in front of the originals.

But so many paintings and so little time—time, again, the whore that urges you to come as fast as you can, the carnival attendant who tells you the ride is over, the waiter who makes you feel like you're staying at the table too long after you've finished your meal. Time that passes too slowly when you're a child and itch to be an adult, time that passes too fast when you're old, rushing you to your death. Fucking time.

But time was not going to rob him of what he had really wanted to do in Berlin—visit Hegel's grave and go to the Pergamon Museum.

After a long walk, they finally found the Dorotheenstadt Cemetery. It was a cool October afternoon, and after much searching among graves, Edith finally came upon Hegel's tomb. With trepidation he stood next to it—how much he had read and thought about this philosopher! It was the spring of 1974 when he had taken a course on Hegel's *Phenomenology of Spirit*, Dr. Walter Koppelman sitting on the edge of the desk smoking a Camel as he thundered against "the worst book ever written on Hegel, *The Open Society and Its Enemies* by Karl Popper." Then the *Science of Logic* and other works, so many years spent with Hegel's books, and now he stood next to the tombstone of the great thinker.

Hegel, the philosopher of determinate negation, recognition and unity, had, after many years of struggle, acceded to the chair of philosophy in Berlin in 1818 and taught there until his death in 1831. He had asked to be buried next to Johann Fichte, who with his wife was buried to the left of Hegel. The old man was surprised to see the grave of Herbert Marcuse nearby. Lloyd Farrar, the old man's former history professor and friend, had taken courses from Marcuse at Columbia. Marcuse taught at the University of California in San Diego from 1965 to 1970, tempestuous years when the local newspaper, the American Legion and politicians demanded he be fired and the KKK sent him death threats. The old man's thesis chairman, Andrew Feenberg, had worked on a PhD under Marcuse. So much time spent reading and thinking about *One Dimensional Man*, *Eros and Civilization*, *An Essay on Liberation* and other works, and the old man now stood in front of the philosopher's grave.

The playwright and poet Bertolt Brecht's tomb lay in front of a red brick wall. It was simple: a rough triangular rock with the great writer's name in white written in front. Below it, on the soil, among leaves and a bouquet of purple carnations, ballpoint pens of different colors were stuck in the ground.

Dietrich Bonhoeffer, the Christian theologian executed by the Nazis in 1945, was also buried there. The old man had read in his youth Bonhoeffer's *The Cost of Discipleship*. Memories of books, ideas, left by human beings long gone; stones with names, and under them the mortal remains of those men once alive who thought and wrote. The old man wandered among the graves; it was cold, silent. Somehow he felt closer to those thinkers who spoke to him from the past.

∽

THE DAY OF DEPARTURE ARRIVED. They had to catch a flight in the afternoon, but in the morning they went to the Pergamon Museum.

Throughout the years, perusing art books, he had admired works housed in this museum, and for decades he had wanted to go there, to stand in front of the great altar of Pergamon. Unfortunately, the altar was being restored and therefore unavailable. Just like the time when he had stood in line for hours at the Vatican to see Raphael's fresco *The School of Athens*, only to look at a tarp covering the work and a sign that said it was being restored. They had to leave Berlin in just a few hours; they could only stay in the museum for an hour and a half.

The Ishtar Gate, built by King Nebuchadnezzar in the sixth century BCE, fifty feet high, transported him back in time. He wanted to stand in front of it as it had been 2,600 years earlier, and experienced again the passing of time as painful loss, erasure, annihilation. And yet, how bizarre that after so much time, due to thousands of fortuitous events he was born and was now looking at it in a museum in Germany. Glazed blue bricks with bas-reliefs of dragons, bulls and lions adorned the walls. He wished he could read the king's inscription in Akkadian cuneiform. When this part of the great Babylonian gate was built, pre-Socratic philosophers in Greece were beginning to move away from mythological thinking. Thales, Anaximander, Anaximenes.

He noticed the Law Code Stele of King Hammurabi, which he had seen in books and documentaries: seven feet tall, with a depiction in relief of Hammurabi receiving the laws from the sun god Shamash and below it, in cuneiform, the laws. he wanted to meditate in front of these works for a long time, feel something that could connect him to those artifacts from thousands of years past, but there were people around, and time was short.

Just before leaving, his eyes rested on the robed head of a priestess of Athena, and the priestess met his eyes. If he could have traveled back to 120 BCE, if he could have spoken her language, what could she have told him? What did a priestess of Athena do? Probably take care of temple duties: cleaning, keeping the sacred fire lit? Jung would have said he projected his anima in that marble head.

On the plane back home, the old man kept thinking about what he had experienced, and was even more certain of what he used to tell his students in the humanities course back in 1992 at Southwestern College. Statues, paintings, frescoes and architectural forms are synthesized history, culture, ideas, feelings, values, hopes and dreams. They are gifts left on the shore of the present by the waves of time, like the coconut the sea had offered Stephanie and him at Torrey Pines Beach, when they had broken it and eaten it in celebration of their love.

28

SAN DIEGO, 2017

The old man stopped looking at photos and glanced at Berry, who slept soundly in his little bed at the foot of the bookcase. It pained him to think the dog was deaf and blind. If it were possible, he would have gotten the dog hearing aids and taken him to have cataract surgery.

The old man got up and went to bed. It took him a long time to fall asleep; then the haunting began.

The laughing face of the French philosopher Julien Offray de La Mettrie. "It's all mechanism, hormones, enzymes, glands, needs, stinking flesh and bad breath, digestion, piss and shit," De la Mettrie whispers and disappears. The old man feels something in his nose and starts to pull it out. It's a bloody throbbing thing with tentacles and a head covered with veins and nerves. He screams in the void at the thing falling in the darkness. A woman lying naked on a bed laughs as she bends over her legs and starts to devour her feet.

After he had taken a hot shower and dressed, after coffee, in the light of day, the old man's sense of the world regained a certain stability. He proceeded to go about the usual everyday tasks, and in their familiarity the sense of "being me" carried him through the hours. But as the sun set and the day withdrew, the world closed in, and when the time came to go to bed, as he glanced at his parchment paper skin, at his crooked fingers, he shrank into himself and was once again locked in, doomed, condemned.

He sat on the sofa in the family room, the TV ten feet in front of him, and glanced at the collection of films on discs in the wall niche to his right. All the films referred to the human condition. They had to do with the doings of people. And wasn't everything else also a reflection of human beings? Philosophy, history, art, the sciences—all expressions of humanity. Was there anything outside of the human? Even nature and other animals were perceived and understood through human lenses. Even God.

And if he wanted to go beyond human representations, if he wanted to talk of the ground of being, of the mystery, it was still in human concepts and language that he could frame the questions and answers, which would have been a particular perspective; he yearned for a "cosmically objective point of view," for the Truth. He began to feel the walls closing in. He was not just a consciousness trapped in an old body, he was trapped in a particular way of perceiving, in a historical, socially and linguistically structured reality. He had understood this for most of his life, but at certain moments, that realization expanded inside of him to fill him up like a balloon that could burst.

When he taught the course on the world's religions, he had asked the students to keep a spiritual journal. Most of the entries dealt with the ups and downs of their relationships, especially with boyfriends or girlfriends. Their thinking was in response to bodily and emotional needs, and if they thought about religion or the meaning of life, it was shaped by their conditioning, by the ideology they had been indoctrinated with. Their goals were to earn as much money as they could, get married, buy a house and a new car, have children and buy all the toys everybody wanted.

He wasn't surprised, but it saddened him to think that human beings were embedded in their cocoons of bodily demands and ideology; they were in the Matrix, content to provide the capitalist machine with power. But wasn't he also in the Matrix? To be a human being was to be locked up in a cage, forever. But there was an escape—non-being. When he died, he would be free of the cage. Was that the ultimate liberation? To escape the wheel of samsara? A kind of nirvana? Nothingness?

While watching the news, he saw photos of well-known people who had died in advanced old age, images that brought to mind what he had seen decades earlier and felt when he had gone to visit his grandfather at the convalescent hospital. Men and women who had been squeezed by time into twisted, shriveled husks. He had been seventeen at the time, and what he had seen was an apparition from hell, something that had nothing to do with him; but now, in his seventies, he wasn't very far from hell.

He glanced at a card of the Virgin Mary propped up on a shelf of the bookcase adjacent to the chair.

Ricardo Jimenez had given it to him the day he went to see him a few months after the retreat at Redlands, back in 1992. He had told Ricardo of his interest in mysticism, and the old accountant said he would call one of the monks at the retreat and have *The Dark Night of the Soul* by Saint John of the Cross and Saint Teresa's *Interior Castle* sent to him. A few weeks later the middle-aged man received the books, and now the old man wondered if he had ever thanked Ricardo for them. The old man had recently found out Ricardo had died in 2003, and he didn't remember visiting him after 1992. He saw him sitting behind his desk, smiling like Anthony Quinn, the first time he met him in the summer of 1963, and now he was dead.

I should have gone to see him, or at least written to him, sent him a card, he thought, and felt a pang of regret. The same pain he had felt when he found out Larry, who had been his best friend for many years, had died in 2019 in a hospital bed in Indiana. In the mid-nineties, Larry's meth addiction caused him to be fired from his job. He couldn't repair his car, was evicted from his apartment and had no other choice than to accept an offer by his sister to move to Indiana to live with her and her husband. He left his cat, books and collection of record albums behind, and a few months later, had converted to Christianity and found salvation in Jesus. The old man and Larry had talked a few times on the phone and had exchanged a couple of letters, but years passed without any communication.

Larry eventually moved into his own apartment, worked as a clerk in a bookstore and then as the manager of a Jiffy Lube until he retired. The last time the old man had talked to him was years earlier, on the phone. Larry wanted to move back to San Diego; he longed to see the ocean, walk on the Ocean Beach Pier, go see a film at the Ken. Then there were no more calls or letters. Why hadn't he written to Larry? He remembered when Larry was in his early twenties, how open to the world he had been, eager to read literature, listen to music, go see films by Bergman and Fellini. Now he was dead, and that was the end of the story. He experienced the same feeling of having been a bad friend, when he had delayed calling Lloyd, and then on the day he had planned to do so, Lloyd had shot himself.

As he sat there, reclining in his chair, looking at the *Expulsion from Paradise*, what he called the inexorable began to seep into him. There was no way to stop it, except by ending his life. Sartre would have said he was still free, free to go on living or to kill himself, but it didn't feel like freedom to him. Impermanence. All things must pass. *Panta rei*. He turned his head toward the bookcase on the left side. On the topmost shelf he spotted Lucretius's *On the Nature of Things*. He got up, retrieved it and sat down again. He opened the book to the page he had marked with a Post-it note years earlier and read: "Why moan and wail at death? If your life's been happy and blessed, and all those blessings haven't been poured into a leaky pot to spill away, with nothing left to give thanks for, why not, as a man who's feasted full of life, retire contented—fool!— and rest in peace?" Then the author has nature speak to the old man who is afraid of death and wants to go on living: "Give it up, old man, it doesn't become your years. Come, be content! Give way to your heirs! You must."

But it's easier to accept the thought of old age and death when one is young. When he was in his twenties, old age was in the distant future, fifty years away, an unthinkable amount of time; but when he got there, it was a different story. What Lucretius said made sense, but the actual process was not going to be so clean and neat. The wear and tear on the old man's body was going to continue until something gave out. His body at some point was going to betray him, and the end might be slow and painful.

The old man was thankful for having lived a long life, but he refused to take the impending end stoically. Like Jons the squire at the end of Bergman's *The Seventh Seal*, he would do so under protest. There were people who faced their deaths with grace and equanimity, but he wondered how many who scoffed at his attitude, those who told him they did not fear the end, would still be unafraid when death was so near they could feel its breath on their faces. Or would the ultimate truth explode inside of them like a supernova, a blinding flash where everything dissolved, their relationships, projects, the foundations of their lives?

In hospitals and in patients' homes he had seen how the story ends, and often it didn't end well. There was palliative care, morphine, and according to Kübler-Ross, acceptance. Death could be made painless. But at the end of the journey, as we lay dying, the past gone and the future canceled, all we would have left is the realization that the curtain was about to fall. The theoretical physicist Carlo Rovelli ends his book

The Order of Time by saying that at the end of our lives, "we can close our eyes, rest. This all seems fair and beautiful to me." Perhaps that was the way it has to be: death is part of life, a cold, logical necessity. But beautiful?

The old little dog slept peacefully next to the Wittgenstein works; the warm light shimmered on the books on the shelves. The old man shifted his weight in the chair, laid his eyes on the *Expulsion*. He moved his head and felt his neck creak. More than half a century had passed since that night when he stayed up to read *Nausea*. Then at the university, he read *Being and Nothingness,* and accepted Sartre's claim that we are radically free. As his eyes ran over the spines of Sartre's books, his thoughts returned to the French existentialist, slick hair combed back, his wandering eye staring, a pipe in his mouth.

When the old man thought back over his life, he understood that in many circumstances he had not been free. He was determined by genes, social and cultural inputs, the biochemistry of his brain, by so many layers of *facticity* that resulted in his having acted as he did. Besides genetic determinants, his parents' educational-social-economic conditions, how others related to him, and the cultural shock he had undergone when he found himself suddenly in a small desert town in California, when overnight his linguistic eloquence disappeared and he struggled in shame to speak in a new language with a heavy accent —all this shaped his personality and behavior.

Divorced, pacing back and forth in mental health units, behind bars in county jail, unemployed and living in his parents' house, the question had presented itself with increasing force: what was he going to do with his life? First question to answer, did he want to live? *Let's not speak falsely now, for the hour is getting late.* Yes, he did. Then the question became, how? Did he want to live in and out of mental health units, find himself in middle age living in a rehab center someplace, perhaps on disability, alone? No, if he was going to live, he wanted to live in his own place, and he wanted to have a long-lasting relationship with a woman. That meant he needed a job, and so he began to force himself to do what he could not do before: suffer through the pain and fear of social interactions, until slowly, he began to feel more self-confident, more able. And when his maintenance needs were met, when he could pay the rent and have reliable transportation, like Abraham Maslow showed in his hierarchy of needs, he could think about his self-actualization, hence his efforts at finding a significant other and a philosophy teaching position. There were times when he could have told himself, "I suffer from depression and severe anxiety disorder, I cannot work," but he wanted a different life. Perhaps, given all his genetic, physiological determinants and all his environmental inputs, he could not have done otherwise. But he chose to see it as an instance of existentialist freedom.

The old man took a sip of water from the bottle he kept on the table next to the easy chair, and in putting it back something fell on the floor. It was the Nakaya fountain pen he had bought in Tokyo two years earlier, and he began to think about his grandparents' native land.

As a child, he became aware of Japan by contemplating his father's photo on the bedside stand, and by his mother telling him his father was a Japanese American; by people staring as if he had been a funny animal at the zoo, by kids throwing rocks as they chanted "little Chinaman," by the priest calling him Chou En-lai, by the sound of his last name, by hiding in the dark space between the school building and the wall, afraid to walk in. To many people who didn't even know Japan existed, he was Chinese. He had almond eyes and big ears, and his last name was a source of derision. Just walking to school and going to the store for his mother were often frightening tasks; what were people going to think and say when they looked at him?

When his father came to Genova from his journeys on the merchant ship USS *Exchester*, and they went to a bar for an ice cream or a Coca-Cola, some people stared with an uncomprehending expression, as if their world had been put in question, threatened, and he felt the blood rushing to his face. He shrank in the chair as he sipped his glass of warm soda and felt as if he didn't belong, as if there was something wrong with him, as if he was guilty of having been born.

When they moved to El Centro, he had met the Japanese side of the family: his grandfather, uncles, aunts and cousins. His grandmother had died the year before, so his only memory of her was of some old photos. When his grandfather became too ill to live by himself, he moved in with them, and when the boy found out he had to share his room with him he became despondent. His grandfather rubbed Ben-Gay ointment on his legs, and as the boy lay on his bed at night, he hated the pungent smell. His grandfather had worked for the Santa Fe Railroad in New Mexico, then moved with his wife and children to Imperial Valley, where he grew lettuce, tomatoes and cantaloupes. He lived with them for a year, until he suffered a stroke and moved to a convalescent home.

The boy was now in America, his country, the land of freedom and equality. But in high school his last name was still a source of mockery, and he was often mistaken for a Mexican. At times people started speaking to him in Spanish and he felt embarrassed. He lived with the Japanese in him as if it were a congenital disease, a kind of mark of Cain that he tried to push out as if it had been embedded inside him.

It wasn't until much later that the young man began to think more about the land of his grandparents' birth. At the university he had read Yasunari Kawabata's *The Sound of the Mountain,* the story of an older man who must learn to accept the unhappy lives of his son and daughter. Meditative and lyrical, the story had impressed him with the quality of the writing, and when he reread it thirty years later, he understood more deeply the protagonist, with his feelings of regrets and disappointments. The next time he went to the campus bookstore, back in 1975, he found a small paperback novel by Kawabata, *Snow Country,* which he finished in a day. A love story between a married man and a geisha, the short novel lingered in him and wouldn't leave him alone. It read in parts like haikus: "The train moved off into the distance, its echo fading into a sound as if of the night wind. Cold air flooded the room." He liked how Kawabata made the reader feel the characters' states of mind through descriptions of nature: "She seemed on edge like some restless night beast that fears the approach of the morning."

His cousin Gary, a student at UCSD, had given him a book by Yukio Mishima, *Confessions of a Mask*. A novel about a man who from childhood is attracted to members of the same sex, and through adolescence and adulthood has to hide his feelings behind a mask of conventionality, the book allowed the reader to enter into the psyche of the protagonist, and to see how hard the struggle is to conform to societal expectations, especially in the protagonist's time, militaristic, Imperial Japan.

The young man then read other books by Mishima, including *The Sailor Who Fell from Grace with the Sea*, a short novel about a sailor who falls in love with the widowed mother of a boy. He enchants the boy and his friends with tales of his glorious exploits at sea, but when the sailor marries the widow and decides to renounce his adventurous life, the disappointed boy and his friends kill him.

When the young man read the novel, he hadn't liked it because he had wished for a different ending, with the sailor and the widow living happily together. But the book challenged him to go beyond his distaste for unhappy endings and to think about what drove the characters. The teenage boy and his gang were motivated by their nihilist philosophy, and they projected on the sailor their dreams of adventure and glory. When the sailor gave up his life at sea, they felt betrayed, and by killing the sailor they not only avenged their dreams but also kept him from becoming just another married man living a conventional life. The more the young man thought about the ideas and feelings moving the characters, the more he liked Mishima's novel.

He used to scoff at his father's interest in *chambara* (sword-fighting) movies, but after seeing Akira Kurosawa's *The Seven Samurai* and *Rashomon*, he rented most of the films by Kurosawa, who besides samurai movies also crafted fine dramas set in the postwar period. The young man became more interested in Japanese cinema and started to look at the works of other Japanese film directors. Kenji Mizoguchi showed women's struggles in Japan, and Yasujiro Ozu, who began his career in the silent movie era, made films based on family relations. He used mostly a static camera at a low height.

Stephanie, the middle-aged man's wife, rented a VHS copy of a movie by Hayao Miyazaki, *Totoro*, for his son to watch. The middle-aged man loved the animation and music of the magical film about two little girls who move with their parents to rural Japan. They discover under a tree a huge, magical bearlike creature. The middle-aged man rented other films by Miyazaki and watched them over and over again. Unlike Hollywood animated films, Miyazaki's were hand drawn, and they were more nuanced and delved deeper into the psychology and emotions of the characters, who were mostly children. All the Japanese books and films he collected boosted his interest in the land from which half of his genes came. He wanted to go visit the land of his father's ancestors.

His father was dead, as were his uncles and aunts, so he couldn't ask them questions concerning their past. He knew his grandparents had been born in Fukuoka, but he didn't know if they grew up in the city or one of the surrounding villages. His grandfather had immigrated to the United States in 1904, his grandmother in 1915.

It was almost two in the afternoon on October 23, 2018, when he and Stephanie departed San Diego for Tokyo. Ten hours later, in the early dawn, the plane neared Narita International Airport. The sea was a cerulean vastness as they flew over the curved coast of Chiba Prefecture, with its green fields and white buildings. Over the roar of the plane's engines, they heard the overhead announcement of the final approach, then the landing. Hours later, after taking the Narita Express to Tokyo Station and a taxi ride, they were finally able to rest. The next day, from their Richmond Hotel room in the Asakusa district, a new cityscape presented itself: plane and dogwood trees, temples with arched roofs, high-rises dwarfed by even taller buildings and the Skytree tower looming in the background.

He still felt jet-lagged when they went to see a play at the National Noh Theatre. The name of the play was *Chikubu-shima*, which meant nothing to the old man, who had never seen a Noh play before. The inside of the theater, built of polished cypress, had a soothing effect. His eyes rested on the stylized pine tree painted on the front wall as spectators streamed in and sat down; then from the side stage actors wearing masks and colorful customs walked in. Players sat on stools and began to play flutes and drums, and the actors danced, spoke and chanted under the warm overhead lights. The old man felt transported to another world. An emissary of Emperor Daigo goes to Lake Biwa to pray at the shrine of Benzaiten, the Buddhist goddess of wisdom and the arts. On the lake's shore he meets a woman and then an old fisherman, who takes them on a boat to Chikusu island, home of the shrine. As the emissary admires the scenery, the fisherman and the woman tell him the history of the island, and when they arrive, the woman says she's a spirit and enters the shrine, while the old fisherman reveals himself to be the spirit of Lake Biwa and disappears. As the emissary is praying in the shrine, the goddess Benzaiten appears in a vision, and as the moon shines over the lake, a dragon god emerges from the waves and offers the emissary precious gems and a blessing. Then they vow to rescue all living beings from suffering. The celestial maiden enters the shrine, and the dragon god returns in the lake. After the performance, the old man and his wife walked around the theater's garden and talked about the play and how mesmerizing it had been.

They visited temples with landscaping shaped into art and went on a night walking tour of the Asakusa district with Satoru, a guide and sake sommelier. He was a pleasant middle-aged man with a slight limp who spoke English well. He showed them small temples and the old red-light district, and he brought them to the top floor of a skyscraper where they could admire the view. At the end of the tour, he took them down a deserted side street where a single lamp shone above a burlap curtain. They walked into a small eatery, where they were greeted by a smiling older woman who brought them rice cakes and beer.

Ueno Park, covering more than 130,000 acres, with nine thousand trees and a small lake, had been the site of a major battle in the Boshin War of 1868 and in the cool of evening, the old man and Stephanie walked through it to the National Museum of Western Art, where he was surprised to see paintings by Van Gogh, El Greco and Renoir, along with many artists he hadn't heard of, such as Léonard Tsuguharu Foujita, a Japanese French painter. Many of his paintings included cats, and his portraits showed a synthesis of Japanese and French influences that were uncanny.

The old man and his wife visited other museums and art galleries and the Imperial Palace grounds, and walked around the Ginza at night, the restless bright neon signs on the sides of skyscrapers making one forget it was late and time to get some sleep. One night they went up to the top floor of Skytree, one of the world's tallest towers, and from the observation deck a phantasmagoric view of the city surrounded them. The old man felt inconsequential. Fourteen million people lived and worked down there, in that ocean of lights.

They devoted the day before leaving Tokyo to the Ghibli Museum. The old man had collected the films made by Miyazaki, and going to the Ghibli was a visit he had looked forward to for many years. They joined a day tour guided by a friendly woman named Mikko. As part of the tour, they stopped for lunch at the Hotel Gajoen, because Miyazaki drew inspiration for his Oscar-winning film *Spirited Away* from its luxurious interior with its double-tiered stories, ancient art silkscreens and koi ponds. After an exquisite lunch they rode on to the museum, where they spent a couple of hours seeing Miyazaki's original artwork and movie props.

IT TOOK several hours on an old diesel train to get to Takayama, a town in the Hida region of Gifu Prefecture, renowned for its healing hot springs. From the apartment in their hotel they had a grand view of the town and the mountains in the distance. In the evenings, soaking in the *onsen* bath with the window open, the steaming hot water and the cold air took their fatigue and worries away.

The next day they walked under dark clouds on a pedestrian street along the Miyagawa River, lined on the left side with shops and restaurants and on the right, by stalls with canvas canopies. Women and men bundled up in jackets sold cabbages, green onions, pomegranates, persimmons and apples. Other vendors offered jackets and gloves. At the end of the street, Stephanie noticed a restaurant. "Look, *Hida Beef, Takayama Ramen*, the sign says—let's try it," she suggested. Inside, they ordered at the counter and sat by a window overlooking the river. On the windowsill, two potted plants framed the view. The turbulent, muddy water flowed below, and from the window's left side he could see double lantern posts and electrical wires crisscrossing the pearl sky. At the bottom, a black retaining wall ran down to the insistent water. The waitress arrived with two steaming plates of Japanese beef curry, but he kept looking at a tall white building. It reminded him of ancient Greece. Who designed it and when, and for what purpose? And then the other buildings, tall, short, narrow and wide, alcoves, brown and charcoal-gray walls, the TV antennas, the air-conditioning boxes—he was looking at a blend of different historical periods and cultures, and they had congealed in the view out the window. "Eat your curry—it's the best I've ever had," Stephanie said. She was right, it was delicious, and as he ate he marveled at how history revealed itself in the scene out the window.

THEY HAD fun walking from the town to the hotel. It was a steep climb, but they were rewarded by the small vegetable gardens that dotted the hilly landscape. As they rounded a bend, one in particular caught his attention. It had rows of dark green onions, ornamental bamboo with crimson flowers, purple, white and pink asters, more rows of turnips and cabbages and a small gray wooden shed with a faded red roof in a corner. It could very well have been part of a Miyazaki film. He expected a couple of children to start running across it, maybe followed by a Totoro. The houses looked different from the stucco and wood structures so popular in Southern California, and later as they relaxed in their hotel apartment after an *onsen* bath, sipping sake and admiring the fiery, brooding sky hanging over the mountains, the old man wished he could have lived in that place. He loved the red maples and tall yellow ginkgoes, the aquamarine skies and white clouds. They had gone to Shiroyama Park, and as they walked up the trail, with each step on the light brown soil and gray roots, minuscule green ferns, yellow and burgundy leaves, he felt part of a Monet painting.

They saw an advertisement on a bulletin board about a Hiroshige exhibit at the Hikaru Museum, so one morning they decided to go. In 2011 they had gone to the San Diego Museum of Art and some prints by Hiroshige were on display. He had been enchanted by the colors and the compositions, and his wife had bought him a book of postcards of the artist's famous *One Hundred Famous Views of Edo*, which he never sent to anyone, because he liked to sit in his chair late at night, look at the prints and dream about crimson skies and white cherry blooms on trees, temples' white roofs and red walls, white foxes and fires around a tall tree at night, stars in the bare branches, people hurrying on a wooden bridge under a heavy rain. He would imagine himself in the scenes, living in a different world, a world of beauty. Hiroshige had influenced many European painters, including Monet, Manet and Van Gogh.

Built on a hill overlooking the town, the Hikaru Museum was a wide, squat multileveled building with small windows and geometric decorations. It took a long bus ride to reach the white structure that from a distance reminded the old man of the Mayan ruins he had seen in art books. Inside, the Mayan motifs continued, with long, wide stairways, white and light brown stones, high multilevel ceilings and imposing halls with geometric designs.

They admired the fifty-three stations of *Tokaido Highway* by Utagawa Hiroshige, who died in 1858. The highway connected Edo (present-day Tokyo) to Kyoto and had fifty-three rest areas with government stations. It must have taken travelers, who mostly went on foot, weeks to cover the 320 miles. Hiroshige made the journey in 1832 and recreated the trip in splendid woodcuts depicting the countryside, bridges, people on the roads, stylized pines and mountains. It was easy to get lost in them, to take the journey oneself.

He felt a tinge of sadness when the time came to leave Takayama. After a four-and-a-half-hour Shinkansen bullet train ride, they arrived in Kyoto. Sitting in the back of the taxi on the way to their hotel in heavy traffic, he looked up in disappointment at the skyscrapers. He had associated Kyoto with the films he had seen, with gardens and temples, not with a modern, bustling city of a million and a half inhabitants.

Yes, the temples and gardens were there, but they were crawling with tourists. At the Temple of the Golden Pavilion, which he had read about in Mishima's novel and seen in the Paul Schrader film on Mishima, he and his wife had to wait their turn to take a few photos of the facade. Exuding timeless beauty and peace, its reflection trembled on the pond's surface. A crazy monk had burned it down in 1950, and this was the rebuilt temple. As they walked away, the old man glanced at the bronze phoenix at the roof's peak. He felt like he had entered into Mishima's novel, understood how the temple's beauty had driven the monk to madness.

They continued on the "Philosopher's Path." Extending for a mile along a canal, it was given its name because the philosopher Kitaro Nishida often took this path for meditation. The old man had read some of Nishida's works and was now taking steps on the same path the philosopher followed on the way to the university. Clear water flowed in the canal and cherry trees, maples and gingkoes lined the path. "Look at that coffee shop," said his wife. "'The Philosophy Cafe'—we have to go in there," replied the old man. They were surprised by the barista, a young man who said he was from Austin, Texas. After drinking their cappuccinos, they continued the walk.

After Kyoto, they took the train to Hiroshima. Mountains covered with green trees and red maples, ravines and rivers, fields and farmhouses passed by the window. They had arranged to go on a day tour and spent the morning visiting Miyajima Island. As they waited in line to board the ferry, he thought the island trip a waste of time, but as the ferry approached the little harbor, they saw the red torii gate standing in the water. On land, they were greeted by friendly deer, who walked around among the tourists. They visited the Itsukushima Shinto Shrine, built in the twelfth century. After a lunch of *okonomiyaki*, oysters, scallops and beer, they ate a dessert of "maple leaf" waffles, bought a bottle of sake and returned to the city. They visited the Peace Park, with its monuments and the museum, which was emotionally painful to go through. In a glass enclosure was a rusted little tricycle. It had belonged to a four-year-old boy who was riding in front of his house the morning the atomic bomb detonated over the city. The boy died of radiation burns but his trike was still there, and the old man found it difficult to look at it. He pictured the little boy enjoying the sunny morning when suddenly an intense flash left him blind and burned. After several hours in agony, he mercifully died.

They visited the famous Genbaku Dome in Chuo Park. As a child, the old man had seen the A-bomb Dome in old newsreels, then in documentaries and books, and in Alain Resnais's *Hiroshima mon amour*. He stood in front of the ruin, forcing himself not to cry. A palpable sadness entered into him, as if the pain and suffering of tens of thousands still lingered in the air. From a bridge over the Motoyasu River, he turned to see the Dome duplicating itself on the water while trees, rusty red and golden, partially hid the ruin, as if protecting it.

Hiroshima had its beginning as a fishing village in the eleventh century, and it grew in size and importance in the succeeding centuries. Warlords establishing castles and then industrialization and trade turned it into a major city. The old man remembered that in high school, he had been taught that an American invasion of Japan would have resulted in half a million American casualties, so dropping the atomic bomb on Hiroshima and then on Nagasaki had saved lives. But he no longer accepted that rationalization. According to some historians Japan was on the verge of surrender, and the bombs didn't have to be dropped. There were always going to be apologists who claimed the US had no choice, but what happened in Hiroshima and Nagasaki were the most hideous acts of terrorism ever perpetrated. No crass utilitarian calculus could erase the bloody stain on the stars and stripes.

The old man remembered how proud he had been of America, the land—he had believed—of the just and the brave, a strong country confident in its values, built on the principles of fairness, equality and freedom. As he walked around the museum, looking at displays of human beings reduced to etched shadows on walls, seeing clips of the living dead, of men, women and children wandering around with their flesh melting off their bones, reading about the tens of thousands who survived the blast only to die later of leukemia and other cancers brought on by radiation exposure, he felt anger at America.

And then on to Fukuoka. The largest city on Kyushu, the southernmost of Japan's four largest islands, Fukuoka is the capital of a prefecture with several cities, towns and villages.

Did his grandparents live in the city itself or elsewhere in the prefecture? Dating from the stone age, Fukuoka had been invaded twice by Mongols who were defeated by bad weather, including a typhoon the second time, which the grateful citizens called a divine wind (*kamikaze*). Unfortunately, no divine wind kept American planes from firebombing Fukuoka in June 1945, wiping out almost a quarter of the city and killing at least one thousand civilians. The old man wondered if any long distant relative of his had succumbed to the raid.

From their hotel room in the Nakasu district he

could see buildings, white, gray and brown, dotted with windows of different shapes and sizes, roofs with satellite dishes and air-conditioning boxes, and as he looked down, red and yellow signs above shops, dark streets and the faint silhouettes of mountains in the distance.

They took long walks along the promenade by the Naka River, seagulls flying low over bridges, the sky azure, wispy cloud strands like halo rays above businesses and hotels, some with amusing names like "Hotel Amare" and "Hotel Sweety." In the cool of night by the river, walking past the brightly lit food stalls where people sat on chairs and benches eating and drinking beer, mesmerized by the buildings lining both banks that had come alive and restless with bright white, yellow, red and green neon signs reflecting on the shimmering surface, he wondered about his grandparents. Even if they had been born and lived in a nearby town or village, they must have come to the city, but how different it would have been in the late 1800s and early 1900s. Maybe they had walked along the river, had laid their eyes on the old temples before leaving forever for America in search of a better life. After decades of toil, they became successful farmers in the Imperial Valley of Southern California, only to lose everything after Pearl Harbor and be imprisoned in a relocation camp in Poston, Arizona. If they hadn't left this place he wouldn't have been born, but there he was, walking along the river, as they may have done more than a hundred years earlier. A part of themselves had come back to Fukuoka.

THE OLD MAN stretched as he sat in his chair, the warm lamp's glow and all the books keeping him safe. His eyes ran over the shelves where on the edges he had put trinkets and photos. He saw the card advertising the sumo wrestling competition they had gone to on their last day in Fukuoka and felt a pang of nostalgia. As he was growing up, Japan had been what made him different, somehow the reason children had laughed at his almond-shaped eyes and his last name, but when the old man came back from the trip, he felt proud of his Japanese ancestry. He was intrigued by the contrasts: state-of-the-art technology and ancient temples, bustling cities and heavily forested mountains, and by the food, the cleanliness and the politeness of almost everyone. If he had been younger, he would have liked to live in Japan, at least for a few years, to learn the language and experience what it meant to be Japanese, but it was too late.

IN MARCH OF 2021, the old man had lunch with Karim and Gerald, two colleagues from Santa Ana College who were also retired. They talked over plates of Middle Eastern food. Gerald announced that he and his wife were going on a cruise to Hawaii, and Karim said he was thinking of buying a farm in Slovenia, where real estate was cheap, and raising sheep. They promised to meet again in a couple of months, but three weeks after their lunch, Karim suddenly died. The old man and Karim had talked at the college over coffee in the morning, before classes, and often went to lunch or dinner at the Nordstrom restaurant or Luigi's in Anaheim. Karim's funeral service had been videotaped and posted on Facebook. As the old man watched it, he could see Karim's body in the open casket. *What the hell, Karim!* thought the old man. *I just saw you a few weeks ago; we're supposed to get together next month. What are you doing in that casket?* Time marched on, mowing down his friends. Walter and Frank, his high school buddies, were the most recent ones to suddenly die. People got old and died, there was nothing unusual about it, and yet he felt as if time, malevolently, was moving on, inexorably, and he wondered when he would be next.

29

SAN DIEGO, 2022

In October of 2022, the governor of California announced that the state of emergency for Covid-19 would come to an end. There was no longer a shortage of toilet paper or hand sanitizer in stores, and as the pandemic became less threatening, much of the old man's anxiety abated.

In November, the old man and Stephanie flew to Traverse City, Michigan, to visit Renée. He hadn't seen his daughter since 2003, when she came to San Diego with her husband and children. Renée was now 53 years old, thin and frail, and as he hugged her, he closed his eyes for a moment and stopped thinking, because he wanted that hug to last forever, to somehow steal it from time. He remembered the night she was born, the little girl who liked dolls and Walt Disney cartoons. Now that little girl was a middle-aged woman who had lived with multiple sclerosis for twenty-eight years, had seen two of her infant children die, had gone through two divorces and the death of her mother. "I'm so happy you came. It's been too long," she said.

Renée lived in a spacious apartment with Lily, a cute little dog, and liked to collect costume jewelry. She kept a small dish full of peanuts on the floor next to the balcony and loved to watch a chipmunk come in the living room, fill his cheeks with the nuts and run away. She got around with a walker and a woman came twice a week to help her. Lexi, Renée's daughter, had just graduated from the university and was soon going to begin working as a special education teacher. She was a warm, bright young woman, and the old man was proud to have a granddaughter like her. They went to restaurants, gorged themselves on sample dried cherries at the Cherry Republic store, explored pumpkin patches and outdoor markets.

He and Stephanie stayed in Traverse City for five days, and when they left, as he hugged his daughter again, he wished they could have lived closer. "Come back soon," Renée said.

"I will," answered the old man.

BACK HOME, the old man resumed his routine—he tried to get some exercise every day, did chores, participated in family events, had doctors' appointments. Every night, in his easy chair, he exchanged a few texts with his son Michael, who had moved up North to work in social services. Then he read until he felt sleepy, and even though he didn't want to, he dragged himself to bed.

FRIEDRICH NIETZSCHE MATERIALIZES in an easy chair. He's a small man, the burning eyes and mustache those of a strange animal. He's silent for a long time; then he says, "You have accepted the death of God, but only intellectually I'm afraid. Deep down in your guts you're still a Christian wishing for transcendence. You disappoint me." He crosses his right leg over his left and rests his hand on the chair arm. "What the hell are you talking about?" the old man let out, irritated, but in the back of his mind realizing Nietzsche might be right.

He woke up with the burning eyes of Nietzsche still in front of him. It was almost six, time to get up. As he made coffee, he kept thinking about the dream. Was he still a Christian wishing for transcendence? He was not a theist nor a deist; he did not believe in an "ultimate reality," whatever that meant, but deep down he still searched for truth with a capital T. By the Truth he had always meant the way things actually were, the answers to all his big questions. Why is there anything at all, rather than nothing? What is energy, what is the universe, is there any transcendent meaning and purpose for life?

When as a child he rushed to the newsstand in Genova to buy the weekly installment of the encyclopedia, when he read the short essays on Socrates and Plato and looked at the illustrations of what they may have looked like, he thought that if he read enough books, if he studied what those philosophers wrote, he would be able to find out. But the more he read and studied, the more the answers receded in the distance until he realized he was never going to find them. He had started his quest as a child, thinking about life and death, and was now an old man, still wondering. He hadn't found the Truth, but holding the books he had been reading and studying for fifty years—feeling their heft, running his fingers over the cloth covers and smelling the pages—became a kind of truth.

Life was absurd for Sartre and Camus, but for the latter we must imagine Sisyphus happy as he walks down the hill to his rock. Sisyphus is eternally young as he pushes the boulder up and then is able to rest as he walks down, feel the breeze cool his face, rest his eyes on the blue dome of the sky as he hears the buzzing of bees and fills his nostrils with the scent of flowers.

But he was not like Sisyphus. The old man grew sicker and feebler as he pushed his boulder, and his senses grew dim as the fist of time squeezed. "There is thus a will to live without rejecting anything of life, which is the virtue I honor most in this world," says Camus, which is what the guru had told Joseph Campbell during their meeting. As he thought about it, a surge of negation began to swell in his chest. *No, sorry, life is a horror show, the living devouring each other, a phantasmagoric hell, a most cruel game.* A game hidden by the veil of civilization and culture, but as Nietzsche said, "...how much blood and horror is at the bottom of all good things!" But would he have wished not to have been born? No. It was a sort of miracle to be a human being standing on this small planet, gazing at the stars. Yes, there was pain and death but there was also beauty, goodness and love.

He stood on the patio in the backyard and glanced at the pine tree he had raised from the seed he brought back from Albinia almost thirty years earlier. Two doves perched on a lower branch were looking at him. *It's a good day for a ride*, he thought.

It was a cool spring morning as the old man slowed down, approaching a stop sign. The sky above clear, with a few white clouds, the light warm. At the Julian Pie Company he had the usual slice of goodness and a cup of coffee, and now he was going to drive through the Laguna Mountains.

He turned left from State Route 79 to Sunrise Highway and sped up on a stretch of straight road until he reached one hundred miles per hour. The air rushed through the cabin of the Miata, scrambling his hair, and he started to think of the possibility of getting a ticket or even worse, of a tire blowing out and the flimsy roadster going off the road, tumbling over and over in the barren wasteland. It would probably mean instant death, it would keep him from getting older and having to face the indignities and horrors of decrepitude, but he slowed down. Was he prolonging his life out of weakness? The road began to snake around, rise up and drop, and soon on the left side was the barren desert, and in the distance, Anza-Borrego State Park and beyond it the Salton Sea. On the right side stood majestic pines and cedars, rolling grassy meadows and half-hidden cabins. The air carried the scents of pine and sage, and he took a deep breath; the engine hummed, and through the chassis he felt the road. He raised his hand from the steering wheel and looked at it. Yes, like Antonius Block, the knight in *The Seventh Seal*, he could say that blood was still pulsing through his veins, but he wasn't playing chess with death, or was he?

As the car passed the Laguna Mountain Lodge he remembered when he and Stephanie had rented a cabin in the winter of 1992. They had gone for a hike, the ground covered in white, and it had started to snow. Heavy flakes fell just like the day when as a boy in Sella he had walked alone in a field and it began to snow. He had felt alone back then, now he was with a woman he loved and who loved him. Then further down he recalled driving his 1964 blue Chevrolet Bel Air on a snowy winter's night, slowly, as the car kept sliding. What was he doing up there at night, alone? Who knows; he was young. He didn't need a reason to go places. The Chevy could easily have slid off the road, crashed into trees or careened down the mountainside. But when he was young he couldn't imagine his own death.

At the foot of the mountain, he stopped at the Pine Valley County Park to go to the restroom. No one was there that morning, and as he walked back to the car he paused for a few minutes to look at the grass, the tall firs and oaks, at the cement tables and benches. He had been there so many times with parents, friends, wives and children. Just before entering the freeway he put the car's top up, then drove home, his head full of memories.

~

AND SO HE was back in the study, it was almost midnight, and even though tired and sleepy, he couldn't bring himself to go to bed. Here, surrounded by his books, in the warm golden glow of the lamp, he felt protected. His eyes moved toward the *Expulsion,* and he saw himself standing in the Brancacci Chapel in Santa Maria del Carmine; then he recalled the Sunday morning at the Mission de Alcalá Church, during communion when he stood in the pew, and as he told himself that it was all meaningless, joy swept through him. Couldn't this be such a moment? He was in his easy chair, admiring the multicolored spines of the books; it meant nothing in the scheme of things, but in its meaninglessness, wasn't it like a resplendent sand mandala? Wasn't it wonderful? Yet he could imagine so many moments of despair, terror and pain that would not have been wonderful. The hundreds of thousands who died due to Covid-19 and the countless men, women and children who were that very instant being tortured, murdered or abused somewhere in the world negated the thought that every moment, even if meaningless, can be beautiful and joyous. Weak ego boundaries? Perhaps, but no matter how many moments were redeemed by love, beauty and joy, so many others were not. And the time of suffering would come to all.

He sat in the chair, the back of his arms feeling the soft, warm texture of the blanket. He heard the insistent, pitiful barking of a dog up the street. The sound of an occasional vehicle driving by. The hum from the air vent, the background hiss in his ears. He saw the books on the shelves, the angel with the sword hovering over Adam and Eve, naked, walking beyond the gate. His hands, bony, the thick veins protruding. He felt his chest inflating and deflating, his toes warm in the socks. Memories, thoughts, hopes, expectations, regrets, guilt, sorrow, the harlequin patches that made him up—that thin surface dissolved at the realization that each moment dies as it is born, most moments to be lost forever, some to be preserved, distorted, embalmed, mummified in memories. But as his brain aged, as the synapses became more difficult to make, even those embalmed corpses, those mummies, those ghosts, would deteriorate and unravel. Each moment swallowed up, each moment lost, gone, sixty funerals per minute.

Dogen and Heidegger said *we are time*. The old man could retain in memory the moments past, could leap forward to future plans and expectations, could act in the present, an existential sense or experience of entropy made possible by the kind of being he was, but there was something else about time that wasn't him, something that was structural, the very essence or backbone of being. Was it the big white whale of Captain Ahab? The more he thought about Ahab, the more he felt like he understood him. The whale was the mask of time, and like Ahab, he wanted to throw his harpoons at it. *Towards thee I roll, thou all-destroying but unconquering whale; to the last I grapple with thee; from hell's heart I stab at thee; for hate's sake I spit my last breath at thee.*

But wasn't time also what made his very being possible, what made possible the world, life? Wasn't time the giver of life and the destroyer? Dancing Shiva? He glanced at the bronze statuette of the Hindu god he kept on a bookshelf next to the chair. Shiva was surrounded by a circle of fire, holding the tambourine of time in one hand and a flame to annihilate it in another. *Don't be afraid, it's a dance, but in order to dance you have to subdue your ego demands to crave, to want.* What did the old man want? Eternal youth? To live forever? He would not have been human then, but a god. His eyes moved up to Adam and Eve as they walked out of Eden in despair. They had lost immortality but gained the world. Would he want to walk in, remain in Eden forever and be immortal? What would he do there?

He took a deep breath. Maybe Bruno, one of the characters in Dino Risi's film *Il Sorpasso*, was right when he said, "You know what the best age is? I'll tell you. The age you are, day by day, until you croak." *Yesterday is gone and tomorrow is not yet; this is the day in which you can be.* Authentic existence for Martin Heidegger meant to courageously face death, and in the realization of one's limited time, to act based on what one truly values and considers important. The old man wanted to pay more attention to his relationships, let go of much that society and the culture distracted him with, deepen his interior life and cultivate the bond he had always felt with nature.

And perhaps, before the end he would once again walk down the Arno in Florence under the rain, hike the Monet trails in Takayama, sit at a café in Piazza de Ferrari in Genova as the spray from the fountain refreshed his face, wander in Highgate Cemetery in London, have a coffee and a Campari at the bar by the beach in Albinia, sit on a bench in Piazza Italia in Perugia with his sister. Visit his daughter in Michigan, see his son Michael again. Travel to new places. Hopefully, he would have time to reread his favorite books and many of the ones he hadn't delved into yet, watch his most beloved films and listen to his records, peruse his art books. And with luck, he would die at just the right time. Berry slept in his little bed next to the bookcase, and the scent of jasmine entered the room from the partially opened window. He reclined even more in the chair and closed his eyes.

HE OPENED them to the warm early-morning light blazing through the window. He lay still listening to voices coming from below—his aunt had arrived the night before from Genova to visit, and now her voice and laughter danced in the air. He jumped up from the old army cot and ran out of the room, down the stairs. His grandmother sat by the kitchen table with her eyes closed and lips slowly moving, as she recited the rosary she held in her trembling hands. Out on the terrace, Sandrina, his sister, sat on the floor playing with a doll as his mother and aunt, wearing robes, lounged on deckchairs, drinking coffee. "Here's my little guy, come give me a kiss," his aunt said. He walked up to her, and she hugged him close to her blue robe and kissed him on the cheek, her long black hair tickling his face. She smelled of coffee and cigarettes. "Good morning," he mumbled, rubbing his eyes. His mother smiled as she hugged and kissed him. As they went in the house to fix breakfast followed by his sister, he lay down on the warm cement propped on his elbows and took a deep breath. He turned to look at the tall fig tree that stood by the left side of the house, then gazed into the distance. The green mountains seemed like the folds of a blanket, and the highway a faint white string on which tiny beetles slowly climbed. He gazed often at those mountains—so far away and at times shrouded in mist or haze. The whole world was out there, and his future.

ACKNOWLEDGMENTS

Cornelia Feye's editing was instrumental in bringing this book to life. I am grateful for her patience and suggestions. Many thanks to the family members and friends who shared their memories with me and to Chris Edwards, who read portions of an early draft and offered helpful comments. I would also like to thank Stephanie, my wife, who read the final draft and provided constructive criticism, encouragement, and support.

ABOUT THE AUTHOR

Ted Shigematsu was born in Rome and grew up in Genova, Italy. When he was 15 he moved to California with his parents and sister. He received a Master of Arts in philosophy from San Diego State University, and after working as a respiratory therapist and a high school English teacher, he taught philosophy at Santa Ana College. His novel, *The Cracks in the Life of Mike Anami* was published in 2020. In September of 2021 he was selected by the San Diego Public Library as Author of the Month, and he was featured as a local author in Imperial Valley newspapers.

For more information and images go to:
tedshigematsu.wordpress.com

www.ingramcontent.com/pod-product-compliance
Lightning Source LLC
LaVergne TN
LVHW091654070526
838199LV00050B/2172